The Social Drama of Da

The Social Drama of Daily Work

A Manual for Historians

Sarah Schneewind

Amsterdam University Press

Cover illustration: Farid al-Din ʿAttar, "Funeral Procession", Folio 35r from a Mantiq al-Tayr (Language of the Birds), Iran, 1486 CE. Courtesy of the Metropolitan Museum of Art (New York).

Cover design: Coördesign, Leiden
Lay-out: Crius Group, Hulshout

ISBN	978 90 4855 953 4
e-ISBN	978 90 4855 954 1 (pdf)
DOI	10.5117/9789048559534
NUR	696

For Everett Cherrington Hughes and Helen MacGill Hughes

Table of Contents

Acknowledgements   11

Preface   13

Introduction   15
     Why Study Work?   15
     Why Use the Sociology of Occupations?   17
     What Counts as Work?   20
     Works Cited   22

Chapter 1   Technique and Object of Technique   25
     Splitting, Lumping, and Bundling   27
     Example: Blacksmiths   31
     A Rough Typology   33
     Technique and the Body   37
     Workshop, Body, Self   40
     Works Cited   43

Chapter 2   The Players in the Social Drama of Work   47
     Clients   48
     Colleagues   51
     Coworkers   52
     What about the Boss?   57
     Hierarchy within the Occupation   60
     Works Cited   63

Chapter 3   Dirty Work   67
     Pollution and Social Distaste   68
     Messy Work Practitioners Don't Mind   70
     Status Pain   71
     Unpredictability and Status Pain   73
     Works Cited   76

Chapter 4   The Path into the Occupation   79
     Sorting Workers on the Path into the Occupation   80
     Social Mobility and Its Discontents   83
     Apprenticeship   86

Example: The Conversion of Nursing Students   91
Commitment and the Game   95
The Path Out of the Occupation   98
Works Cited   99

Chapter 5   Self-Regulation and Public Relations (Code and Policy)   103
Policy   104
Code   106
Code and Technique   109
Works Cited   112

Chapter 6   Social Authority (License and Mandate)   115
License   116
Mandate   119
Example: Jazz Musicians   123
Works Cited   126

Chapter 7   Technique and Danger (Guilty Knowledge)   129
Symbols of Distinction   130
Flavors of Guilty Knowledge   132
Example: Master Jacques of the Journeymen's Companies   137
The Dilemma of Routine and Emergency   139
Fraud and Corruption   141
Works Cited   145

Chapter 8   Mistakes at Work   149
Flow and Error   151
Mistakes, Colleagues, and Coworkers   153
Danger and Charisma   156
Mistakes at Work Create Culture   157
Example: Mistakes in !Kung San Hunting   161
Works Cited   163

Chapter 9   Pace and Discipline   167
The Assembly Line and the Anthropologist   168
Rethinking Pace   169
The Group and the Pace   172
Works Cited   174

Chapter 10   The Family Workshop 177
    Works Cited 182

Conclusion 183
    Stonemasons in Early Modern Italy 183
    Why Study History through the Social Drama of Work? 186
    Works Cited 187

Index 189

Acknowledgements

This book began as a way to explain the Hughes framework to my undergraduate students in a course on Ming history at the University of California, San Diego, and their creative responses suggested that it would work for my own research and that of other historians. I would like to thank Cathy Gere, Anne Gerritsen, Micah Muscolino, Felipe Pait, Dagmar Schäfer, and Qiao Yang for helpful comments on drafts. The Max Planck Institute for the History of Science (MPIWG) in Berlin supported my work in the academic years 2020–21 and 2022–23, and I thank the members of the Working Group on Ability and Authority there for using the framework, demonstrating its possibilities and limitations, and commenting on the manuscript. The members of Ming In Southern California (MISC) provided thoughtful comments when I sandboxed the framework with them. Dagmar Schäfer's faith in the project has meant a lot to me, and so has the encouragement of Professor John H. Stanfield in Mauritius. Philippe Vienne's close reading, his suggestions for further reading, and especially his enthusiasm got me back on track after a difficult year. Martha A. L. Schulman read the penultimate draft with great attention, raising questions about logic and evidence that I have tried to answer. Cathleen Paethe of MPIWG managed the image permissions, and Tim DeBold of Atramenti Editing speedily and thoroughly cleaned up the footnotes and bibliography, and compiled the index. Most of all, I am grateful to my family, past and present.

Preface

Do you want to research everyday life and ordinary people? This manual is for you! Since the advent of agriculture 10,000 years ago, most people have spent most of their days – for most of the years of their lives – working. Work has always mattered to people's thoughts, feelings, and identities. Sociologists have called the human interactions that work involves "the social drama of work."

Whatever the place and time you study, the concepts laid out here will lead you to see more in your sources. Whether you are interested mainly in a particular sort of worker – Apothecary? Blacksmith? Cardsharp? Doctor? – or want to move outward to broader social questions, this manual will guide you. You'll move from understanding the tasks and knowledge of an occupation, to drawing connections to clients, coworkers, and colleagues, to developing new insights into social and cultural developments.

Work interactions create emotional tensions for the individuals holding occupational roles. But since these tensions occur over and over in similar work-related transactions within a given society, they both take cultural and social forms and also affect the broader society and culture of the place-time. The culture of a given place-time may, to a large degree, be created by the sum of the cultures of its occupations; the social drama of work may inform the broader social drama of the place-time. Using this manual, historians can test these propositions.

The manual introduces key ideas of the Chicago-school sociology of occupations. It provides a framework that moves beyond stilted ideas of "social status" that often replicate the limited viewpoint of primary sources, mainly written by a small literate elite. The sociology of occupations does not replace systemic analyses of class domination or labor exploitation; rather, it gives us an approach to research that adds texture to those analyses. In this manual, I illustrate the key ideas with examples from a variety of place-times. And to help you connect your sources and those concepts, I include suggested research questions for each chapter.

You may be starting an entirely new project – from a high-school paper to a master's thesis to a Ph.D. dissertation to a third monograph. You may have collected a body of source material, but be unsure how best to approach it. Or perhaps you have masses of notes on a particular occupation in a long-ago place-time, but have not figured out how they all hang together. Whatever stage you are at, the questions in the boxes will initiate a practical research program linked to the concepts that will help you do your own analysis.

If you are starting fresh and are still looking for a topic, first choose a story, object, or image. Figure out all the workers who are lurking in its the crevices. Let's take Cinderella. Forget about Cinderella, the handsome prince, and the ugly stepsisters. What about the shoemaker and the seamstress who sewed the ballgowns? What about the carriage-driver and the four footmen? What did they know that got Cinderella safely to the ball? What did they talk about while waiting for her to run back out? Who built the carriage? Who laid those marble stairs? Who decorated the ballroom and who handed round the champagne? Any starting point can lead you to generate a list of people who contributed to the social, the material, and even the personal and religious lives of the literate elite who wrote most of the sources, and whom historians usually spotlight.

Pick one occupation. Then read a chapter of the manual, and start answering some of the research questions provided. Although Chapter One makes the argument for starting with "technique" – the skills and knowledge of the occupation – any piece of the framework will lead to other pieces. Where a key concept appears in passing before the manual discusses it in detail, it is in **boldface**. Use the concepts that illumine your material and discard those that do not; or, in your writing, propose a revision. The concepts are hypotheses, not straitjackets: a new pair of glasses to help researchers see more about those people of the past who are often hidden.

Introduction

Abstract

Historians and history students researching daily life and ordinary people of any place and time can learn a great deal by investigating work, since most people have spent most of their time working to earn a living. Whether as wage laborers in a market economy, as independent farmers, or as enslaved persons in various arrangements, people learned skills and developed their consciousness of self through work as well as through family, religion, and other aspects of life. The sociology of occupations offers a set of concepts and questions for the historian that can illuminate the working lives and identities of practitioners of any occupation, including their relations with colleagues, coworkers, clients, and other members of society. Those relations shaped culture.

Keywords: daily life, ordinary people, work, identity, society, culture

Why Study Work?

Many social and cultural historians today want to dive deep into the lives of ordinary people in the places and times they study. When they look at ordinary life, what do they find? Not only religion, not only family, but also work. Work usually changes more slowly than politics and constitutes a more fundamental layer of life. As anthropologist Herbert Applebaum points out:

> Work is such a pervasive activity that it influences and affects all individuals and all social phenomena. Until recently most people had to work most of their waking hours to earn their livelihood ... Thus, work is a significant part of the human condition.[1]

---

1   Applebaum, *Work in Non-market and Transitional Societies*, 39.

Schneewind, S.K. *The Social Drama of Daily Work. A Manual for Historians.* Amsterdam: Amsterdam University Press, 2024
DOI: 10.5117/9789048559534_INTRO

Work occupied at least a third of most people's time in the past. Therefore, the first reason to study work in the past is that nearly everyone did it, and they spent much of their lives doing it. Even in historical, non-egalitarian societies with a rank system, only a few people engaged in no productive labor at all.[2]

A second reason to study work is that it is inherently social: it necessarily involves relations between people that are arguably more fundamental than their ideological relationships. Since work must go on, while ideology may be ignored or even flouted, it is a good place to start trying to understand society. Applebaum argued that the study of work is even more important for studying societies less governed by the market, for work was embedded in their kinship structures, religion, taboos, and political leadership.[3]

Third, work often occurred in public and took the form of observable action. Even if the elite writers of the past ignored them, the details of work were not usually taboo, so information about it is less likely to be distorted than, say, the details of sexual relations. And this information may appear not only in standard textual sources, but in pictures, jokes, songs, calendars, and any other trace of the place-time. Fourth, work is at the heart of the economy: to understand the economy we must understand production as it really occurred. Fifth, as state and society change, work changes, so studying work illuminates historical change and continuity, again at a nitty-gritty level.

A sixth reason to look at work is to strive for a bottom-up history, filtering out the elite bias.[4] The history of work offers a way to look away from political and economic domination for a while, see what emerges, and then look back at domination again with better questions.[5] Seventh, just as stories reach students and other readers by humanizing the past, so readers may be drawn into an embodied history that connects the details of daily work to larger social patterns.

For the historical questions that matter to you, what kinds of work were involved?
Which kinds of work appear or are hidden within the cracks of myths and ideas central to the place-time you study?
Which of those occupations interests you most?

2   Nash, "Anthropology of Work," 46.
3   Applebaum, *Work in Non-market and Transitional Societies*, 2.
4   Berger, *Invitation to Sociology*, 46.
5   James Scott's scholarship, informed by the details of agricultural work, is an example of this scholarly process. See, for instance, *Weapons of the Weak* and *Moral Economy of the Peasant*.

Brainstorm about sources that might include information about that line of work.
What do you know about positive or negative stereotypes of those workers?
How essential was the occupation to other members of the community, both overall and in terms of regular availability?

Why Use the Sociology of Occupations?

The essential problems of [people] at work are the same whether they do their work in the laboratories of some famous institution or in the messiest vat room of a pickle factory ... [Scholars can] make comparisons between the junk peddler and the professor without intent to debunk the one and patronize the other.[6]

Once the historian has decided to study work, the Chicago-school sociology of occupations, developed from the late 1930s onward primarily by Everett C. Hughes and his colleagues and students, offers a well-developed set of concepts and questions that we can adopt and adapt as observational tools.[7] The sociology of occupations provides a comprehensive set of concepts and questions that are intrinsically flexible. The "sociological imagination" requires a kind of free association "guided but not hampered by a frame of reference." Together, these characteristics make the Hughes framework suitable for historians to borrow; and as literary scholar Michael Fuller wrote recently, "Poaching [from other disciplines] ... is one of the ways in which disciplines are reinvigorated."[8] This manual illustrates how historians can use the framework and adapt it as we go – for, naturally, not every concept developed in twentieth-century North America will apply in every other place-time. Historians may add nuance and new generalizable insights to the framework that the occupational sociologists created.

The team of sociologists behind a major early study on the **path into the occupation** – focusing on medical students – described an approach that historians can appreciate. Using a social psychological theory of "symbolic interaction," they decided to look at "the more conscious aspects of human

---

6   Hughes, "Work and the Self," 48. I suspect that the pickle factory refers to Bessie McGinnis van Vorst's experience as recounted in van Vorst and van Vorst, *The Woman Who Toils*.

7   For the origins, development, and legacy of the sociology of occupations discussed here, see inter alia Chapoulie, *Chicago Sociology*; Helmes-Hayes and Santoro, *Anthem Companion to Everett Hughes*; and Becker, "The Chicago School."

8   Fuller, "Digital Humanities," 261.

behavior and relate them to the individual's participation in group life."[9] That meant paying particular attention to topics that (1) mattered to the medical students and those around them, as shown by the fact that they talked about – or at least around – those topics; (2) produced "tension or conflict"; (3) connected clearly to other elements in the social system of the school; and (4) were common to cohorts of students, rather than representing individual variation.[10] This approach makes sense for historians. For we deal mainly with texts and images on topics of explicit social interest, reading both for what they say and what they do not say; we agree that conflict and tension are a common and revealing part of society; and we want to understand not just individuals but institutions, cultures, and social systems, generation by generation.[11] The Hughes framework thus fits well with what historians already do.

The historian, like the occupational sociologist, as Louis Kriesberg wrote,

> ranges widely for data … In conceptualization, he manages to capture significant aspects of a broad phenomenon, yet retains a concreteness which never lets one forget the people and their conduct upon which the abstractions are based … [and] the ways in which aspects of social life are interconnected, in disorder as well as in order. Dilemmas, inconsistencies, and paradoxes, consequently, are frequently noted.[12]

It is people's efforts to resolve dilemmas and inconsistencies that generate culture itself, and because so much of people's time has been spent on work, work dilemmas are among the most productive engines of culture-creation.

Individuals vary, of course, but the framework assumes that **practitioners** in the same occupation will often act similarly in the same place-time, because they face the same conditions and problems.[13] A second fundamental assumption, at the next level of abstraction, is that "a feature of work behavior found in one occupation, even a minor or an odd one, will be found in others," in analogous form.[14] This "perspective by incongruity," lets investigators "learn about doctors by studying plumbers; and about prostitutes by studying psychiatrists."[15] The results include what sociologist Fred

9   Becker et al., *Boys in White*, 19. The key figure here is Anselm Strauss.
10 Becker et al., *Boys in White*, 18–21.
11 Likewise, anthropologists see "blaming and criticizing" as "essential social processes." Douglas, *Thought Styles*, 36. Conflict is not always about economic advantage.
12 Kriesberg, "Internal Differentiation," 141.
13 Solomon, "Sociological Perspectives on Occupations," 6–7.
14 Hughes, "Sociological Study of Work," 425.
15 Hughes, "Mistakes at Work," 88.

Davis calls "mind-jolting similarities" among disparate social phenomena.[16] Transferring a concept from its original context to a new one helps uncover social dynamics that **colleague code** and **policy** may have concealed, or that **laypeople** (those outside the occupation) may have covered up.[17] By the same token, "perspective by incongruity" helps historians break out of both the ideology of the place-time under study and their own biases.[18] This creative approach also invites the historian to consider together different occupations in the place-time she is studying: instead of taking for granted the great gulf between them, we may ask, for instance, what the priest and the peasant shared in their working lives. As sociologist Lewis Coser comments, perspective by incongruity subverts "habitual sequences of ideas" and offers new ones.[19]

When historians study lines of work that particularly interest them, in a way that can connect with research on other occupations, the resulting comparisons and contrasts can both reveal more about the object of study and better show its importance to larger social, political, economic, and cultural structures and developments. Neutral terms that apply to all work facilitate the study on equal terms of people of different ranks, genders, ethnicities, and so on. They help us see through the ethical and ideological assumptions of our sources, and let us see more broadly, looking past the specifics to the way they generate culture that contributes to the social order overall. The standard terminology and set of concepts of the Hughes framework help researchers circumvent official stories about society to reach something deeper and more surprising. Shared terminology will also facilitate comparison across place-times.

This manual offers the first systematic account of the key concepts in occupational sociology, along with historical examples and research questions. The manual is meant as a practical guide for teachers, historians, and history students at any level researching the working lives of people in any place and time. I strongly recommend reading Hughes's fascinating original essays, referred to in the footnotes. For some readers, tracing his line of thought as he lays it out will bring the concepts to life more fully than the way I have systematized it.[20]

---

16 The phrase is used to describe Hughes in F. Davis, "Professional Socialization," 236.
17 Hughes, "Mistakes at Work," 88.
18 Coser, "Introduction," 11 (the phrase came originally from Kenneth Burke); Hughes, "Mistakes at Work," 88.
19 Coser, "Introduction," 11.
20 For a comment on becoming accustomed to Hughes's style, see Coser, "Introduction," 7–8. Coser also briefly recounts Hughes's life and career.

Is there scholarship on the occupation in other place-times, for comparison?
What kinds of social differentiation (gender, race) occur in the place-time that
might affect work, especially the occupation you have chosen?
What is the "official version of community life," or ideology, of your place-time?

What Counts as Work?

Work, in this manual, means a person's **occupation:** "the role of an individual
in an ongoing system of activity, through which s/he makes a living."[21] Both
practitioners and **laypeople** of the place and time under study must have
recognized the occupation as a category. People work and value work for
reasons beyond the purely economic, in ways that vary by place-time. But
since the occupation is defined as the practitioner's means of making a
living, historians may first ask about wages or other remuneration.[22]

Because remuneration for work has taken many forms, that inquiry
immediately raises cultural questions.[23] French artisanal journeymen in
the eighteenth century were paid not only in cash wages and advances, but
also in meals, non-monetary rights including "informal marks of esteem"
from the masters, and "other forms of irregular income."[24] Men bound to
Buddhist monastic lineages in India from about 200 CE worked as clerks,
craftsmen, soldiers, and builders, and earned both worldly remuneration
and spiritual merit.[25] Medieval university students paid master teachers
partly in spices and sweetmeats.[26] The peasant family's recompense for
labor may be no more than the recognition that they have fulfilled their
obligations to the lord and survived another year. That is still working for
one's livelihood. In addition to wages, salary, fees, piece-rates, advances on
the cost of raw materials, or payment for objects, remuneration may include
consumption of what one grows and makes, discharge of a tax obligation,
or receiving an honor that comes with tax exemptions, a residence, or
other perquisites.

---

21   Solomon, "Sociological Perspectives on Occupations," 7 and footnotes 5–8.
22   Josef Ehmer explains that from about 1900 onward, the history of work has focused on
questions of wages, working hours and conditions, and work discipline. This multifaceted history
took up the (incomplete) transition from small workshop to factory, the industrious revolution,
etc., but paid less attention to forced labor of various kinds. "Work, History of," 16572–73.
23   For complications in terms and arrangements see for example Caracausi, "Just Wage," 113–15.
24   Sonenscher, "Mythical Work," 58–59.
25   Chatterjee, "Locked Box," 153.
26   Huisman, "L'étudiant au Moyen Âge," 51.

Workers' freedoms and obligations varied widely, and the specifics affect how the various concepts in this framework might apply. For enslaved people, the historian will have to think through, based on the facts at hand, whether or not any part of the framework applies. Labels like "slave," "peasant," or "free worker" may obscure as much as they illuminate lived experience.[27] Under some regimes, slaves were worked to death, as in Shang China, for instance, and a good linen spinner in Scotland in 1751 working twelve-hour days still could not earn enough to cover grain, clothing, fuel, and rent.[28] Yet even under slavery, in the USA for instance, some highly skilled enslaved practitioners may have shared aspects of occupational culture with free **colleagues.**

The definition's requirement that the practitioner "make a living" by his work raises three caveats. First, amateurs may often do or make the same things (there are amateur musicians, carpenters, cooks, even healers). Historians of technology will track their technique even if the makers are producing things purely as gifts, for friends or family, as amateurs and for no kind of recompense. Second, some historians consider "work" to include any application of effort to meet any need, including "emotional work" among kinfolk and friends.[29] Delimiting "work," in other words, is as complex as delimiting "sex."[30] The approach here focuses on the social relations among **colleagues, coworkers,** and their **clients,** so it requires that the work be performed to make a living. The third caveat is that an occupation may include practitioners who are so unsuccessful that they cannot survive on their earnings. Since failures have social relations around work as much as the successful and the fairly paid, they are part of the occupation. In fact, as we will see, **mistakes at work** play a central role in the social drama of work.

Asking questions about remuneration and conditions of employment will yield a range within any occupation. The sociological framework does not replace other explanations and sets of questions about labor mobility, shortages, and control, but suggests ways to look for complex, emotional human relations as well as relations that can be expressed in numbers, or subsumed under general terms like "exploitation."

27 Huang, *Peasant Family*, 105. On the problems with the term "peasant" see M. Cohen, "Cultural and Political Inventions."
28 Schneewind, *Outline History of East Asia*, 16; Berg, "Women's Work," 78–79. The primary source does the math and concludes, "Therefore she must starve."
29 Frevert, "Trust as Work," 93, adopting Kocka's definition: "the purposeful application of physical and mental forces in order to fulfil needs."
30 Hinchy and Joshi, "Selective Amnesia," 9.

How was the occupation you are studying referred to in its place-time? Some languages offer synonyms. Terms may not translate easily to modern languages.
Were practitioners remunerated by time, by piece, or by long-term arrangement?
Were practitioners paid in cash or in kind?
Were they recompensed with honor or spiritual merit?
Did their work discharge a tax duty or a duty to an overlord?
Did their work feed themselves, their family, or others?
Did the remuneration for work suffice to support the practitioner's life?
Did amateurs also do the same work?
Where in the sources might you find accounts of failures in the line of work?

Works Cited

Applebaum, Herbert, ed. *Work in Non-market and Transitional Societies*. Albany: SUNY Press, 1984.

Becker, Howard S. "The Chicago School, So-Called." *Qualitative Sociology* 22, no. 1 (1999):1–7.

Becker, Howard S., Blanche Geer, Everett C. Hughes, and Anselm L. Strauss. *Boys in White: Student Culture in Medical School*. Chicago: University of Chicago Press, 1961.

Berg, Maxine. "Women's Work, Mechanization and the Early Phases of Industrialization in England." In *The Historical Meanings of Work*, edited by Patrick Joyce, 64–98. Cambridge: Cambridge University Press, 1987.

Berger, Peter L. *Invitation to Sociology: A Humanistic Perspective*. Garden City: Anchor Books, 1963.

Caracausi, Andrea. "The Just Wage in Early Modern Italy: A Reflection on Zacchia's *De Salario seu Operariorum Mercede*." *International Review of Social History Special Issue* 56 (2011): 107–24.

Chatterjee, Indrani. "The Locked Box in *Slavery and Social Death*." In *On Human Bondage: After* Slavery and Social Death, edited by John Bodel and Walter Scheidel, 151–66. Hoboken: Wiley, 2016.

Chapoulie, Jean-Michel. *Chicago Sociology*. Translated by Caroline Wazer. New York: Columbia University Press, 2001.

Cohen, Myron. "Cultural and Political Inventions in Modern China: The Case of the Chinese 'Peasant'." *Daedalus* 122, no. 2 (1993): 151–70.

Coser, Lewis. "Introduction." In *On Work, Race, and the Sociological Imagination*, edited by Lewis Coser, 1–17. Chicago: University of Chicago Press, 1994.

Davis, Fred. "Professional Socialization as Subjective Experience: The Process of Doctrinal Conversion among Student Nurses." In *Institutions and the Person:*

Festschrift in Honor of Everett C. Hughes, edited by Howard S. Becker, Blanche Geer, David Riesman, and Robert S. Weiss, 235–51. Chicago: Aldine, 1968.

Douglas, Mary. *Thought Styles: Critical Essays on Good Taste.* London: Sage, 1996.

Ehmer, Josef. "Work, History of." In *International Encyclopedia of the Social and Behavioral Sciences*, vol. 24, 16569–74. London: Elsevier, 2001.

Frevert, Ute. "Trust as Work." In *Work in a Modern Society*, edited by Jürgen Kocka, 93–108. New York: Berghahn Books, 2010.

Fuller, Michael A. "Digital Humanities and the Discontents of Meaning." *Journal of Chinese History* 4 (2020): 259–75.

Helmes-Hayes, Rick, and Marco Santoro, eds. *The Anthem Companion to Everett Hughes*. London: Anthem, 2016.

Hinchy, Jessica, and Girija Joshi. "Selective Amnesia and South Asian Histories: An Interview with Indrani Chatterjee." *Itinerario* (2021): 1–16.

Huang, Philip. *The Peasant Family and Rural Development in the Yangzi Delta, 1350–1988.* Stanford: Stanford University Press, 1990.

Hughes, Everett C. "Mistakes at Work." In *Men and Their Work*, 88–101. Glencoe, IL: The Free Press, 1958.

Hughes, Everett C. "The Sociological Study of Work: An Editorial Foreword." *American Journal of Sociology* 57, no. 5 (1952): 423–26.

Hughes, Everett C. "Work and the Self." In *Men and Their Work*, 42–55. Glencoe, IL: The Free Press, 1958.

Huisman, Michel. "L'étudiant au Moyen Âge" [Students in the Middle Ages]. *Revue de l'Université libre de Bruxelles* (1899): 45–67.

Kriesberg, Louis. "Internal Differentiation and the Establishment of Organizations." In *Institutions and the Person: Festschrift in Honor of Everett C. Hughes*, edited by Howard S. Becker, Blanche Geer, David Riesman, and Robert S. Weiss, 141–56. Chicago: Aldine, 1968.

Nash, June. "The Anthropology of Work." In *Work in Non-Market and Transitional Societies*, edited by Herbert Applebaum, 45–55. Albany: SUNY Press, 1984.

Schneewind, Sarah. *An Outline History of East Asia to 1200*, 3rd ed. eScholarship, 2022. Retrieved from https://escholarship.org/uc/item/9d699767

Scott, James. *The Moral Economy of the Peasant: Rebellion and Subsistence in Southeast Asia.* New Haven: Yale University Press, 1976.

Scott, James. *Weapons of the Weak: Everyday Forms of Peasant Resistance.* New Haven: Yale University Press, 1985.

Solomon, David N. "Sociological Perspectives on Occupations." In *Institutions and the Person: Festschrift in Honor of Everett C. Hughes*, edited by Howard S. Becker, Blanche Geer, David Riesman, and Robert S. Weiss, 3–13. Chicago: Aldine, 1968.

Sonenscher, Michael. "Mythical Work: Workshop Production and the *Compagnon-nages* of Eighteenth-century France." In *The Historical Meanings of Work*, edited by Patrick Joyce, 31–63. Cambridge: Cambridge University Press, 1987.

Van Vorst, Mrs. John, and Marie van Vorst. *The Woman Who Toils: Being the Experiences of Two Ladies as Factory Girls.* 1902, 1903; facsimile reprint Carlisle, MA: Applewood Books, n.d.

I.   Technique and Object of Technique

Abstract

In studying a particular occupation in a particular place-time, the historian should investigate precisely what tasks it encompassed, and what skills and knowledge it required – which together are called "technique." Exactly what the occupation worked on, or the "object of technique," along with bodily and mental experiences of work, also varied. The same occupation in different cultures and societies had different technique and object of technique. Tasks and skills were divided among occupations or lumped together into one occupation in different ways, as examples demonstrate. Further, technique encompassed both direct producing activities, such as healing or making swords, and supporting activities, such as knowing how to acquire raw materials or find clients. The chapter also offers a rough typology of occupations.

Keywords: skill, knowledge, daily work, ordinary people, body, experience

I say to thee, Nazarene, that an accomplished cavalier should know how to dress his steed, as well as how to ride him; how to forge his sword upon the stithy as well as how to use it in battle; how to burnish his arms, as well as how to wear them; and above all, how to cure wounds, as well as how to inflict them.[1]

"Technique" refers to the skills and knowledge of the occupation. "Object of technique" refers to what practitioners worked *upon*.[2] Historians must take the details of technique seriously, just as the savvy boss hires and fires on the basis of technique, considering the specific dangers of the "workshop" – the space, of any kind, in which practitioners do their work – and the tools they use.

---

1   So says Saladin to the Knight of the Leopard in Sir Walter Scott, *The Talisman*, 298.
2   Hughes, "Personality Types," 35. Benjamin Franklin's early theoretical considerations of work, picked up approvingly by Karl Marx, focused on humans as tool-makers, so historians of work created a grand narrative of work history divided according to technological advances (the agricultural, industrial, and electronic revolutions). See Ehmer, "Work, History of," 16571.

Schneewind, S.K. *The Social Drama of Daily Work. A Manual for Historians.* Amsterdam: Amsterdam University Press, 2024
DOI: 10.5117/9789048559534_CH01

For instance, a scholarly article reports that a Maine lumber camp foreman in the 1920s and 1930s described his method of hiring as "Just take right off and hunt 'til I found some men." Yet in fact, the foreman did not take just anyone of the right gender. The historian who wrote the article was not thinking about technique, so he described as "arbitrary" the foreman's rejection of an applicant who wore a long-tailed coat, knocked on the door of the office instead of walking right in, and hit his head on the lintel coming in.[3] But the rejection was not arbitrary. It was perfectly reasonable: long clothes that could get caught in a saw, excessive refinement in a camp with no privacy, and clumsiness disqualified the applicant. Likewise, smoking tobacco instead of chewing it was a dangerous practice in a camp of wood and canvas, so a worker who smoked would be fired immediately; but because a person turned out into the woods alone risked being attacked by bears, a Minnesota foreman also fired whoever was standing around nearest the smoker.[4] Even if bear attacks were the rationale, it is easy to see that peer pressure would come to bear on smokers pretty heavily. Thinking about technique shows that the lumber camp foreman's decisions made sense, and reveals the rationale behind aspects of occupational culture.

To understand what technique for an occupation in a given place-time consisted of may require in-depth work. R. L. Miller, researching physicians for ancient Egyptian tomb-builders, uncovered their technique in a combination of texts, visual representations, archaeology, and epidemiology.[5] The basics of technique and object of technique may seem obvious. Doctors heal people; lumberjacks fell trees. But complexities arise immediately, and generate research questions that deepen understanding of the occupation.

What tasks, knowledge, and skills did the occupation encompass? List them and revise the list as your research progresses.
Where – in what sort of space – did the practitioners work?
How much physical skill or strength did each task require?
What knowledge did each task require?
On what basis were practitioners selected or rejected?
What personality traits might help or hinder success?
What did practitioners work on, using what tools?
How much coordination of tasks among coworkers was required?

3   Tomczik, "He-Men," 701.
4   Tomczik, "He-Men," 701–2.
5   Miller, "Paleoepidemiology," 16.

Splitting, Lumping, and Bundling

The first complication is that labels may lack precision: not only the scholarly labels for occupations (such outsiders' categories and labels are called "etic"), but even the labels used in the place-time under study (insiders' categories are called "emic"). On the one hand, labels may split categories of occupation wrongly. As Michael Sonenscher writes about eighteenth-century France:

> The names of the trades have a very misleading precision and most historians of the *compannonnages* [journeymen's associations] have assumed that words like *menusier* [joiner] or *serrurier* [locksmith] meant something technically precise about the work done by members of such trades. Journeyman locksmiths made springs for carriages, made or repaired the wrought iron used on railings, staircases and shop signs, installed the complicated clusters of needles and rods used in stocking frames, and also made the metal clamps and hinges needed for doors and shutters. Some of them actually made locks ... There was therefore no rigid correlation between the nomenclature of the trades and the work which journeymen could do. A [journeyman] farrier could be employed by a [master]locksmith; a [journeyman] wheelwright or turner by a master joiner.[6]

Journeyman "locksmiths" did far more than make locks, while master locksmiths might employ a journeyman with a quite different label, such as "farrier." Looking for specifics of technique and object of technique will lead to more accurate historical understandings than relying on emic labels that suggest spurious distinctions among occupations.

Second, emic labels may lump categories wrongly. In thirteenth- and fourteenth-century China, the government considered "silk-weaver" an occupational category. But other Chinese nomenclature identifies separate specializations such as "preparing the loom" (for which the object of technique is the loom with its warp and woof threads) and "beating textiles" (for which the object of technique is the woven cloth requiring smoothing).[7] Similarly, a description of occupations in Venice in the same period explained that weaving wool involved so many different skills that "among weavers themselves those doing one job do not know or understand what the others

---

6   Sonenscher, "Mythical Work."
7   Based on comments by Dagmar Schäfer, September 2020.

do," and "the person doing one type of weaving cannot do another type, nor even understand it."[8]

Armed with a clearer delineation of technique and object of technique, the historian will ask how far social interactions and work culture were shared among all "weavers," or on the other hand, how social interactions and work culture differed between textile-beaters and loom-preparers. Did one group outrank the other in the **hierarchy within the occupation?** Did they interact differently with shop-bosses or master weavers? Did practitioners move from one set of tasks to another as they progressed from apprentice to journeyman to master weaver? Asking about technique and object of technique, rather than assuming that they aligned with *a priori* labels, allows historians to raise and then consider these questions.

A third complication is that technique may even be much broader, not only than what the scholar expects, but than what the occupation explicitly advertises. The classical West African griot was a historian and advisor to royalty. Reciting the genealogies and deeds of the social elite, griots advertised their reliability: "My word is pure and free of all untruths; it is the word of my father; it is the word of my father's father." But although, like historians everywhere, they stressed their reliability, the griots' technique included not only memorizing histories, but also "praise-singing, stage entertainment, artistic narration, diplomacy, state etiquette and the like."[9] In about the year 2000, both Manhattan apartment building doormen and their **clients** said that doormen were in place primarily to provide "security," yet they almost never did anything to keep tenants safe from dangerous outsiders. Instead, they greeted and announced visitors; received packages, rental movies, dry-cleaning, and food deliveries; cleaned the lobby and the space in front of the building; watered plants and shoveled snow; operated elevators, and did other tasks.[10] Practitioners' **policy** or self-presentation may not match their real technique, and clients understand technique still less.

Fourth, although historians have correlated higher degrees of specialization in technique with market societies using money and lower degrees of specialization with lower commercialization, that cannot be taken for granted in the study of a particular occupation. A large literature shows that in non-market societies, most people do a wide variety of tasks (i.e.,

8   Mocarrelli, "Attitudes to Work," 95.

9   Camara, *Is There a Distinctively African Way of Knowing*, 33–36. Camara does not always give a date for the phenomena he discusses.

10   Bearman, *Doormen*, 5, 68, 113–15. "Only a few doormen can *ever* recall a single [security-related] event at their building" (113; emphasis in the original).

their technique includes many skills) as families mostly feed themselves; in Herbert Applebaum's example, each women makes her own baskets as well as using them, and each man his own bow and arrows.[11] Often, even the craftspeople with specialized technique (carving, ironmongery, weaving, pottery, boatbuilding) and who tend, in practice, to do just one part of a long production process *can* competently do every part of the process.[12] And, even as commercialization increases specialization, it also requires practitioners in many occupations to *add* skills in what are called "supporting activities" to the technique of direct producing activities: specifically, business skills like knowing how to buy raw materials and how much to pay for them, how to respond to changing markets, how much to charge for one's products or services, how to attract customers, how to keep books, and so on. Commercialization may also affect the division of labor differently, as manifested in occupational technique and object of technique.

In fact, starting with technique and object of technique, instead of with a label like "market" or "non-market," tells us more about the division of labor as a human experience. For instance, by closely examining who was doing what when in the village of Tenía in Mexico in 1948, anthropologist Charles Erasmus and his (unnamed) wife realized that the residents could work and rest as they pleased precisely because they mostly did the same things. That is, the whole economy of the village rested on tasks done by men and women depending on their age; even if some people did specialize, it was socially accepted that their tasks *could* be done by others (i.e., in the terms of the Hughes framework, they lacked **license**). Only the two shopkeepers kept anything close to regular hours, and since their livelihood rested not on their shops but on their herds, even they closed up when they felt like it. By comparing Tenía with nearby towns that had many specialized occupations, the Erasmusses concluded that standard hours arose when work was both specialized and integrated enough that some workers relied on others for their products to be available on schedule. Standardization of work hours was not a disembodied or top-down process, but one that arose from technique and client relations.[13]

A fifth complication is that, as Hughes argued, one occupation might encompass "a bundle" of different objects of technique. That might happen if the technique required was similar; or if the activities shared a workshop (massage, barbering, and sex work in a bathhouse, for instance); or if one

---

11   Applebaum, *Work in Non-market and Transitional Societies*, 22.

12   Applebaum, *Work in Non-market and Transitional Societies*, 21–22.

13   Erasmus, "Work Patterns in a Mayo Village," 179.

technique and object would not provide enough business for a worker's livelihood.[14] Isolation within a small population would be another cause, a kind of throwback within a commercialized economy. Consider, for instance, the isolation of the ship. In 1849, Herman Melville wrote:

> A thorough sailor must understand much of other avocations. He must be a bit of an embroiderer, to work fanciful collars of hempen lace about the shrouds; he must be something of a weaver, to weave mats of rope-yarns for lashings to the boats; he must have a touch of millinery, so as to tie graceful bows and knots, such as *Matthew Walker's roses* and *Turk's heads*; he must be a bit of a musician, in order to sing out at the halyards; he must be a sort of jeweler, to set dead-eyes in the standing rigging; he must be a carpenter, to enable him to make a jury-mast out of a yard in case of emergency; he must be a sempstress, to darn and mend the sails; a rope-maker, to twist *marline* and *Spanish foxes*; a blacksmith, to make hooks and thimbles for the blocks: in short, he must be a Jack of all trades, in order to master his own.[15]

Bundled skills may be very dissimilar but necessary to carry out the work, as for Melville's sailors. Musician Ron Carter explained that three skills were essential for a career playing double bass in New York: musicianship, which demanded that one worked on physical and emotional skills, and read scores really thoroughly to understand what the parts meant in the music; promptness, to the extent that arriving at 7:15 p.m. for an 8:00 p.m. gig meant one was an hour late; and keeping one's instrument ready and in wonderful playing condition, even when the weather was playing its tricks. All were in aid of his larger technique: making the other musicians, who had hired him, sound great.[16] Or bundled skills may be linked by tools: for instance, the barber-surgeon of medieval Europe both shaved beards and cut flesh with his sharp tools. Historians should expect lines between occupations to fall in unexpected places in the division of labor; they should investigate what the people they are studying did all day as a solid foundation for understanding other aspects of their lives.

What words referred to the occupation then? Now?
What occupations referred to by other words did the same or related tasks?

14   Hughes, "Study of Occupations," 30.
15   Herman Melville, *Redburn*, quoted in Thomas, *Oxford Book of Work*, 363–64.
16   Carter, "Legendary Jazz Bassist."

Did one practitioner carry out a number of different tasks, or did practitioners specialize?
Did the degree of specialization change over time?
Did specialization vary by place?
Did practitioners specialize in very particular products or services?
Did different tasks give some practitioners more power or prestige within the occupation?
Did those doing different tasks enter the occupation differently?
Or did practitioners do different tasks along the path to mastery of technique?
Did technique include abilities needed in other occupations, too?
How did the occupation affect and how was it affected by commercialization?
Did technique overlap with the specialized technique of other occupations?
Do the specialization and bundling require revision of the scope of research?

Example: Blacksmiths

Blacksmiths exemplify the complexities of technique and object of technique. For it turns out that we cannot simply consider iron the object of technique.

The Gadulia Lohars of northern India in the 1960s worked on the scrap iron that villagers collected year-round in expectation of their next visit. They forged their own tools, but what they offered clients were special techniques for repairing agricultural tools and for cold-hammering small objects like ladles and scrapers. Other blacksmithing tasks were done by sedentary village smiths, who obtained iron from outside the village.[17] With different technique and object of technique, the two types of blacksmith could be classified as two different occupations, and indeed, their relations with colleagues and clients differed.

In contrast to this splitting of tasks, blacksmiths in West Africa in recent times controlled the whole production process, from mining to smelting to making tools and weapons. Furthermore, because they could create such a strong material out of "wild dirt," they also carried out the ritual circumcisions that made boys into strong men. The West African blacksmiths' bundled technique thus included what we might label a medical or ritual procedure.[18]

In commercialized late imperial China, some occupations relied on blacksmiths to make their specialized tools. For instance, the fishermen

17 Misra, "Gadulia Lohars," 130–31.
18 Camara, *Is There a Distinctively African Way of Knowing*, 12–13.

of Wenzhou on the southern Zhejiang coast preserved fish by slicing them
open, drying them for three or four days on a bamboo frame called a "fish-
drying hat," and salting them. Since the best season for catching plentiful
yellow croaker was also the rainy season, fishermen prayed to a patron
god for dry weather, and it was this god – called "Old Man Yangfu" or "The
Marquis of Dried Fish" – who had designed the special curved-bladed,
fish-shaped "dried fish knife" used to split the fish; he was also the first to
ask a blacksmith to forge such a knife.[19] Other late imperial occupations that
used iron tools, however, did not rely on blacksmiths. Inkstone quarriers'
technique included being able to *make* the tools of the trade. Every night
upon returning home, the miners would make their four types of iron chisels
for the following day. Historian Dorothy Ko explains that the chisels wore
out so quickly in mining stone that quarriers had to be able to repair their
own, so they understood wood and iron well enough for that. Ko comments
that the quarriers' "bundled skills ... straddle[ed] fields that in the modern
academy would be divided into smithy, metallurgy, carpentry, stratigraphy,
and mining geology."[20]

Knowing about an occupation in one place-time is only a rough
guide – perhaps no more than a set of questions – when the historian
is considering what it was like in another. Even when fundamental
technique – say, of smithing – is shared across place-times, the bundle
of skills of occupations, and their relations with clients and laypeople,
may differ dramatically.

> What can we learn from reading about the occupation in different place-times?
> Did different occupations use similar technique on a different object of tech-
> nique?
> Or did they use different techniques on the same object of technique?
> Did they have different clients, or offer different products or services?
> How were they differentiated in their workshop or lifestyle?
> Did they align with different ethnicities, genders, or religions?
> Did some potential clients carry out an occupation's tasks themselves, rather
> than calling on practitioners?
> Which skills were part of the practitioners' bundle?
> Did practitioners advertise some technique and keep quiet about some?

19   Zhang K., "Temples in Jinxiang Guard," 76. While some thought that Old Man Yangfu had
been an official during his lifetime, others said that he had been captain of a fishing boat who
had saved many people from drowning; see Muscolino, *Fishing Wars*, 40.
20   Ko, *Social Life of Inkstones*, 52.

A Rough Typology

Societies fall on an analytical spectrum with respect to how people enter their occupations: from societies in which most people were born into their daily work, career path, wealth, and other aspects of life practice and understanding, to those in which people had a lot of choice.[21] If those paths are well-established, and if wealth, rank, and occupation align neatly, as for instance in a caste system,

> the right and duties pertaining to each are well understood and generally beyond doubt and discussion. The ways by which an individual is assigned to and enters a given status are likewise well defined: by descent, sex, social learning, and accomplishments of various kinds, arriving at a certain age, or by certain rites of passage, such as initiation and marriage. In such a case, one would expect – and the evidence on such societies seems to warrant it – that persons of a given status would exhibit a whole complex of social attributes ... unconsciously woven into a seamless garment. Finally, everyone would know exactly who he is. His status identification would be unquestioned by himself or others.[22]

But so perfect an alignment of wealth, rank, and occupation is rare, if not unknown, in human history. Indian caste was complicated and changing, and even in England, in 1583 a writer distinguished the three vectors by complaining that people were wearing fancy fabrics despite being "base by birth, mean by estate and servile by calling."[23] As an ideal type, sociologists say that such a caste system has a "sacred division of labor." ("Sacred" in this sociological sense does not necessarily mean that there is a connection to the divine; rather, "sacred" refers to that which people largely do not question, which they perceive as being just how the world is.[24] I will discuss below how the existence of such a category underlies one kind of **guilty knowledge**.)

The secularization of the division of labor, therefore, refers to the move away from the inheritance of occupation, away from an unquestioned alignment of family standing with a person's proper work. Sociologists link it to societies becoming more complex, but we need not accept a progressive

21   Hughes, "Personality Types," 27, quoting C. C. North, *Social Differentiation* (Chapel Hill: University of North Caroline Press, 1926), 255.
22   Hughes, "Social Change and Status Protest," 173.
23   Philip Stubbes, quoted in Mitchell, "Silk Trades in Restoration London," 188.
24   Hughes, "Personality Types," 27.

model.[25] More Chinese people were legally permitted to choose their occupations under the Song dynasty (960–1279) than under succeeding regimes up to about 1500. Furthermore, within the same society some people may have great freedom in choosing an occupation and others none: the social structure of the USA in the nineteenth-century rested on the labor of enslaved people, for instance. Legal regimes enforcing occupational rigidity for some people were one way that the path into certain occupations was narrowed. Finally, some work is seasonal; that may mean that workers' technique includes bundled skills they use in different seasons, that they shift from one occupation to another over the course of the year, or that they are unemployed in the off-season. The availability of work might fluctuate with weather, or with fashion among consumers. These factors have different implications for their identification with the occupation and their work experiences.

To move from a systemic perspective to one centered on experience, Hughes offered a rough typology of occupations in approximately ascending order of personal choice, training and commitment, and social status. The categories are jobs, trades, arts, enterprises, professions, and missions.[26] This very rough grouping of different occupations may or may not be useful for different historical place-times and certainly cannot be mechanically applied. It will mainly suggest questions, comparisons, and contrasts, perhaps with larger implications.

1. A mission is an occupation to which a person feels "called" or is "converted." S/he feels convinced that s/he has a special place, different from others' in society, perhaps inspired by a communication from a god, but perhaps just a total commitment to a larger cause. It means that the practitioner thinks s/he can save the world or the nation, or save people's souls, lives, or health. The classic example is charismatic religious leaders, but the key thing is that the call is a deep, emotional experience that is unusual and keeps the person committed to the occupation in a way that s/he thinks sets her apart from others. Missions usually have a special language and way of thinking really understood only by the few who have "partaken of the emotional experience common to the group." With so

25 Hughes, "Personality Types," 30. In a secularized division of labor, the work of the parents may still influence the work of the children, but indirectly – an example is that many sons of ministers and rabbis, people who had to understand the dynamics of their congregations, became sociologists. Hughes himself is an example.

26 As late as 1968, the scheme had not been applied. Solomon, "Sociological Perspectives on Occupations," 12.

few colleagues, there may be no **code**. The **missionary** founds his or her identity mainly on the occupation.[27]

2. Hughes went through various stages of thinking about the professions.[28] Were they those that required a long period of training, "prescribed by the occupation itself and sanctioned by the state"? Or, since more and more occupations were claiming the label "profession," was it just a bid for high social status?[29] Since a sociologist's proper technique is to analyze, and not to judge, Hughes decided to use "profession" as a category for occupations that had both **license** and **mandate**, because they were likely to hold **guilty knowledge** and have a long **path into the occupation.**

3. An enterprise possibly makes and definitely sells things: it involves a commodity, something bought and sold. An enterprise *may* involve a sense of mission, for instance selling meditation cushions or medicinal tea that the entrepreneur thinks will save people's health, or make them happy, or save the world. But the entrepreneur must be agile and flexible, unhampered by either a sense of mission or conservative attachments, ready to switch to another commodity. Entrepreneurship may require lots of training – selling machines to a factory, for instance, may require some training as an engineer; and marketing medicines in early modern China required a great deal of technical knowledge about gathering and storing plants.[30] But if the training prevents the entrepreneur from shifting to a new enterprise, then s/he is more like a professional.[31] The entrepreneur's identity may spring less from his/her occupation than from faith, ethnicity, place of origin, family roles, and so on. For the entrepreneur, the object of technique is the market, rather than a particular commodity.

4. "The arts are presumably entered by a combination of a special talent or ability plus a training in a technique," wrote Hughes.[32] This category in particular may not transfer well to all historical societies, in which even the definition of "art" may be unclear. For some art was a calling, for others a business. While nowadays we think of the arts as the epitome of *choosing* an occupation, in the past many people were born into families that specialized in painting or sold into theatre troupes, for instance. Training might come from kinfolk from birth onward, or through apprenticeship,

---

27 Hughes, "Personality Types," 33.

28 For discussion see Hughes, "Work and the Self," 45–46.

29 Hughes, "Personality Types," 33.

30 Bian, *Know Your Remedies*, 137–42. I applied the Hughes framework to Bian's work in Schneewind, "Chinese Physician-Pharmacist."

31 Hughes, "Personality Types," 34.

32 Hughes, "Personality Types," 34.

as well as through paid lessons. Each of these paths might affect a person's relationship to colleagues and clients, the degree of his commitment or devotion to the occupation, and so on.

5. A trade is entered mainly by acquiring a skill through training.[33] Whether a certain technique and object of technique qualify the occupation as an art or a trade is hard to specify. Arts and the trades were distinguished differently in historical times: for instance, workers on medieval cathedrals were in the trades of stonemasonry, glazing, carpentry, and so on, but created what we now view as "art." The path into the occupation might be hereditary, or one might have had a special knack for it to start out with. Being a practitioner of a trade may entail ownership of the means of production – the tools of the trade. Again, the trade may or may not set one's identity and relation with colleagues, etc. Cabinet-maker Peter Korn wrote, "It was not just *making* furniture that I loved, but also *being* a furniture-maker."[34] Davis's participant-observer account of painting Victorian houses in San Francisco describes beautifully how some, but not all, painters identified with the occupation as a mission.[35]

6. Jobs require no training to enter, although one may acquire skills through experience. Hughes says: "The method of acquiring a job of the more casual sort is simply to present one's self at the proper time and place when manpower of a certain age, sex, and perhaps a certain grade of intelligence, is wanted." A certain grade of physical strength, flexibility, or size might also be wanted; only small people can be chimneysweeps, or slide through windows to assist burglars, as Oliver Twist learned. But the point is that getting a job requires no special training, involves no sense of mission, and does not define the person's sense of self. As Bernard Karsh writes, "If [the hourly worker] is to fulfill himself as an individual, he will have to do it on his own time."[36]

This typology will not transfer neatly to all historical place-times, but it highlights some of the aspects of occupations analyzed below. It facilitates a preliminary analytical grouping of occupations that may suggest hypotheses about the transferability of findings from one occupation in a particular place-time to others.

33   Hughes, "Personality Types," 34.
34   Korn, *Why We Make Things*, 45.
35   E. Davis, *Hidden Dimensions*, 141–54.
36   Karsh, "Human Relations versus Management," 44.

Did individuals choose this occupation, or if not, who chose for them?

Were they born into it?

Was work seasonal?

Did it depend on weather? Or social trends?

How did practitioners find employment?

How did they manage unemployment or underemployment?

As a starting point you might question later: into which of the six categories would you place the occupation you are studying? You might ask:

Did practitioners usually belong to a particular gender, ethnicity, or religion?

What role did talent play in selection?

How much training was required?

How far did practitioners travel for work and by what means?

Did they travel alone or with colleagues, coworkers, clients, or family members?

Did entering the occupation require capital?

Did practitioners say they had a calling?

Did they identify chiefly with their occupation or with other aspects of social being?

Did laymen identify practitioners chiefly with the occupation?

Did practitioners rely on their occupation for their whole livelihood or part of it?

Technique and the Body

Technique and object of technique form the foundation for figuring out other aspects of occupations. That does not mean that the historian *first* completes a study of technique: rather, aspects of technique will emerge as the historian investigates other topics. This circular process is desirable, for sociologists and social historians alike study technique to understand culture and social relations, not as an end in itself. For example, the 1961 sociological study of medical school students explains quite a lot about the dissection of corpses, but only to allow the reader to follow the descriptions of how medical students prepared for their examinations: a process that, it turned out, structured the group's interactions and mentality.[37]

Technique and object of technique undergird an occupation's social relations and culture. Their details matter. They may matter even for mere measurement and arithmetic: for instance, some land deeds in China still

37   Becker et al., *Boys in White*, 83–85.

describe amounts of land not in acres, but in terms of how much seed must be used to plant the field or how much human or animal labor power is needed to work it.[38] The details of technique and object of technique matter to the mind: one manager warned participant-observer Bessie McGinnis Van Vorst against requesting handwork over operating a sewing machine, because she would not be able to let her mind wander as she could with the machine.[39] And technique's details matter to the body: different kinds of work produce different muscles, sensitivities, strengths, fatigue, and injuries. Because human bodies have remained relatively similar across time, studies made on recent workers' bodies can be used to hypothesize about how technique affected people in the past, and once one is looking for it, evidence may appear in the primary sources. For instance, R. L. Miller has pointed to ancient Egyptian portrayals of porters stooped under their loads, noting that they may have suffered from swollen abdomens and necks, as well as humped backs. He combines his primary sources with an eighteenth-century Italian work, *De morbis artificum* (Diseases of workers), which talks about the permanently rounded backs of porters, and observations of nineteenth-century London's porters.[40]

An example of the specifics of work linking body and mind involves one of the most common farming tools of the past: the mattock. Archaeologist Alexander Langlands decided to try breaking ground with a mattock and wrote this description.

> Mattocking the ground is a relentless process. Working in three-foot strips, you gradually plod your way up and down the plot. Each clod broken free of the ground is the result of lifting a seven-pound block of iron above your head and bringing it crashing down, shattering the earth beneath your feet. It's not long before your hands are on fire with blisters. The sweat stings into the creases around your eyes and a numb, menacing twinge develops in your lower back. This is a job that tames you. Having started out with all the vigour of youth, boldly hammering away at the ground, you very quickly tire. The swinging motion becomes wilder and less controlled as your muscles weaken. If you're not careful, the mattock will drop short of your target, skid off the surface and swing dangerously

---

38   Szonyi and Zhao, *Chinese Empire in Local Society*, 10.

39   Van Vorst and van Vorst, *The Woman Who Toils*, 111.

40   Miller, "Paleoepidemiology," 7. He cites D. Hunter, *The Diseases of Occupations*, 6th ed. (London: Hodder & Stoughton, 1978) at 11; see 12 for a doctor's examination of porters' bodies and bones published in 1886; and 14 for B. Ramazzini, *Diseases of Workers* (W.C. Wright's translation of *De morbis artificum*, 2nd ed., 1713) (Chicago: University of Chicago Press, 1940).

close to your shins. You stop. Panting, you survey the pitiful results of your power burst ... Gradually, your pace slows and, like a horse brought in from the plains, you are tamed into the work. You resign yourself to it. Your breathing moderates as you become more methodical, more controlled ... Your breaks are regular, but short. You give yourself time to straighten up, stretch your back and clean the blades of the mattock with your raw hands ... My father's mantra – always "let the tool do the work" – rings in my ears whenever I wield a mattock.[41]

Langlands worked alone; Tolstoy gives a vivid portrait of how the details of cutting a field with scythes deeply shaped the workers' shared social experience.[42]

Historians of work should try out the tools their subjects worked with, if possible. Art historian Henry John Drewal wrote that he learned about artistic concepts from a Yoruba artist named Sanusi, in 1965, and an Ilaro mask-maker named Ogundipe, in 1978, not only by listening to and watching them and asking questions, but also by trying to *do* what they were doing. Carving was a "bodily, multi-sensorial experience" that transformed him and his understanding: "Slowly my body learned to carve as my adze-strokes became more precise and effective and the image in my mind took shape through the actions of my body." Historian Mohamed Saliou Camara comments that of course, Drewal's experience differed from that of insiders because of different prior experiences. But, as an outsider, Drewal could better articulate the process of "knowledge transfer, knowledge acquisition, and knowledge codification."[43]

If it is not possible to closely observe or use the tools and techniques we study, historians can practice physical empathy: trying to imagine what it is or was like spending hours at a time reeling silk, for instance, or working in a thundering textile factory. Every aspect of bodily experience also affects the mind and may connect to social interaction: as novelist Daphne du Maurier put it, "There is nothing so defeating to ease of manner as being uncomfortably seated."[44] This exercise applies not only to work that is overtly physical; bodily movement is important for language interpreters, for example. In some clearly tiring work, the practitioner may have the ability to control his own timing, whereas an interpreter, although the motions

41 Langlands, *Cræft*, 300–301.
42 Tolstoy, *Anna Karenina*, chapter 4, 268–71.
43 Camara, *Is There a Distinctively African Way of Knowing*, 51–52.
44 Du Maurier, *My Cousin Rachel*, 73.

themselves are gentler, may be at the mercy of the speakers' choices about time, and have no chance to take a break. Since our historical subjects worked with their bodies, we need to think with our bodies.

> Be thinking about which aspects of technique you will explain to your reader.
> Do the historical sources yield or hint at details of the physical side of technique?
> Could you observe comparable tasks or read about them for other place-times?
> Could you learn to use the tools of the trade?
> How will you best convey to readers the physical aspects of technique?
> How much room for creativity lay within simple tasks?
> How much attention did technique require?
> If practitioners used machines, did that require more or less mental attention than handwork?
> What was the relation of technique to time?
> Did the work require a particular posture?
> What muscles and senses did technique require?
> Did the work entail sounds, smells, tastes, temperatures, or other physical feelings?
> How might technique have affected practitioners' bodies?

Workshop, Body, Self

Some effects on bodies seem simple. There are injuries, which can be traced in surprising sources: Miller found illustrations in ancient Egyptian murals of dislocated shoulders, eye injuries, a mallet dropped on a foot, and so on, as well as depictions of how some injuries were treated. From a literary genre known as "satire on trades," he also learned about how "jewellers and wall builders have cramped arms and aching joints, weavers spend their time in a darkened workshop squatting with their knees against their belly, [and] tenant farmers and messengers are worn out with long journeys."[45] He went on to compare these comments with studies of living or recently dead workers. Workers' ailments, such the gardener's humped back, were portrayed in Egyptian tomb reliefs to add verisimilitude, he argues.[46] June Nash wrote about the incredible din in the assembly room in the automobile factory she studied and the distance between the working spaces and the

---

45   Miller, "Paleoepidemiology," 14.
46   Miller, "Paleoepidemiology," 7–8; the account of a hump-backed gardener operating a well-sweep is at 10.

cafeteria. The first caused hearing loss and the second, given the very short lunch break, caused accidents when workers ran.[47] Noise and short lunch breaks crop up again and again in Van Vorst's participant study; hands are cut and ruined; lint and bronze dust settle in lungs, and sewing harms vision.[48]

But some effects might be difficult to predict. Many workers across time have had severely limited diets, and at a certain level historians can measure misery and suffering by calorie intake.[49] Calories do not tell the whole story, however. What people wanted to eat varied, and was not the same as what they got to eat; nor were their food desires independent of technique. Van Vorst observed that the very fatigue of non-stop factory work

> steals the appetite. I can hardly taste what I put in my mouth; the food sticks in my throat. The girls who complain most of being tired are the one who roll up their newspaper bundles [of lunch] half full ... I did not want wholesome food, exhausted as I was. I craved sours and sweets, pickles, cake, anything to excite my numb taste.[50]

The physical effects of the workshop environment and the requirements of technique changed bodies and desires.

Work environments produce work culture. Noise led cotton-mill workers in North Carolina, desperate to communicate with one another above the din, to develop a semaphore language, speaking to one another by hand and body signs: a striking example of occupational culture. A former jazz musician told fellow musician and sociologist Howard Becker:

> I'm telling you, musicians are different than other people. They talk different, they act different, they look different ... Musicians live an exotic life, like in a jungle or something. They start out, they're just ordinary kids from small towns – but once they get into that life they change ... You live that kind of life long enough, you just get to be completely different.[51]

What changed them? The inverted working hours and the occupational culture (see below), to be sure, but the physical workshop also contributed to the sense of difference.

---

47   Nash, "Anthropology of Work," 53. Solution: they carpooled to work and talked then.
48   Van Vorst and van Vorst, *The Woman Who Toils*, 41 and 141 (hands), 136 (bronze dust), 75 (eyeglasses).
49   See for instance, Miller, "Paleoepidemiology," 5.
50   Van Vorst and van Vorst, *The Woman Who Toils*, 40.
51   Becker, "Dance Musician," 137.

Being on stage removed musicians from conventional morality and from their conventional identities. A musician who identified himself as Jewish said,

> When you sit up on that stand up there, you feel so different from others. Like I can even understand how Gentiles feel toward Jews. You see these people come up and they look Jewish, ... and they ask for a rumba or some damn thing like that, and I just feel, "What damn squares, these Jews," just like I was a *goy* myself. That's what I mean when I say you learn too much from being a musician. I mean you see so many things and get such a broad outlook on life that the average person just doesn't have.[52]

The physical removal from laypeople created an objectivity that is the heart of **guilty knowledge**. Work culture develops based on technique; relations with clients, colleagues, and laypeople; and the workshop space. In turn, occupational culture shapes practitioners' selves.

The workshop, technique, object of technique, and tools of an occupation form the groundwork of analysis. Some aspects of technique may necessarily be common to occupational culture across different place-times, so that (for instance) carpenters from eighteenth-century France and second-century China might share not only the physical aspects of their work but also work relations. In other cases, technique may vary dramatically from one place-time to another, and work relations with it.

How did colleagues talk about technique and object of technique?
What effects did technique have on the practitioner's body?
How did workers or healers manage harm to the body?
Did practitioners get enough to eat? Did they eat differently from laymen?
What physical effects did the work environment have?
Who determined the layout of the workspace?
How was the workshop laid out?
Were there shared leisure spaces within the work compound?
Where there rest or meal breaks, and if so, when?
Were workers separated from others by barriers, sound, equipment, or in other ways?
How did that separation affect their relation with coworkers? With clients?
Did separation change workers' relation to laymen or the wider culture?

---

52 Becker, "Dance Musician," 143.

Works Cited

Applebaum, Herbert, ed. *Work in Non-market and Transitional Societies.* Albany: SUNY Press, 1984.

Bearman, Peter. *Doormen.* Chicago: University of Chicago Press, 2005.

Becker, Howard S. "The Professional Dance Musician and His Audience." *American Journal of Sociology* 57, no. 2 (1951): 136–44.

Becker, Howard S., Blanche Geer, Everett C. Hughes, and Anselm L. Strauss. *Boys in White: Student Culture in Medical School.* Chicago: University of Chicago Press, 1961.

Bian, He. *Know Your Remedies: Pharmacy and Culture in Early Modern China.* Princeton: Princeton University Press, 2020.

Camara, Mohamed Saliou. *Is There a Distinctively African Way of Knowing (a Study of African Blacksmiths, Hunters, Healers, Griots, Elders, and Artists): Knowing and Theory of Knowledge in the African Experience.* Lewiston: Edwin Mellen Press, 2014.

Carter, Ron. "At 85, Legendary Jazz Bassist Ron Carter is Still Going Strong." Interview by Celeste Headlee. *NPR Illinois*, August 19, 2002. https://www.nprillinois.org/2022-08-19/at-85-legendary-jazz-bassist-ron-carter-is-still-going-strong

Davis, Edward B. *Hidden Dimensions of Work: Revisiting the Chicago School Methods of Everett Hughes and Anselm Strauss.* N.p.: Xlibris Books, 2011.

du Maurier, Daphne. *My Cousin Rachel.* London: Penguin, 1962.

Ehmer, Josef. "Work, History of." In *International Encyclopedia of the Social and Behavioral Sciences*, vol. 24, 16569–74. London: Elsevier, 2001.

Erasmus, Charles J. "Work Patterns in a Mayo Village." In *Work in Non-market and Transitional Societies*, edited by Herbert Applebaum, 168–79. Albany: SUNY Press, 1984.

Hughes, Everett C. "Personality Types and the Division of Labor." In *Men and Their Work*, 23–41. Glencoe, IL: The Free Press, 1958.

Hughes, Everett C. "Social Change and Status Protest: An Essay on the Marginal Man." In *On Work, Race and the Sociological Imagination*, edited by Lewis Coser, 171–79. Chicago: University of Chicago Press, 1994.

Hughes, Everett C. "The Study of Occupations." In *On Work, Race and the Sociological Imagination*, edited by Lewis Coser, 21–36. Chicago: University of Chicago Press, 1994.

Hughes, Everett C. "Work and the Self." In *Men and Their Work*, 42–55. Glencoe, IL: The Free Press, 1958.

Karsh, Bernard. "Human Relations versus Management." In *Institutions and the Person: Festschrift in Honor of Everett C. Hughes*, edited by Howard S. Becker, Blanche Geer, David Riesman, and Robert S. Weiss, 35–48. Chicago: Aldine, 1968.

Ko, Dorothy. *The Social Life of Inkstones: Artisans and Scholars in Early Qing China.*
    Seattle: University of Washington Press, 2017.

Korn, Peter. *Why We Make Things and Why It Matters: The Education of a Craftsman.*
    Boston: David R. Godine, 2013.

Langlands, Alexander. *Cræft: An Inquiry into the Origins and True Meaning of
    Traditional Crafts.* New York: W. W. Norton, 2017.

Miller, R. L. "Paleoepidemiology, Literacy, and Medical Tradition among Necropolis
    Workmen in New Kingdom Egypt." *Medical History* 35 (1991): 1–24

Mitchell, David. "'What d'ye Lack Ladies? Hoods, Ribands, Very Fine Silk Stockings':
    The Silk Trades in Restoration London." In *Threads of Global Desire: Silk in the
    Pre-Modern World,* edited by Dagmar Schäfer, Giorgio Riello, and Luca Molà,
    vol. 1, 187–222. Woodbridge: Boydell Press, 2018.

Misra, P. K. "The Gadulia Lohars: Nomadism and Blacksmithy." In *Work in Non-
    market and Transitional Societies,* edited by Herbert Applebaum, 127-33. Albany:
    SUNY Press, 1984.

Mocarrelli, Luca. "Attitudes to Work and Commerce in the Late Italian Renaissance:
    A Comparison between Tomaso Garzoni's *La Piazza Universale* and Leondardo
    Fioravanti's *Dello Specchio Di Scientia Universale.*" *International Review of Social
    History Special Issue* 56 (2011): 89–106.

Muscolino, Micah. *Fishing Wars and Environmental Change in Late Imperial and
    Modern China.* Cambridge, MA: Harvard University Asia Center, 2009.

Nash, June. "The Anthropology of Work." In *Work in Non-market and Transitional
    Societies,* edited by Herbert Applebaum, 45–55. Albany: SUNY Press, 1984.

Schneewind, Sarah. "The Work of the Chinese Physician-Pharmacist in He Bian's
    Know Your Remedies." *Pharmacy in History* 62, nos. 2–4 (2020): 168–80.

Scott, Sir Walter. *The Talisman.* London: Thomas Nelson and Sons, 1825.

Solomon, David N. "Sociological Perspectives on Occupations." In *Institutions and
    the Person: Festschrift in Honor of Everett C. Hughes,* edited by Howard S. Becker,
    Blanche Geer, David Riesman, and Robert S. Weiss, 3–13. Chicago: Aldine, 1968.

Sonenscher, Michael. "Mythical Work: Workshop Production and the *Compagnon-
    nages* of Eighteenth-Century France." In *The Historical Meanings of Work,* edited
    by Patrick Joyce, 31–63. Cambridge: Cambridge University Press, 1987.

Szonyi, Michael, and Shiyu Zhao. *The Chinese Empire in Local Society: Ming Military
    Institutions and Their Legacies.* Abingdon: Taylor & Francis, 2020.

Thomas, Keith, ed. *The Oxford Book of Work.* Oxford: Oxford University Press, 1999.

Tolstoy, Leo. *Anna Karenina.* Translated by Constance Garnett. N.p.: Quality
    Paperbacks, 1991.

Tomczik, Adam. "'He-Men Could Talk to He-Men in He-Man Language': Lumberjack
    Work Culture in Maine and Minnesota, 1840–1940." *The Historian* 70, no. 4
    (2008): 697–715.

van Vorst, Mrs. John, and Marie van Vorst. *The Woman Who Toils: Being the Experiences of Two Ladies as Factory Girls*. 1902, 1903; facsimile reprint Carlisle, MA: Applewood Books, n.d.

Zhang Kan. "The Evolution of Temples in Jinxiang Guard and the Localization of State Institutions." In *The Chinese Empire in Local Society: Ming Military Institutions and Their Legacies*, edited by Michael Szonyi and Shiyu Zhao, chapter 4. Abingdon: Taylor & Francis, 2020.

II. The Players in the Social Drama of Work

Abstract

Historians studying work as culture could work comparatively if they shared theoretical framework and vocabulary for what sociologists have dubbed "the social drama of work." The actors include the practitioner of the occupation; clients who consume products or services; colleagues in the same occupation; coworkers in the same workshop; and laypeople, or other members of society. Persons in these roles learn how to express and negotiate the particular aspects of trust and distrust, conflict and cooperation, communication and miscommunication that arise from technique and object of technique. As practitioners move from apprentice to master in the hierarchy of the occupation, they learn both technique and the culture of the occupation: their proper place in the social drama of work.

Keywords: social conflict, daily work, apprentice, teamwork, hierarchy, pace

If occupations comprised no more than technique, studying them would not illuminate society much. But work is inherently social. The occupation is not merely the technique, but relations with clients, colleagues, and laypeople, which generate culture. Since the 1980s, historians have been studying work as culture, focusing on daily relations in the workshop, as well as the symbolic and ritual resolutions and containments of conflicts at work.[1] Sociology offers a consistent vocabulary for discussing such topics.

The occupational sociologists watched what people did as they competed and fought, cooperated and accommodated at work in an effort to "arrive at

[1] Ehmer, "Work, History of," 16573.

Schneewind, S.K. *The Social Drama of Daily Work. A Manual for Historians.* Amsterdam: Amsterdam University Press, 2024
DOI: 10.5117/9789048559534_CH02

a livable human order."[2] Hughes dubbed this **"the social drama of work"**: a drama that plays out among four overlapping groups of actors, with other organizations from the state on down taking a role and the rest of society as a boisterous audience. These neutral terms put study of all occupations, from food server to lawyer to emperor, on an equal playing ground:

> 1. The practitioner is a member of an occupation, who makes a living through its technique.
> 2. The client hires or owns the practitioner or consumes the product or service.
> 3. Colleagues are fellow members of an occupation, but not necessarily in the same workshop.
> 4. Coworkers work in the same workshop, whether or not in the same occupation.
> 5. Laypeople are other members of society, those outside of the occupation.

While the practitioner is the center of study, for the history of work to illumine society and culture, it must focus on social relations. Social roles shape one another in a "mutual dance"; as sociologist Peter Bearman puts it, "Doormen help teach tenants how to be tenants, while at the same time tenants help teach doormen how to be doormen for them."[3] Let's consider the players in a little more detail.

Clients

Many of the insights this manual explains relate to practitioner–client relations, directly or indirectly. Clients take in the goods and services that constitute practitioners' output. The practitioners' producing activities can continue only if someone wants the output and carries on what sociologist Louis Kriesberg called "paying or contributing activities" to get it.[4] Historians should be flexible in looking for and studying clients. If exchanges of "gifts" created by experts in a certain occupation are quantified and contribute to livelihoods, then we can consider their consumers clients for the purpose of asking research questions. But when much of the output is consumed by the practitioners themselves – as with farming families or

2   Coser, "Introduction," 14.
3   Bearman, *Doormen*, 103.
4   Kriesberg, "Internal Differentiation," 142–43.

monasteries – we should not equate consumers with clients. Not every occupation necessarily has a client, or one might say that not every technique in an occupation serves a client; the "purest" scientists, for instance, may serve knowledge and seek to convince colleagues, not clients.[5]

The client may not be obvious. For the twentieth-century United States, Hughes asked whether the client of a schoolteacher was "the child, the parent, the community at large, or some class of people within it."[6] One might assume that the healer's client is the patient. But if the healer's technique includes the diagnosis and curing of illness, the patient is the object of technique; and often not the patient in his or her full humanity (not, for instance, religious beliefs or emotions), but the human body: that is what it is the business of the doctor to understand and manipulate.[7] For medical specialists, the object of technique may not even be the whole human body, but only the skin, the digestion, or a particular disease. Nor is the patient necessarily the client. The client of a Ming elite male physician was probably not the female patient but her husband, and what she wanted may not have mattered to the doctor; but a Ming female healer probably had the elite wife herself as her client.[8] Trying to specify the client is a revealing exercise in beginning to understand a particular occupation's social drama of work.

Relations between practitioners and clients may be quite different in nearby places at the same time. For instance, sociologist Philippe Vienne writes that

> in the medieval Parisian mode of universities the authority is detained by the masters on their "clients," and in the Bologna mode, it is the student who has authority (through the corporation of students) and hires the service of the doctors, and evaluates them and "masters" also. From each side of the frontier, colleagues and students had a "view" of the other, and you can see the Bologna doctors regretting the power that their Parisian colleagues could exercise over their students.[9]

In the two cities at the same time, quite different power relations developed between teachers and students. But since occupational culture develops among colleagues and other players in the social drama of work as a daily social process, it may vary by city or even by workshop.

5   Hughes, "Psychology: Science and/or Profession."
6   Hughes, "Professions," 664.
7   Hughes, "Personality Types," 35.
8   Chen, "Medical Treatment of Women."
9   Philippe Vienne, personal communication, August 2021.

Just as wages are not the only thing practitioners earn by working, so details reveal that money was no universal solvent. Practitioners may reject clients as well as the other way around; for example, fancy shops may discourage people of color, no matter how wealthy, and universities long rejected women as clients. Even beyond such category-based discrimination, Howard Becker comments that there are "good" clients and "bad" clients, reflecting not the color of their money, but "differences in the way people in various segments of the society learn to play the role of client."[10] Fancy shops may reject the shabbily dressed, without knowing what's in her wallet. As Hughes notes, even as commercialization proceeds, "it is very difficult to keep money exchanges free of other kinds" of exchange, and this plays out in social relations with clients, colleagues, bosses, and laypeople.[11] The monetary interaction does not eliminate human feeling about those we work for and with.

By the same token, in less-commercialized economies, identifying practitioner and client may be difficult. Communal work played a larger role and work relationships overlapped more fully with other social relationships. Brothers-in-law among Trobriand islanders in the early twentieth century, by cultural norm, exchanged half of the produce from their respective gardens.[12] Anthropologists have identified "a sense of mutuality" among families and individuals, and between men and women in their gendered work roles as arising from such arrangements. But as the term "prestige economy" suggests, even when work or produce is exchanged rather than recompensed with cash, it may still be quantified.[13] Historians can inquire into the social drama of work even for less-commercial societies and situations of communal work.

Who consumed the goods and services?
Who paid or contributed to keep the workshop or practitioner going?
Was the immediate client the ultimate consumer or an intermediary?
If there was a human object of technique, was s/he the one who paid the practitioner and gave instructions?
Were transactions highly public, open, private, or covert?
How did clients find practitioners?
Did clients seek out practitioners or vice versa?
What characteristics might lead a practitioner to reject a client?

10   Becker, "Role and Career Problems," 42.
11   Hughes, "Study of Occupations," 24.
12   Applebaum, *Work in Non-market and Transitional Societies*, 3–4.
13   The term occurs, for instance, in Suttles, "Coping with Abundance," 110.

Was competition for clients publicized (through advertising, for instance), open, private, or covert?
Did practitioners share output with others rather than selling it all?
Were such non-cash exchanges quantified?
How did colleagues talk about clients?

Colleagues

Colleagues are workers in the same occupation. They or may not share a specific workshop. They often compete with one another for clients. But that competition coexists with deep mutual understanding and deep similarities. The sociologists found that colleagues share not only technique but also a view of their objects of technique, clients, and themselves. I explain below how those occupational views may develop in response to, as David Solomon puts it, "aspects of work, or of work situations [that] are experienced as threatening the sense of dignity or prestige of the workers or ... problems of power."[14]

Together, colleagues create **code** and **policy** to spread out the shared risk of **mistakes at work;** make claims on society to **license** and **mandate**; experience some tasks as **dirty work** and figure out how to manage that; and develop **symbols of distinction** and other ways to handle the **guilty knowledge** with which society entrusts them. Together, colleagues tread and shape **the path into the occupation,** and their daily interactions manifest **the hierarchy within the occupation**. All of these aspects constitute **the culture of the occupation,** embedded in and affecting the wider culture of the place-time. In some occupations, especially those that demand a long period of training, the culture and technique, the skills and the etiquette, the way of doing things, are so deeply engrained in the individual workers that they come to seem like personal traits, even if paths into the occupation varied. For instance, a priest is never really off-duty; same with some professors.[15] At the opposite end of the pay scale, one sociologist studying waitresses found that even though the work is taken up casually – it is

---

14   Solomon, "Sociological Perspectives on Occupations," 9.
15   Sociologist Irving Louis Horowitz posed the question "How many hours a day?" to distinguish three points along a spectrum running from practitioners who restrain their working thoughts to eight hours, to sixteen-hours-a-day practitioners who tend to look at the whole world in professional terms, but also have wider concerns, to 24-hour-a-day practitioners whose work invades not only their time, but their whole attitude to the world, their "reflexes and dreams." Becker, "Professional Sociology," 177, 180.

a job – waitresses in the early twentieth century lived together so much that they came to share "a language and a set of social attitudes peculiar to themselves, individualistic though they be."[16]

The shared culture of practitioners within one occupation is the fundamental object of study in the sociology of work.

Where did the work take place?

Did practitioners compete for clients?

Did brokers mediate competition among colleagues?

What goods or services did the workshop produce as output?

What goods or services supported practitioners' ostensible work? Who did those supporting activities?

Did colleagues cluster together, or work and sell far apart?

Did colleagues share personality traits either before or after joining the occupation?

What risks did practitioners face?

Did technique require trust to manage physical or other dangers?

Did technique require teamwork?

Did practitioners in teams work on the object of technique at the same time or in sequence?

Coworkers

Most human endeavors rely on a group of occupations in the same workshop, not just one. As *Boys in White*, an extended study of the path into the occupation, points out: "Physicians find themselves working with registered nurses, practical nurses, aides and maids, and with several kinds of technicians and therapists, not to mention accountants, personnel [staff], and administrators."[17] Relations among such coworkers may be particularly intense, and where the lines are drawn between occupations is contested and changes over time. The most basic division within an organization is between "direct producing activities" and "supporting activities." Direct producing activities include potters shaping vessels, nurses dispensing pills to heal patients, and professors teaching.[18] Supporting activities include serving

16   Hughes, "Personality Types," 36, citing Frances R. Donovan, *The Woman Who Waits* (Badger: Boston, 1920), 128.

17   Becker et al., *Boys in White*, 8.

18   Kriesberg, "Internal Differentiation," 141.

or advising the producers and maintaining or supplying the material used in production: porters haul prepared clay to the potters' wheels, orderlies bring nurses the pill bottles, and staff clean whiteboards and deal with problems connecting laptops in classrooms.

Policy focuses on direct producing activities, and historians may follow its lead. But sailors in the US Navy in the 1960s cared more about getting their ship safely through a mission than about achieving the mission itself; their **code** focused on that.[19] Supporting activities often take up a great proportion of space and labor. For instance, historian Anne Gerritsen's study of the imperial porcelain manufactory at Jingdezhen in the fifteenth and sixteenth centuries shows that the largest workshop, the greatest number of kilns and workers, and large quantities of clay and fuel were allocated to the production of kiln furniture called saggars – coarse clay vessels that protected the porcelain vessels from the flames and kept them from fusing with one another inside the kilns. The saggars were absolutely necessary, yet they were disposable and rarely appear in the many illustrations of the porcelain process that were popular in both Europe and China in the eighteenth and nineteenth centuries.[20] The many tools used in the manufactory – made of wood, bamboo, metal, stone, and porcelain – were also made on-site, taking up more space and requiring more workers.[21] Those who shaped the imperial porcelains were outnumbered by their coworkers with other technique, yet the more numerous workers had escaped scholarly attention. Reading between the lines to understand work life includes thinking about who is doing the supporting activities, and *their* technique, object of technique, and all the rest, as Gerritsen did.

Relations among coworkers, including those who are also colleagues, exhibit cooperation and amiability, competition and distrust. Emotions may affect work arrangements; or it may be that work arrangements of long standing culturally shape emotions. Farmwork, for instance, may be done alone or with colleagues, creating a different emotional experience. While many historical farming communities cooperate in harvest, building, or other activities requiring a lot of labor power at a particular time, Kapauku farmers in New Guinea in the 1950s worked on their own land, by themselves. They did not trust coworkers, fearing that they would lose credit for work they had done. They worked with such concentration that in wartime they were easy targets for snipers, so they sometimes arranged for a young son or

19 Zurcher, "The Sailor Aboard," 390.
20 Gerritsen, *City of Blue and White*, 144–45.
21 Gerritsen, *City of Blue and White*, 158–59.

Figure 1a. Cameleteer   Figure 1b. Lion-tamers

Source: *Gansu zhen zhanshou tulue.* ©National Palace Museum. Used by permission.[23]

daughter to stand guard. Their habit of self-reliance meant that when hiring or being hired, the unit was the task to be done, not the length of time.[22] Whether the practice of working alone or the cultural trait of distrust of others came first would be a question for a historian; either way it had an impact on structures of remuneration.

Dangerous occupations require a high degree of trust among coworkers. Coworkers may hold each other's lives in their hands. For instance, images from a Ming map of its western province show cameleteers alone with camels, but lions with two handlers (Figure 1).[23] The cameleteer can manage this famously cantankerous animal on his own; managing a lion requires two people. If the lion bounds in one direction with murderous intent, the other lion-tamer can yank on the chain; if the lion gets annoyed and bounds towards him, his partner will pull the lion back again. One person could not do this job, and each practitioner needs full confidence in the colleague and coworker's strength, agility, and vigilance. The historian could guess, and then look for confirmation in written sources, that partnerships, once formed, were long-lasting – that the boss did not switch practitioners in and out of teams unless s/he suspected bad feeling between partners, which could be fatal. Technique must have affected relations between coworkers and thus the broader occupational culture of lion-tamers.

Most occupations lie between the extremes of working entirely alone and the absolute requirement for close teamwork. In most workshops, from universities to factories to homes, some cooperation is required. For instance, the blacksmiths shown at the lower right of Figure 2 include one young person working the bellows for the firebox, one old man holding the hot iron in place on the forge with tongs and indicating where the next blow should come with a wooden mallet, and two large young men

22   Pospisil, "Organization of Labor among the Kapauku," 181.
23   Thanks to Qiu Yihao for this source.

Figure 2. Workers of various trades: sawyers, bricklayers, blacksmiths, and long-gowned official supervisors. *Chui dian baigong tu* 垂典百工圖 [Illustrations for handing down the methods of the hundred trades]. In Sun Jia'nai 孫家鼐, Li Xisheng 李希聖, Zhan Xiulin 詹秀林 and Zhan Bukui 詹步魁, *Qinding Shujing tushuo* 欽定書經圖說 [Imperially endorsed illustrations and explanations of the *Book of Documents*] ([Beijing 北京]: [Neifu 內府], 1905) 2/33a. Reproduced with permission of Staatsbibliothek zu Berlin – Preußischer Kulturbesitz, Germany.

hitting that spot in turn. They wear heavy leather aprons to protect them from flying sparks. On the left are two sawyers working together pushing and pulling one saw; two porters with a load of bricks; and two masons, one shoveling mortar onto the wall and one smoothing it before placing the next brick.

Cooperation within the workshop may be simultaneous or sequential. Shoddy work by one practitioner affects others: a poorly stitched cotton sole will impinge on the task and pride of the woman affixing the upper; mistakes in registration will upset the size of a class and thus the professor's assignment structure. Since coworkers are stuck with one another, sociologist Edward Davis dubs such problems of shoddiness "situational work blockages." He differentiates these from "interactional work blockages" that stem from personality clashes or workers being spatially separated, either of which can weaken communication enough to damage work output. The third type is "structural work blockages," which result when an organization allocates resources unwisely or fosters internal political battles that hinder workers.[24] All these blockages could be examined from the perspective of the institution. But they also both stem from and cause conflicts among practitioners and lead coworkers to develop workarounds or "secondary adjustments" that rely on new forms of cooperation.[25]

Conflict and cooperation involve emotional and social developments that affect both production and the work culture of the occupation.

Who owned or controlled the object of technique?
Did practitioners who owned land (or another object of technique) sometimes work on neighbors' land instead?
How voluntary was such work exchange?
Who exchanged work?
What emotions surrounded work exchange and what cultural form did they take?
How was interdependence of work roles by age or gender recognized?
Did coworkers cooperate simultaneously (teamwork) or sequentially (shift work)?
If some coworkers supported the work of others, whose technique was more dangerous?
Whose work appears more prominently in texts, images, or analysis?
Did the quality or quantity of one practitioner's work affect others' work?

24   E. Davis, *Hidden Dimensions*, 116–17.
25   E. Davis, *Hidden Dimensions*, 113–19.

Can delays in production be traced back to conflicts among coworkers or separation in the workspace?

What support did the direct producers require?

Were supporting items produced on-site or acquired from outside?

How did management coordinate producing and supporting activities?

How did management mediate relations with the outside?

Did different people produce, support, and manage?

What about the Boss?

It took me a while to understand why the sociology of work does not include systematic theory about the boss. I think the reason is that there are so many kinds of bosses. It is not always clear to workers whom to treat as the boss. For instance, even though it was the building superintendent who hired and fired the doorman, on a daily, hourly basis the doorman answered more to the tenants. One doorman said, "I'm the middle-man; [a tenant] wanted to see the supervisor and I had to call him regardless of whether the super wants to be bothered or not ... And, actually, he is my boss, but actually the tenant is bigger boss because this is a co-op and the tenants own the place. And who is stuck in the middle?" Many doormen who have held their positions for a long time (not only in cooperative buildings) say that "they have hundreds of bosses, and that the super is just one of them."[26] There are different, coexisting sorts of bosses, and therefore they do not have one clear role in the social drama of work.

Sometimes, the ultimate boss is the state, or a lesser political power such as a lord. Work relations in such cases are affected by the state's violent and legal power over all subjects. Working for the state could drain a practitioner's time and damage his or her income. In those cases, practitioners with more social resources might attempt to hire or suborn colleagues to substitute for them. But working for the state might also be a stamp of approval that enabled practitioners to gain additional clients. One historian of early modern England has pointed out that expertise – the practitioner's mastery of technique – is both "possessed" and "controlled." Only the practitioner possesses her skills, but she may temporarily transfer control of her expertise to a patron, such as a lord or the state, or such a power may co-opt that expertise.[27]

---

26 Bearman, *Doormen*, 131, 137, 202.
27 Ash, "Expertise and the Early Modern State," 5.

Some bosses are managers, pure and simple. Their chief object of technique is the worker. Such managers may extend control to workers' personal lives,[28] while not knowing how to do the direct producing activities; examples include Chinese imperial civil officials managing state-run artisanal/industrial production and twentieth-century managers in the USA, who took inspiration from Frederick W. Taylor's *Principles of Scientific Management*, published in 1911. Just as civil officials thought themselves best educated to manage others, so Taylorites held that someone other than the blue-collar worker could best plan efficient workflow.[29] But sometimes, the "boss" is the client: that is, he is paying the practitioner for goods or services and is not part of the same institution. Or the boss may be the ship's captain with absolute authority, or the plantation overseer with his whip. Bosses vary so widely that productive questions should focus on precise roles within the workshop.[30] Who answers to whom, and in what circumstances? What powers does each player have?

Whether overseer, manager, or client, the boss's demands may encroach insultingly on practitioners' sense of their own expertise, as we will see below in the discussion of license and mandate. While in twentieth-century North America many workers had the right to choose or leave a job and the right to legal protection against abuse from their superiors, historically this was not so for most workers. Enslaved people endure physical violence, sexual violation, family separation, and other terrible experiences, but in some place-times some enslaved people became expert practitioners in a craft or service field, or even served as stewards managing estates. Enslaved practitioners, in addition to their other woes, may also have faced particularly sharp practitioner–client tensions. Privately owned acting troupes in Ming China, for instance, not only entertained the master and his friends and sometimes had to have sex with them, but sometimes had to submit to being directed, even "trained," by the master, who did not share their skills but wanted to think he did.[31] Their **status pain** must have been intense.

Some bosses, however, are colleagues: they are in the same occupation, with the same technique, but with the additional duty of managing the flow of information and making decisions about when to convert information into action.[32] As superiors in the hierarchy of the occupation, they also

28   Van Vorst and van Vorst, *The Woman Who Toils*, 92.

29   Karsh, "Human Relations versus Management," 35–37.

30   As suggested by Bernard Lahire's discussion of Norbert Elias and his use of habitus in "Elias, Freud, and the Human Science."

31   Shen, "Private Theatre of the Ming Dynasty."

32   On the flow of information see E. Davis, *Hidden Dimensions*, 138.

supervise or manage junior colleagues. Some are more like coworkers, in that they are part of the same institution, with the tasks of managing other workers within it. Expectations of such superior coworkers, even if they are called "boss," are like the expectations of other coworkers or colleagues.

For instance, in 1952 Becker reported that, on one hand, a Chicago schoolteacher said:

> After all, he's the principal, he is the boss, what he says should go, you know what I mean. ... He's the principal and he's the authority, and you have to follow his orders. That's all there is to it.[33]

On the other hand, whenever a teacher faced "interference" from a parent (who might be either the client or the parent of the client), she expected the principal to stand with her. Teachers considered one principal bad precisely because "she really can't be counted on to back you up against a child or a parent."[34] A good principal, on the other hand, according to teachers, would even lie if necessary to support a teacher against a parent, even if he later disciplined the teacher without telling the parents, and would be happy to be feared by the young clients in the interests of supporting teacher authority and keeping classrooms orderly. This is the same kind of backing that teachers expected of one another: they reported that "no teacher should ever disagree with another teacher or contradict her, in front of a pupil ... [not even] raise her eyebrow funny."[35] This is **code**, extended up the hierarchy within the occupation to the principal.

Becker concluded that in the small realm of social control that was a school, the principal and the teachers could all control one another to some degree, creating stability.[36] Regulating workflow and coordinating production and supporting activities – that is, the tasks of management – may not be carried out by a boss. Rather, we might add to bundled technique the part of work that involves communicating with coworkers, including both colleagues and coworkers in different occupations but the same organization or workshop. Communication among coworkers is necessary for effective teamwork; if they speak different languages, coordination may be hindered. Beyond speech, writing, gesture, and song have all been used to coordinate activities in the workshop. Tensions are inevitable, but smooth coordination strengthens

33 Becker, "The Teacher in the Authority System," 133.
34 Becker, "The Teacher in the Authority System," 134.
35 Becker, "The Teacher in the Authority System," 134–35, 139.
36 Becker, "The Teacher in the Authority System," 140.

espirit d'corps, and vice versa. For risky occupations, where coordination had to be smooth, the person deciding whom to hire might require the consent of all team members. Loggers in British Columbia in the early twentieth century could veto hiring decisions made by the company owner when it came to those who coordinated the lifting of enormous logs by means of whistles.[37]

Further, supervision by a higher-ranking figure may not be about control; as depicted for winemaking on a Cypriot pottery vessel from about 2000 BC, colleagues, the wider community, or authority figures observed significant stages of production processes ritually, to honor the process, rather than to manage it.[38] The specific details in any given workshop and occupation will therefore reveal more about the pleasure, pride, tension, and conflict of the practitioners than simply being able to identify the boss.

Whom did practitioners, or coworkers within in one workspace, call "the boss"?
Did the state or another authority assign families or individuals to the occupation?
Could practitioners fulfill obligations to the authority by hiring substitutes?
Were obligations full-time or part-time?
Did the authority's designation allow practitioners to gain additional clients?
If the boss was a manager, who was his/her client (the state, investors)?
Did work groups cohere to oppose or to obey the manager?
Did the boss understand technique?
What did practitioners expect of their superior(s) in the workspace?
Who assigned tasks and who got credit for the work of assigning tasks?
How did coworkers coordinate their work actions?
Did they all speak the same language or technical language?
Did they sing? If so, did work songs arise among practitioners?

Hierarchy within the Occupation

Colleagues and coworkers are not necessarily equals, even if they share code, policy, and other aspects of work culture discussed below. First, individuals vary. Different individuals in the exact same occupation may stand higher or lower in their own eyes and those of others based on experience and ability. Even the lowly pathologist's diener, charged with the dirty work of handling dead bodies, could be either a star who had won recognition and a decent

---

37   Letter from Everett Hughes to Edward B. Davis, quoted in E. Davis, *Hidden Dimensions*, 95.
38   Karageorghis, *Everyday Life in Ancient Cyprus*, 12.

salary and was at home in his professional identity, or a despised or invisible practitioner who, for that very reason, according to a participant-observer, had more freedom in his attire and lifestyle.[39]

But second and more systematically, the path into the occupation may affect hierarchy within the occupation. In the mid-twentieth century US, nurses who went to university looked down on those who had not. In Ming times, a county magistrate who had passed the highest level of the civil service examinations had more prestige and authority than a county magistrate appointed with only a provincial degree or lower. The precise path into an occupation mattered for authority and image within the occupation and might well affect collegial relations in other ways, too. Enlisted men and officers in the US Navy in the 1960s, for instance, wore different uniforms and ate and slept separately, and the enlisted men had plenty to say about their superiors: "They don't say 'officers and men' for nothing!" and "You're worse than that! You're officer material!"[40] Indeed, who eats with whom and who controls mealtimes are key questions in establishing the elements of hierarchy that matter to workers.[41]

At the top of the hierarchy is the one who makes ultimate decisions (the physician, in Hughes's example). But no matter how closely s/he guards the authority of the role, s/he cannot know all, and must have a "lieutenant" (the nurse, in this example). The lieutenant outwardly defers, but sometimes must make decisions and get the decision-maker's approval afterward. To keep the enterprise going, the lieutenant also does tasks that are rightly those of inferiors. The lieutenant's role "is essentially that of doing in a responsible way whatever necessary things are in danger of not being done at all."[42] The lieutenant thus plays a critical role with reference to **mistakes at work**. Moreover, the practitioner at the top of the hierarchy may have to make concessions of minor kinds for the workshop to function smoothly: Erving Goffman observed surgeons jollying along sullen residents to keep the work on track.[43]

Hierarchy within the occupation is rarely based solely on objective criteria. In the United States, race, gender and other factors still affect who outranks whom at work. Changing workshops affects where a person falls in the hierarchy; if management brings in an outsider as shop boss who had

39   See E. Davis, *Hidden Dimensions*, 40, 42.
40   Zurcher, "The Sailor Aboard," 391.
41   See for instance E. Davis, *Hidden Dimensions*, 145, 152.
42   Hughes, "Social Role," 74.
43   Goffman, *Encounters*, 120–25.

been an underling elsewhere, both the newcomer and coworkers have to adjust their identity and social relations. Michael Sonenscher notes that in medieval Europe, "the relationship between a journeyman's age, experience, competence and seniority changed constantly in the passage from *boutique* to *boutique* and, more obviously, from town to town. A man of thirty who had been established for months or years in one *boutique* could find himself working as a newcomer alongside a seventeen- or eighteen-year-old in another," dropping from top dog to the bottom of the heap.[44] Sonenscher argues that the "frequent inversions of age, seniority and precedence" contributed to the development of the rituals of the journeymen's companies, rites that borrowed elements from the army, the law, and the fraternities of better-established journeymen.[45] (Such rules and rites are code.) For instance, any member could randomly charge any other member with a misdemeanor requiring a fine, and the whole group would spend the fines collectively on their trade holidays. Sonenscher calls this equalizing force a "counterpart" to unpredictable workshop inequalities.[46] Naming the journeyman's experience of contradictory identities "status dilemma" permits comparing one cultural solution to this feeling with others and to hypothesizing broadly similar solutions that may appear in our sources once we ask.

Historians must also pose as a research question – rather than assuming they know – where the boundaries between occupations lay and where social relations instead bespeak hierarchy within one occupation. An increasingly complex division of labor creates distinct tracks within one occupation until identities have coalesced around different technique and object of technique. The line that historian He Bian shows developing between doctor and pharmacist in Ming times is just one such division in the medical profession.[47] As Hughes points out, physicians have shared work with undertakers; midwives with abortionists; bloodletters with barbers; bonesetters with smiths; and masseurs with bathhouse-keepers. Increasing specialization has divided the work and the social prestige, and this process continues. As some practitioners abandon tasks that they experience as **dirty work**, new workers take them on.[48]

Here, as in other historical processes, agent and structure interact dynamically. Over time, a hierarchy within the occupation splits into different

44 Sonenscher, "Mythical Work," 59.
45 Sonenscher, "Mythical Work," 60–62.
46 Sonenscher, "Mythical Work," 59.
47 Bian, *Know Your Remedies*, 127; Schneewind, "Chinese Physician-Pharmacist."
48 Hughes, "Social Role," 72–73.

occupations. This process will happen unevenly, so boundaries between occupations may not only be unstable, but probably unclear. On the other hand, initially separate occupations may be gathered in to one hierarchy. Before the medical establishment took its current shape in twentieth-century Europe and America, "the physician, midwife, surgeon, and apothecary were somewhat independent of each other."[49] The historian should investigate the trajectories of related occupations or levels within an occupation over time. One key stimulant to change is dirty work.

Were certain colleagues admired for their performance? For what aspects?
Did all members of the occupation do similar tasks?
If practitioners entered the occupation along different paths, did some lead to lower positions in the hierarchy within the occupation?
Did tasks within technique vary along the hierarchy within the occupation?
How greatly did pay or other compensation vary?
How did the highest-ranked practitioners treat the lower ranks?
Who ate with whom at work? Did they eat the same food?
Who lived with whom? Did they live in equal comfort?
Did they dress the same, worship together, and so on?
Did they socialize with one another?
How did they write/talk/sing about or otherwise depict each other?
Might a practitioner's position in the hierarchy of the occupation vary as he moved from place to place?
Who did the dirty work?
Among coworkers, who made the weightiest decisions?
Did practitioners have organizations, such as guilds or unions, whether within the workshop, within the occupation, or across several occupations?
If so, what problems of authority or prestige did they solve or create?

Works Cited

Applebaum, Herbert, ed. *Work in Non-market and Transitional Societies*. Albany: SUNY Press, 1984.

Ash, Eric. "Introduction: Expertise and the Early Modern State." *Osiris* 25, no. 1 (2010): 1–24.

Bearman, Peter. *Doormen*. Chicago: University of Chicago Press, 2005.

49   Becker et al., *Boys in White*, 8.

Becker, Howard. "Professional Sociology: The Case of C. Wright Mills." In *The Democratic Imagination: Dialogues on the Work of Irving Louis Horowitz*, edited by Louis Filler, chapter 10. New York: Routledge, 1994.

Becker, Howard. "Role and Career Problems of the Chicago Public-School Teacher." Ph.D. diss., University of Chicago, 1951.

Becker, Howard. "The Teacher in the Authority System of the Public School." *The Journal of Educational Sociology* 27, no. 3 (1953): 128–41.

Becker, Howard S., Blanche Geer, Everett C. Hughes, and Anselm L. Strauss. *Boys in White: Student Culture in Medical School*. Chicago: University of Chicago Press, 1961.

Bian, He. *Know Your Remedies: Pharmacy and Culture in Early Modern China*. Princeton: Princeton University Press, 2020.

Chen, Yunü. "Buddhism and the Medical Treatment of Women in the Ming Dynasty." *Nan Nü* (2008): 279–303.

Coser, Lewis. "Introduction." In *On Work, Race, and the Sociological Imagination*, edited by Lewis Coser, 1–17. Chicago: University of Chicago Press, 1994.

Davis, Edward B. *Hidden Dimensions of Work: Revisiting the Chicago School Methods of Everett Hughes and Anselm Strauss*. N.p.: Xlibris Books, 2011.

Ehmer, Josef. "Work, History of." In *International Encyclopedia of the Social and Behavioral Sciences*, vol. 24, 16569–74. London: Elsevier, 2001.

Gansu zhen zhanshou tulue: Shaanxi yu tudi renwu 甘肅鎮戰守圖略：附西域土地人物 [Gansu garrison military operations map and outline: Appended, Land and people of the Western area]. 1522–1566. Taipei Imperial Palace Museum.

Gerritsen, Anne. *The City of Blue and White: Chinese Porcelain and the Early Modern World*. Cambridge: Cambridge University Press, 2020.

Goffman, Erving. *Encounters: Two Studies in the Sociology of Interaction*. Indianapolis: Bobbs-Merrill, 1961.

Hughes, Everett C. "Personality Types and the Division of Labor." In *Men and Their Work*, 23–41. Glencoe, IL: The Free Press, 1958.

Hughes, Everett C. "Professions." *Dædalus* 92, no. 4 (1963): 655–68.

Hughes, Everett C. "Psychology: Science and/or Profession." *The American Psychologist* 7, no. 8 (1952): 441–43.

Hughes, Everett C. "Social Role and the Division of Labor." In *Men and Their Work*, 69–77. Glencoe, IL: The Free Press, 1958.

Hughes, Everett C. "The Study of Occupations." In *On Work, Race and the Sociological Imagination*, edited by Lewis Coser, 21–36. Chicago: University of Chicago Press, 1994.

Karageorghis, Vassos. *Aspects of Everyday Life in Ancient Cyprus: Iconographic Representations*. Nicosia: A. G. Leventis Foundation, 2006.

Karsh, Bernard. "Human Relations versus Management." In *Institutions and the Person: Festschrift in Honor of Everett C. Hughes*, edited by Howard S. Becker, Blanche Geer, David Riesman, and Robert S. Weiss, 35–48. Chicago: Aldine, 1968.

Kriesberg, Louis. "Internal Differentiation and the Establishment of Organizations." In *Institutions and the Person: Festschrift in Honor of Everett C. Hughes*, edited by Howard S. Becker, Blanche Geer, David Riesman, and Robert S. Weiss, 141–56. Chicago: Aldine, 1968.

Lahire, Bernard. "Elias, Freud, and the Human Science." In *Norbert Elias and Social Theory,* edited by François Dépelteau and Tatiana Savoia Landini, 75–89. New York: Palgrave Macmillan, 2013.

Pospisil, Leopold. "Organization of Labor among the Kapauku." In *Work in Non-market and Transitional Societies*, edited by Herbert Applebaum, 180–85. Albany: SUNY Press, 1984.

Schneewind, Sarah. "The Work of the Chinese Physician-Pharmacist in He Bian's *Know Your Remedies.*" *Pharmacy in History* 62, nos. 2–4 (2020): 168–80.

Shen, Grant. "Acting in the Private Theatre of the Ming Dynasty." *Asian Theatre Journal* (1998): 64–86.

Solomon, David N. "Sociological Perspectives on Occupations." In *Institutions and the Person: Festschrift in Honor of Everett C. Hughes*, edited by Howard S. Becker, Blanche Geer, David Riesman, and Robert S. Weiss, 3–13. Chicago: Aldine, 1968.

Sonenscher, Michael. "Mythical Work: Workshop Production and the *Compagnonnages* of Eighteenth-Century France." In *The Historical Meanings of Work*, edited by Patrick Joyce, 31–63. Cambridge: Cambridge University Press, 1987.

Suttles, Wayne. "Coping with Abundance: Subsistence on the Northwest Coast." In *Work in Non-Market and Transitional Societies*, edited by Herbert Applebaum, 95–113. Albany: SUNY Press, 1984.

van Vorst, Mrs. John, and Marie van Vorst. *The Woman Who Toils: Being the Experiences of Two Ladies as Factory Girls.* 1902, 1903; facsimile reprint Carlisle, MA: Applewood Books, n.d.

Zurcher, Jr., Louis A. "The Sailor Aboard Ship: A Study of Role Behavior in a Total Institution." *Social Forces* 43, no. 3 (1965): 389–400.

III. Dirty Work

Abstract

To understand ordinary people's experience of life requires moving away from elite condemnations of occupations on which society in fact depended. "Dirty work" in the sociology of occupations is a generative concept that leads us to ask which parts of *any* occupation its practitioners find degrading. Many occupations include in technique both messy work that practitioners have integrated into their self-concept, and work that seems clean to outsiders (both laymen and the historian) yet offended the practitioners' self-concept. The former is not "dirty work"; the latter is. Every occupation includes dirty work. The historian cannot predict what it included, but must investigate it, and investigate how practitioners have created culture to manage their experience of doing work they themselves despised.

Keywords: hierarchy, caste, pollution, dirt, ordinary people, social role

Textbook writers Tony Watson and Marek Korczynski offer a definition that is far too limited when they write that "dirty work" is "an occupational activity which plays a necessary role in society but which is regarded in some respects as morally doubtful" and align it with "deviant occupations."[1] This judgmental term runs contrary to the whole spirit of occupational sociology. In fact, dirty work in the Hughes framework has a range of connected meanings. The main point of the concept is precisely that *every* occupation experiences some of its tasks as dirty work.[2] Without investigation, the researcher cannot know which parts of technique the practitioners themselves resent. And historians should not forget to ask about which parts of technique brought practitioners pride or joy.

---

1   Watson and Korczynski, *Sociology.*
2   Solomon, "Sociological Perspectives on Occupations," 9.

Schneewind, S.K. *The Social Drama of Daily Work. A Manual for Historians.* Amsterdam: Amsterdam University Press, 2024
DOI: 10.5117/9789048559534_CH03

Pollution and Social Distaste

One kind of dirty work, of course, is unpleasant or ritually polluting (defiling) work that society needs done.[3] Practitioners in occupations whose object of technique is physically dirty, like garbage or manure, may indeed be looked down upon by clients and other laypeople. A ranking of nine crafts recorded in an Indian village in 1968 puts goldsmiths at the top because of the nobility of the material; carpenters next, as they built temples; blacksmiths next, since iron weapons kill; and the coppersmiths next, because women's use of copper for cooking makes it inferior to iron. The last three categories are the barber, who risks pollution; the washerman, who handles dirty clothes; and the leatherworker, since leather pollutes.[4] Society needs all these crafts, yet laypeople despise (or are instructed to despise) the practitioners of the lower ones.

A contemporary US example is prison guards. Because they manage those whom society has dubbed criminals, they are essential to the penal system we have created. Activists or politicians may reprimand guards from time to time for treating prisoners too harshly, but delegating our duty to assure the decent treatment of others to prison guards allows us, the broader public, to shut our eyes, believe in our own goodness, and say, "That's not my job."[5]

The researcher cannot assume, but must investigate, which occupations laypeople considered "dirty." For one thing, not everyone agreed. Third-century rabbis, for example, differed over whether cameleteers were respectable and sailors deeply pious or whether both were so likely to be dishonest that a father should forbid his son from taking up those occupations.[6] Historian of medieval Europe Jacques Le Goff offers a list of the occupations most frequently despised or condemned:

---

3   Solomon, "Sociological Perspectives on Occupations," 9.
4   K. Ishwaran, *Shivapur: A South Indian Village* (London: Routledge & Kegan Paul, 1968), quoted in Thomas, *Oxford Book of Work*, 365.
5   Hughes, "Good People and Dirty Work," 186. In the eighteenth century, workers who had been donated to a Hindu deity had come to include "those who worked with waste products," including barbers, cobblers, and sweepers. Though the work is distasteful, laypeople cannot do without it, and in this case, despite their low "moral" standing, these workers were still entitled to tax exemption because of their religious bondage (Chatterjee, "Locked Box," 157–58). Might the sense that something was polluting have arisen from a particular occupation's long-ago feeling that it was dirty work, rather than just from the causes laid out in Mary Douglas's *Purity and Danger*?
6   The third-century text reports one view that "A person may not teach his son the trades of a donkey driver, a camel driver, a pot maker [misprint for caravan driver], a sailor, a shepherd, or a storekeeper, as their trades are the trades of robbers"; and another that "Most donkey drivers are wicked, and most camel drivers are decent, and most sailors are pious." The twelfth-century

Innkeepers, butchers, jongleurs, mountebanks, magicians, alchemists, doctors, surgeons, soldiers, pimps, prostitutes, notaries, merchants, fullers, weavers, saddlers, dyers, pastry makers, cobblers, gardeners, painters, fishermen, barbers, bailiffs, game wardens, customs officers, exchange brokers, tailors, perfumers, tripe sellers, milliners.[7]

Le Goff explained that in each case the cause for condemnation was either an old, "primitive" taboo surviving in early medieval thinking or a new Christian dislike (the latter influenced by Jewish and classical thought). The blood taboo stained butchers, executioners, barbers, apothecaries, surgeons, and even physicians; sometimes it extended to soldiers. The taboo on uncleanliness sullied fullers, dyers, cooks, laundrymen, and dishwashers. The money taboo tarnished merchants, brokers, and, according to some, all wage-earners. Association with any of the seven deadly sins was grounds for Christian condemnation, so lust, for instance, tainted not only sex-workers and their pimps, but also innkeepers, bathhouse-keepers, minstrels, and so on. Le Goff adds that a list that included all contemptible occupations mentioned in any source would "include virtually all medieval professions."[8]

In saying that *someone* wrote disparagingly *somewhere* of almost every medieval occupation, Le Goff points us to the problem of perspective. It is unlikely that all these people heartily despised their own work and that of their families. As historian Peter Shapinsky argues in discussing the "others" against whom the land-bound Japanese elite defined itself, the elite picture of those who worked on the sea, like fishermen, salt-makers, sailors, and masters-at-arms reflected not only layers of land-based thinking, but also the "work cultures" of seafarers themselves, as land-based clients interacted with them.[9] The sociological understanding of dirty work goes beyond

---

commentary explains: "*Donkey driver, a camel driver, a caravan driver* – all those trades involve robbery, since when they stay on the road they go in and pick up wood and fruits from the vineyards, and in addition, when a person hires them they never keep the conditions [i.e., they charge more than was agreed upon]. *A shepherd* – lets his animals feed in the fields of others. *A Storekeeper* – is known to add water to the wine and dried twigs to the wheat. *Most donkey drivers are wicked* – on account of robbery [as above, they charge more than agreed upon]. *Most camel drivers are decent* – because they go to the desert, where there are animals and brigands, and so they fear for their lives and subdue their hearts to God. *Most sailors are pious* – since they go to a place of danger and they are always in fear, even more so than the camel drivers." Tractate Kiddushin of the Mishnah (emphasis in the original). Mira Balberg, personal communication, August 2022.

7   Le Goff, *Time, Work, and Culture*, 59, as summarized in Applebaum, *Concept of Work*, 244.

8   Le Goff, *Time, Work, and Culture*, 59.

9   Shapinsky, *Lords of the Sea*, 34, 39, 43.

work that is literally dirty or tasks that laypeople want to offload. Labeling whole occupations as "dirty" reveals less about a society than considering the dirty work of every occupation, as defined primarily by the thoughts and feelings of the practitioners themselves. But this is not simple, either.

> How central was the occupation's work to society's operation?
> How did laypeople disparage or praise the occupation?
> With what other occupations did laypeople associate it?
> How did they explain those attitudes and categories?
> Were those attitudes and categories changing at the time?

Messy Work Practitioners Don't Mind

A first complication is that practitioners in some occupations may integrate physically dirty work into a positive self-conception. Butchers in the US in the mid-twentieth century, doing work others despised, and which butchers themselves hoped their sons would avoid, had their own sense of occupational honor: among other things they were proud of their strength and skill, and ability to endure the cold of meat-lockers.[10] Some Buddhist monks in Song-era China (960–1279) had to deal with sick bodies and dead bodies, clean latrines, and raise money. Because they conceptualized these potentially polluting tasks as steps to enlightenment, they did not push the tasks down the occupational hierarchy to novices or servants.[11] Even very prestigious occupations may not delegate all physically dirty work: surgeons – even those who drive a Mercedes-Benz and are sought after as marriage partners – cannot avoid blood. Hughes hypothesized that they had successfully "knit it into some satisfying and prestige-giving definition of role," and that it had even become part of the occupation's charisma.[12] Thus, even if practitioners continue to do tasks others reject, they may succeed in guiding a "divesting process" in which they shuck off the demeaning implications of their role and create a new consensus around its value and standing.[13]

But a surgeon asked to mop up the blood in the operating room would be deeply offended. The physically dirty work that surgeons have incorporated

10   Meara, "Honor in Dirty Work."
11   Phillip Bloom, communication in meeting of Ming In Southern California (MISC), January 2021.
12   Hughes, "Work and the Self," 52.
13   Davis, *Hidden Dimensions*, 59–61.

into their self-conception as an acceptable part of technique is dealing with blood as they operate on their object of technique; dealing with the very same blood once it has spilled on the floor is excluded from technique. A surgeon forced to mop up the blood he has just spilt will experience what is called "status pain," a sign of dirty work.

What aspects of technique did practitioners take pride in and enjoy?
How does specifying who thought what change the conception of pollution?
What tasks in the occupation were literally dirty?
How did practitioners talk about those tasks?
Who in the occupation carried them out?

Status Pain

To understand dirty work, why not ask the janitor of an apartment building? That is just what sociologist Raymond Gold did: in 1949 and 1950, he interviewed thirty-seven janitors in Chicago. They had no direct supervisors, but they also had no one else helping them clean the building. Their ideas of dirty work turned out to be fascinating and complex. As one might expect, they bitterly hated garbage (this was before plastic trash bags). Just as deeply, however, they resented physically cleaner, more skilled work – doing repairs – when they were asked to do it at all hours, outside of the schedule they had set for themselves. Being at the tenants' beck and call was dirty work, because it offended their pride in their professional autonomy.[14]

Practitioners in an occupation find some tasks in their technique to be beneath their dignity. The painters of Victorian houses in San Francisco in the mid-twentieth century considered all of the exterior work before the final coat inappropriate for artists; yet only a few of them aspired to move up, beyond the dirty work that constituted most of each stint – using blowtorches and scrapers to remove a century's worth of layers of (leaded) paint, sanding down the surfaces, applying primer, sweeping up, cleaning brushes, and so on.[15] Cleaning up may be dirty work.

Pierre Bourdieu comments on the dirty work of sociology itself: "many sociologists of high social or academic origin invent every possible way of avoiding the tasks to my mind most imperatively required of the researcher

14   Gold, "Janitors Versus Tenants." Goffman borrowed from Gold's Master's thesis, *Presentation of Self*, 155. See also Hughes, "Work and the Self," 50–51.
15   E. Davis, *Hidden Dimensions*, 150, 153.

... [such as] personally administering a questionnaire."[16] Likewise, historian Arunabh Ghosh shows that in China during the late 1950s, statistical workers (some full-time, some part-time) perceived the importance of different tasks – collection of data, collation, research, and supervision – as unequal. The fact that collation and research could not proceed without data collection did not deter workers from preferring research and supervision. The frustrated director of the State Statistics Bureau wrote:

> If, in order to supervise or [carry out] research, one were to become relaxed about the collection and collation of statistical work, this is akin to destroying the foundations of one's own work; exactly like the scholar who, having lost his pen, takes a sword to a [literary] competition at a colleague's home.[17]

But the director's frustration could not change what his colleagues further down the hierarchy perceived as dirty work and tried to avoid. Likewise, editors in late imperial China perceived copyediting as dirty work; they pushed it down the hierarchy of the occupation, as we know because both sets of workers are named, and they do not overlap.[18] In these two cases, the work is in no way literally dirty. Rather, practitioners have decided certain tasks are beneath them.

Some parts of technique offend the practitioner's highest idea of himself. Why do university professors hate grading so much? It is not merely that assigning grades is tedious and unrewarding. Rather, grading injures our relations with our students, whose minds are our object of technique. It feels beneath us, for we believe that our calling is to educate and enlighten. But, further, it brings to the surface the unequal power relation that we would like to pretend is not there all the time, always potentially hampering the free discussion we value. All this makes grading dirty work for teachers.[19] Likewise, doctors, with (at least in their highest self-concept) a calling to heal but a necessity to earn, find discussion of fees to be dirty work, so they have pushed it down the hierarchy to receptionists and financial administrators and ensure that it takes place in a different space in the doctor's office.

---

16   Bourdieu, *Sketch for a Self-analysis*, 101–2.
17   Ghosh, *Making it Count*, 136.
18   Allan Barr provided this example in the MISC meeting, January 2021.
19   Hughes made the point that teachers describe themselves in various ways but rarely as "graders of papers," according to E. Davis, *Hidden Dimensions*, 136.

Dirty work affects relations among colleagues and coworkers. Pathologists in the USA in the mid-twentieth century pushed down the hierarchy of the occupation the preparation and evisceration of the corpse, the opening and closing of the skull, and the sewing the body up again. When no diener was available – there was high turnover – medical residents had to do these tasks, and they felt it so beneath them that they would fall far behind in their cases. They did not mingle socially with dieners, even to the extent of eating lunch together, and even if a diener was dressed in a tie and white coat. The diener was forbidden to wear his apron outside the autopsy room even in an emergency; he had to take it off even, for instance, when all the lights had gone out and he was going to change the fuse.[20] Medical residents deal with blood and bodies living and dead, so there is nothing particularly obvious or rational about the extreme pollution that surrounded the dieners' technique and its practitioners.

Did practitioners clean themselves when the workday ended?

Which tasks led practitioners to sulk or express anger?

What aspects of the work did they complain about and on what grounds?

What tasks did practitioners avoid if possible?

Which aspects of the work did laymen and clients admire or despise?

Did rituals surround certain tasks?

Were some tasks delegated down the hierarchy?

If so, did colleagues or coworkers refuse to eat with the one doing the dirty work?

Did signs of distinction marking dirty work require covering up, even in an emergency?

Were some coworkers overlooked by visitors to the workspace?

Unpredictability and Status Pain

The outsider, whether layman or researcher, cannot necessarily predict what members of the occupation will consider dirty work. For instance, in William Westley's participant-observer study of the army, he writes that one day,

> I fled into the company office to escape the rain and mud. The company clerk seemed to have an ideal job, and I congratulated him on this. To my

20 E. Davis, *Hidden Dimensions*, 43–44.

surprise, he responded, in effect, "So who wants it?" Then he told me that this was not what he had come into the army for, to waste his time sitting in a lousy tent. They had said he would become a soldier, so why didn't they let him stay out on maneuvers? Questioning revealed his dream of brawn and invulnerability.[21]

Whereas Westley found the rough side of army life uncomfortable, the recruits expected to be toughened up into he-men and resented the softening aspects of the newer army. To them, clerking inside, out of the rain, was dirty work.

It is the emic, insiders' perspective that determines dirty work. Even the pickle-factory girls, who cheerfully worked ten hours a day, grumbled about the end-of-week task of scrubbing the floors on their hands and knees. Participant-observer Mrs. Van Vorst wrote, "There is but one opinion among the girls: it is not right that they should be made to do this work. They all echo the same resentment."[22] Scrubbing tables was fine; getting down and scrubbing floors was dirty work. Dirty work, in a nutshell, includes whatever work insults the occupation's highest image of itself, causing status pain: the thought that "I am above this," or "this isn't what I was thinking of when I got into this occupation!" Determining what really constituted dirty work in the eyes of practitioners requires research.

Dirty work hurts: hence the term status pain. As David Solomon explains,

People in the occupation usually feel the need to make their peace with the [dirty] work, with themselves, and with others. This may involve developing a terminology to make the work seem less dirty, concealing the dirty aspects, referring the dirty work to less-favored colleagues, or sloughing it off onto members of other occupations.[23]

21   Westley, "Organization of the Army," 205.
22   Van Vorst and van Vorst, *The Woman Who Toils*, 34. Van Vorst was curious about whether the men had to scrub, and found out that they managed the task with a hose and brooms. She commented on it to the boss of that room, staffed by men, and he said, "I won't have no scrubbing in my place. The first scrubbing day they says to me, 'Get down on your hands and knees' and I says – 'Just pay me my money will you; I'm going home. What scrubbing can't be done with mops won't be done by me.' The women wouldn't have to scrub, either, if they had enough spirit all of them to say so" (35). A social sense even among factory management that scrubbing floors was not fit work for white men, and even among the uppity young factory women that it *might* be fit work for them as women, may have accounted for the difference. Van Vorst did not figure it out.
23   Solomon, "Sociological Perspectives on Occupations," 9.

One way to manage dirty work is colleague **code** requiring concealment. Language can help. For instance, universities have replaced the terms "Pass/Fail" with "Pass/No Pass" to soften and conceal the brutal necessity for teachers to grade. Sociologist Erving Goffman points out (citing Hughes), "We tend to conceal from our audience all evidence of 'dirty work'."[24]

Another way to manage status pain is "role distance," a term Goffman uses to describe how a practitioner acts out his dissatisfaction with his dirty work: a clerk sneering at customers, for instance, or a resident sulking in the operating room.[25] These performances are essentially a refusal of "conversion" – balking on the **path into the occupation**. In the case of jobs, which demand no emotional commitment, role distance may continue. In the case of professions, the apprentice must overcome his resentment: either making his peace with the dirty work of the profession by integrating it into his self-concept or learning how master practitioners offload or conceal it.

Dirty work may be pushed off onto other occupations or down the hierarchy within the occupation. Gold's Chicago janitors worked alone – they could not push the dirty work down an occupational hierarchy. But cleaning up blood and gore was pushed down from surgeon to orderly. This is a dynamic process in which new roles arise to take on rejected tasks, and those new, lowlier occupations in time develop their own occupational culture, integrating, concealing, or pushing down the dirty work again.[26] This social process in the drama of work makes it hard to delineate the boundaries between related occupations.

Did practitioners have saints or heroes who did tasks others despised and rose above it?

Did practitioners enter the occupation from non-elite strata with cultural values that might lead them to view tasks differently from those who wrote the sources?

Did practitioners use euphemisms to describe certain tasks?

Did practitioners act rudely to clients or other people in certain situations?

Did the occupation subdivide over time?

---

24 Goffman, *Presentation of Self*, 44. For new light on the Goffman–Hughes relation, see Vienne, "Enigma of the Total Institution."

25 Goffman, *Encounters*, 113–14, 120–24.

26 Hughes, "Social Role," 72–73. E. Davis, *Hidden Dimensions*, 27–72.

Works Cited

Applebaum, Herbert. *The Concept of Work: Ancient, Medieval, and Modern.* Albany: SUNY Press, 1992.

Bourdieu, Pierre. *Sketch for a Self-Analysis.* Translated by Richard Nice. Cambridge: Polity, 2007.

Chatterjee, Indrani. "The Locked Box in *Slavery and Social Death.*" In *On Human Bondage: After* Slavery and Social Death, edited by John Bodel and Walter Scheidel, 151–66. Hoboken: Wiley, 2016.

Davis, Edward B. *Hidden Dimensions of Work: Revisiting the Chicago School Methods of Everett Hughes and Anselm Strauss.* N.p.: Xlibris Books, 2011.

Douglas, Mary. *Purity and Danger: An Analysis of Concepts of Pollution and Taboo.* Abingdon: Routledge & Kegan Paul, 1966.

Ghosh, Arunabh. *Making it Count: Statistics and Statecraft in the Early People's Republic of China.* Princeton: Princeton University Press, 2020.

Goffman, Erving. *Encounters: Two Studies in the Sociology of Interaction.* Indianapolis: Bobbs-Merrill, 1961.

Goffman, Erving. *The Presentation of Self in Everyday Life.* New York: Anchor Books, 1959.

Gold, Ray. "Janitors Versus Tenants: A Status-Income Dilemma." *American Journal of Sociology* 57, no. 5 (1952): 486–93.

Hughes, Everett C. "Good People and Dirty Work." In *On Work, Race and the Sociological Imagination*, edited by Lewis Coser, 180–91. Chicago: University of Chicago Press, 1994.

Hughes, Everett C. "Social Role and the Division of Labor." In *Men and Their Work*, 69–77. Glencoe, IL: The Free Press, 1958.

Hughes, Everett C. "Work and the Self." In *Men and Their Work*, 42–55. Glencoe, IL: The Free Press, 1958.

Le Goff, Jacques. *Time, Work, and Culture in the Middle Ages.* Chicago: University of Chicago Press, 1980.

Meara, Hannah. "Honor in Dirty Work: The Case of American Meat Cutters and Turkish Butchers." *Sociology of Work and Occupations* 1, no. 3 (1974): 259–83.

Shapinsky, Peter D. *Lords of the Sea: Pirates, Violence, and Commerce in Late Medieval Japan.* Ann Arbor: Center for Japanese Studies, University of Michigan, 2014.

Solomon, David N. "Sociological Perspectives on Occupations." In *Institutions and the Person: Festschrift in Honor of Everett C. Hughes*, edited by Howard S. Becker, Blanche Geer, David Riesman, and Robert S. Weiss, 3–13. Chicago: Aldine, 1968.

Thomas, Keith, ed. *The Oxford Book of Work.* Oxford: Oxford University Press, 1999.

van Vorst, Mrs. John, and Marie van Vorst. *The Woman Who Toils: Being the Experiences of Two Ladies as Factory Girls.* 1902, 1903; facsimile reprint Carlisle, MA: Applewood Books, n.d.

Vienne, Philippe. "The Enigma of the Total Institution: Rethinking the Hughes–Goffman Intellectual Relationship." *Sociologica* 2 (2010): 1–30.

Watson, Tony and Marek Korczynski. *Sociology, Work and Industry*, 5th ed. Abingdon: Taylor & Francis, 2003.

Westley, William A. "The Informal Organization of the Army: A Sociological Memoir." In *Institutions and the Person: Festschrift in Honor of Everett C. Hughes*, edited by Howard S. Becker, Blanche Geer, David Riesman, and Robert S. Weiss, 200–207. Chicago: Aldine, 1968.

IV. The Path into the Occupation

Abstract

People entered particular occupations in various ways, ranging from orders from the master, to inheritance, to more or less free choice, depending on location and on culturally-informed sorts along the path in by gender, race, ethnicity, and so on. The path into the occupation begins with learning technique, but ends by shaping the practitioner's identity and social relations to a greater or lesser degree. When the self is greatly changed, or "converted" to the occupation, that may alienate the practitioner from his or her original social milieu. Historians must attend to status contradictions and status dilemmas, in which the practitioner or others perceive a mismatch between the practitioner's occupation and other social characteristics, as well as to dropouts and retirement: different paths out of the occupation.

Keywords: education, retirement, conversion, status, social mobility, ordinary people

The division of labor is often discussed in terms of the economy or society as a whole. But as individuals or families sharing a specialization, people experience the division of labor as defaults, compulsions, choices, and failures, as well as successes, on the path into the occupation. The path into a person's occupation varies greatly among place-times, but also by occupation in one place-time: some people enslaved, others free to choose, still others who tried for one occupation but failed and settled for another. People may be sorted into occupations by gender, age, inherited rank, or another ascriptive criterion, or by choice and talent.[1] The choice of work, whoever makes it, matters immensely to individuals' life experiences and in some cases to their core identity, so the emotional stakes are high. Further,

---

[1]   Gender has been a salient topic within the history of work. Ehmer, "Work, History of," 16573–74. For rank, see Hinchy and Joshi, "Selective Amnesia," 7.

Schneewind, S.K. *The Social Drama of Daily Work. A Manual for Historians.* Amsterdam: Amsterdam University Press, 2024

DOI: 10.5117/9789048559534_CH04

some who start on the way into an occupation drop out, and those who stay the course may find themselves dramatically altered, so much so that leaving the occupation is difficult. All these aspects of the path into the occupation generate social dynamics well beyond the individual.

Sorting Workers on the Path into the Occupation

Many societies far from a caste mentality still hold sacred aspects of the division of labor, in the sense that factors other than physical and mental fitness for a particular occupation set the path into the occupation. It may be customary for people of certain ethnicities or religions to go into some lines of work and be excluded from others because of social prejudice – that is, fixed and irrational conceptions about how fitness lines up with gender, skin color or ethnic origin, and so on. Just to give one example, Ron Carter started by studying cello, but there were no jobs for classical black cellists, so he switched to double bass and to jazz.[2] Even when there is no social prejudice, families and individuals may choose well-trodden occupational paths. Of course, across time, many people have had little choice; for instance, at one moment in ancient Egypt, sixty men were randomly demoted from a construction crew to become mere porters for the others.[3]

Employers have often relied on gender to sort workers on the path into the occupation. Bessie McGinnis Van Vorst found numerous listings Chicago newspapers under "Wanted, Females" – a kind of practice that continued into the 1970s in the USA – and she offers interesting comments on the male/female differences in the pickle factory.[4] In late eighteenth-century Birmingham, "Girls were specifically requested in advertisements for button-piercers, annealers, and stoving and polishing work in the japaning trades."[5] Women's and girls' smaller hands and experience with stoves were cited as reasons for their recruitment, but there is no evidence that hiring managers measured hands or asked if a girl knew how to cook. An English poem of about 1597 describes moving through the rooms of a wool cloth manufactory. By two hundred looms stood as many men, weaving, attended by two hundred boys with a different task;

2   Carter, "Legendary Jazz Bassist."
3   Miller, "Paleoepidemiology," 11.
4   Van Vorst and van Vorst, *The Woman Who Toils*, 109, 45–46.
5   Berg, "Women's Work," 85.

a hundred women carded wool in the next room; in the next two hundred maidens did the spinning; children picked over the wool to divide it by quality.[6] Gender has often facilitated a rough sorting on the path into the occupation.

Customary occupations depending on ethnicity may arise from social prejudice or because of family and community networks and shared knowledge of how to manage specific businesses – or the two may reinforce one another. In the USA in the late twentieth and early twenty-first centuries, there were Korean grocers, Indian motel owners, Vietnamese nail parlor attendants; and we have already met the Gadulia blacksmiths. If those doing the hiring in an occupation are of various ethnicities, the occupation may reflect this, and yet specific workshops may be segregated. For instance, a long-time doorman on the Upper East Side noted shifts in the ethnic makeup of apartment building employees over time from Irish to South American, and reported that his own building had initially had a Romanian superintendent who hired mainly Romanians, then a Hispanic super who hired mainly Hispanic men, and so on.[7] On the other hand, ethnic identity may be fabricated to ease the path into the occupation: David Robinson has shown that some Han-Chinese bandits in North China attired and accoutered themselves as Mongols, who were especially feared both as foes and as members of the Ming army.[8]

But family background that is occupational, not specifically ethnic, may also affect the path into the occupation. Steel erectors in the USA in the twentieth century, who raised and placed the beams in skyscrapers, usually came from families who had done the same work. This was so that their coworkers would trust them. As Hughes put it, "It is not so much a long training that the other workers want; they want a man who has it in his bones – that is, a man who is accustomed to this kind of risk as a way of life."[9]

An occupation may be difficult to enter in the sense that most people who want to enter fail to do so, yet still be entered casually by most practitioners. Manhattan doormen around the year 2000 earned better salaries than teachers and policemen, but to enter the occupation required no particular education, skill, or strength. Many applied in vain, yet those in

6   Thomas Deloney, *The Pleasant Historie of John Winchcomb* (H. Lownes, 1619), cited in Thomas, *Oxford Book of Work*, 351–52.
7   Bearman, *Doormen*, 56–61.
8   Robinson, "Banditry."
9   Letter from Everett Hughes (1972) to Edward B. Davis, quoted in E. Davis, *Hidden Dimensions*, 95–96.

the occupation had often entered with no forethought, through connections – sometimes quite distant – to an apartment building superintendent.[10] The precise path into the occupation may vary by practitioner and the ease or difficulty of starting out does not necessarily correlate with lax or stringent qualifications.

Finally, location often determines occupation: many of those born in sheep country raised sheep, and even those who did not were affected by that dominant occupational culture. In eighteenth-century France, career paths and workshop conditions in Paris, Lyon, and Marseilles differed from those in other towns. Hatters in the cities worked with beaver; those in towns worked with wool. In the cities, some journeymen were sufficiently well established to use the law to prevent the hiring of migrants; in the towns, the hierarchy within the occupation did not take this form.[11] Broad-brush generalizations about class or economic systems cannot capture the daily reality of the social drama of work.

If colleagues have followed a path into the occupation based on ethnicity, gender, religion, or a similar factor, so that they share language and culture, that may reinforce their solidarity, but make it especially hard for a lone practitioner of another background to fit in; or to put it another way, that practitioner may have to modulate aspects of his personality and habits more than others do to follow colleague code. If laypeople despise a practitioner's ethnicity or gender but revere his occupation, he may face a "status contradiction" (a mismatch in the eyes of other people) or "status dilemma" (the person's own subjective feeling of contradictory identities). One example is Jewish moneylenders in medieval and early modern Europe, who were both despised and flattered by Christian aristocrats who needed their money. Another is Chicago janitors: they earned more than many of the tenants whose garbage they had to sort by hand, which increased their resentment at having to interrupt their own lives for tenants' emergencies.[12] Likewise, upper-class women held considerable authority over working men even when patriarchal norms dominated society.[13] Status dilemmas and status contradictions in such situations may never be resolved.

10   Bearman, *Doormen*, 39.
11   Sonenscher, "Mythical Work," 55, 60–61.
12   Gold, "Janitors Versus Tenants," 487–88.
13   Hughes, "Dilemmas and Contradictions of Status"; and "Social Change and Status Protest." On gender, at least in China, there may have been "no universal category of 'woman' before the twentieth century"; roles as daughters, wives and mothers defined people instead. Tani E. Barlow, "Theorizing Woman: *Funü, Guojia, Jiating*," in *Body, Subject and Power in China*, edited

Did men or women normally enter the occupation?

Did practitioners tend to come from a particular place?

Did law or custom prescribe drawing practitioners from a certain ethnic, religious, or other group?

How strictly were others excluded?

What were the exceptions?

Was it possible to "pass" and join the occupation?

What rationales for the linkage of ascriptive identity and occupation were given?

Might technique or business networks explain such a link?

Did a need for trust among coworkers affect who could enter the occupation?

Was the occupation hard to enter just because few practitioners were needed?

Did certain locales produce more practitioners?

What stereotypes of the occupation did laypeople hold?

Social Mobility and Its Discontents

In systems toward the "sacred" end of the spectrum of how societies determine the division of labor, children follow parents' occupations. Inheriting the father's "property of skill" or membership in an occupation was a more common path into the crafts than bound apprenticeship in Bristol in 1813. Colleague code determined whether all sons or just the one could inherit.[14] In Staffordshire, not only did most people work in the potteries, but even in the early twentieth century about 60 per cent of positions in particular workshops had passed down from parent to child.[15]

As the division of labor becomes more secular and children's occupations differ from those of their parents, social mobility increases. What does this term mean when we focus on the social drama of work? First, it may mean that the entire occupation is gaining respect among laypeople; this is what occupations fight for when, for instance, they claim the label "profession." Second, it may mean that an individual or family has changed occupations. Rarely does everyone in society agree on the ranking of occupations; that is, status contradictions litter history. An example is the superstar courtesans of Ming, who legally were mere prostitutes, yet whose every fashion choice was imitated by respectable women. So rather than movement up and

by Angela Zito and Tani E. Barlow (Chicago: University of Chicago Press, 1994), 235–89, cited in Fang, "Priceless, Civilized Applause," 132. We might ask also about occupational roles.
14 Rule, "Property of Skill," 111.
15 Whipp, "A Time to Every Purpose," 228.

down a single scale of social status, historians should, more neutrally, use "social mobility" to refer to movement from one occupation to another.[16] More specialized occupations might not enjoy dramatically better living conditions: the doctors assigned to treat ancient Egyptian corvee laborers lived in the same uncomfortable desert camps as their patients, and ate the same rations (although their sideline work may have brought in more income).[17]

Even within the most secular divisions of labor, an individual's path into his or her occupation depends on factors beyond his or her control. As Hughes explains,

> The individual makes several choices, and achieves the skills which allow him to move to a certain position in the occupational, and thus – he hopes – in the social and economic hierarchy. His choice is limited by several conditions, among which is the social knowledge available to him at the time of crucial decision, a time which varies for the several kinds of work.[18]

In many place-times, the choice made by one member of a family could determine the occupation of younger siblings of later generations. Conversely, one spendthrift *pater familias* may ruin a business that youngsters assumed they would enter.

One family member's new path may have a profound impact on family dynamics and cause conflicts in personal identity. New social or religious practices associated with the new occupation may create a dilemma for the practitioner. If a son or daughter enters a higher-status occupation or one that makes more money, parents may be proud but also feel that they have in some sense lost their child, that he is no longer part of their social circle and is less close to them, even if he lives nearby. Hughes quotes an Irish father in Chicago, whose son entered a seminary. Proud of the achievement, the father nonetheless said,

> The wife is proud of the boy. But he breaks her heart. He ain't our boy anymore. He doesn't talk to us the same way. He never stays home long,

16   Mary Douglas points out how impoverished, how "deplorably thin," is an explanation of taste that "considers only individuals foraging in a field of other individuals of higher or lower status. In the pecking order model, lateral links are not considered, nor groupings, nor alliance nor patronage." *Thought Styles*, 57, 59.

17   Miller, "Paleoepidemiology," 3, 16–17.

18   Hughes, "Work and the Self," 44–45.

and when he does he seems like a stranger. We are going to keep the youngest home. We gave two to the Church already.[19]

Dickens understood this: Pip's great expectations as a gentleman severed him from Joe before they could ever enjoy their larks, the good times they had looked forward to in the blacksmith's forge.

Occupations often alter practitioners' identity and relationships. By the time s/he becomes a master, the practitioner may have taken on characteristics that seem like aspects of personality, as Hughes pointed out and Erving Goffman elaborated:

> In performing a role, the individual must see to it that the impressions of him that are conveyed are compatible with the role-appropriate personal qualities effectively imputed to him: a judge is supposed to be deliberate and sober; a pilot, in a cockpit, to be cool; a bookkeeper to be accurate and neat in doing his work. ... A self, then, virtually awaits the individual entering a position.[20]

Since Goffman's study of roles is not limited to occupations (although all his examples here are), he goes on to point out that an individual has several roles, and thus several selves. "Social mobility" as a macro concept does not suffice to capture the human reality of such changes.

Did practitioners inherit their occupation or particular post?
Was the occupation gaining or losing laymen's respect?
Could individuals or families move into this occupation?
What social knowledge did that require, and when in the person's lifetime did s/he have to acquire that knowledge?
Did adopting the occupation require readjusting lay behavior or outlook?
Did families encourage or discourage moving into the occupation or have mixed feelings about it?
Did laypeople comment on such moves in popular culture?
Did one sibling's choice of occupation affect those of other siblings?
What qualities that assured success in technique aligned with aspects of personality?

---

19 Hughes, "Personality Types," 31–32.
20 Goffman, *Encounters*, 87. See Hughes, "Personality Types," 35–36.

Apprenticeship

Maturation in the career may not line up with a person's chronological age. Sociologist and Professor of Education Dan C. Lortie wrote of the USA in the mid-twentieth century that "a farm youngster may be, to all intents and purposes, a working man at sixteen; medical students [even at 25], are still 'boys'."[21] The path into the occupation, in other words, could be long or short, with many distinct stages or few. Historians can adopt and test the rough traditional terminology "apprentice, journeyman, and master" for stages along the path.[22] Proceeding by stages, a practitioner-in-the-making learns technique and the culture of the occupation, but also new presentations and experiences of self.

Apprenticeship may take a short time or it may take years.[23] In traditional West Africa, for instance, apprentice blacksmiths first studied at home but then studied at another forge, the whole process taking five or even ten years.[24] The Chinese government in Tang times allotted four years for learning casting, engraving, openwork, and inlay in gold, silver, and bronze, but only one year for learning work in bamboo, wood, and lacquer.[25] The length of apprenticeship may be enforced by practitioners themselves: journeymen shearers in early modern England refused to work with those who had not done a seven-year apprenticeship, considering them not "regular." They may have felt that learning technique well really did require that long or they may have been reducing competition.[26] Or they may have understood the way a long apprenticeship teaches not just technique, but the whole culture of the occupation. An early nineteenth-century apprentice in a British silk-weaving factory wrote that he willingly ran errands for the journeymen, who in return showed him things about the business that no one would otherwise have taught him.[27] Long paths in are about more than technique.

---

21 Lortie, "Shared Ordeal," 253.

22 The journeyman stage is "fluid and ambiguous," since in European history many never made it to master, but were paid by the day (*jour*, the origin of the term) for their whole lives. Ehmer, "Artisans and Guilds," 817.

23 Ash, "Expertise and the Early Modern State," 6.

24 Camara, *Is There a Distinctively African Way of Knowing*, 11–12. Another example: Andy Eichfeld, the head of personnel at Discover, the credit card company, said, "A younger person needs apprenticeship in the first 10 or 15 years of their career. And we know how to deliver that in person. I'm not sure how apprenticeship works remotely." Friedman and Browning, "July is the New January."

25 Barbieri-Low, *Artisans in Early China*, 73.

26 Rule, "Property of Skill," 100–102.

27 Rule, "Property of Skill," 110.

A longer path into the occupation is common when the person is most fully identified with the occupational role by virtue of a high degree of occupational **license** and **mandate**, possession of **guilty knowledge**, and striking **symbols of distinction**.[28] Each transition to a new stage of a career comes with a temporary status dilemma as one sets aside an old identity, set of responsibilities, and so on, for another.[29] Further, as the apprentice becomes a journeyman and then a master, s/he must cover the traces of his/her recent learning: in order to feel and inspire confidence, s/he must appear to clients as if s/he had always known technique.[30]

To develop this new self and new self-presentation, apprentices, journeymen, and masters in an occupation may each have different code that must be unlearned and learned as part of the path into the occupation. As sociologist Dan Lortie writes, "Some occupations lay out an elaborate maze for would-be newcomers, while others, perhaps most, make little ado over the arrival of a newcomer."[31] Tracing that maze, or the "induction to work," is a rite of passage or status passage.[32] But Pierre Bourdieu differentiates a general, temporal rite of passage that everyone goes through as s/he ages from a "rite of institution" that distinguishes "those who have undergone it, not from those who have not yet undergone it, but from those who will not undergo it in any sense."[33] Male coming-of-age rites are less about the movement from boy to man than the distinction between man and woman. Investiture (as a knight, president, etc.) sanctifies and perhaps creates a difference by publicizing it, alerting both the new practitioner and others to how the new inductee must act and be.[34]

Induction to work may involve ordeals, whether public or more private. Often, journeymen or masters subject apprentices or new journeymen to

28 Hughes seems to be suggesting this as he mentions the long rite of passage – or "rite of institution" in Bourdieu's more specific phrase – that is medical education, and the need for a long novitiate to assure that there are no marginal priests. Hughes, "Social Change and Status Protest," 173–74; Bourdieu, *Language and Symbolic Power*, 51. For Hughes and Bourdieu, see Vienne, "History of Everett Cherrington Hughes," 108.

29 Hughes, "Social Change and Status Protest," 179.

30 Hughes, "Mistakes at Work," 90.

31 Lortie, "Shared Ordeal," 253.

32 See for instance Strauss, "Status Passage," 265–71. Straus comments that "the straight line of development between [Hughes's] work and this paper should be easily recognizable."

33 Pierre Bourdieu, "Les rites comme actes d'institution," translated as "Rites of Institution," in *Language and Symbolic Power,* 117. Bourdieu is not quite right, in my view, to say that it will "never pertain" to the latter group, because practitioners relate to the category of laypeople who are defined precisely by their exclusion from such rites and the other appurtenances of the occupation. Othering categorizations "pertain" to both in- and out-groups.

34 Bourdieu, *Language and Symbolic Power,* 121.

hazing rituals; new sailors in the mid-twentieth-century US Navy were teased as well as cared for by the older hands as they got their sea legs, when they were promoted, and when crossing the equator for the first time (this last always necessitated a long and entertaining set of rituals, including role reversals that temporarily usurped the captain's authority).[35] Lortie found that when apprentices shared ordeals of induction they developed self-esteem, intergenerational trust, and closer ties with colleagues. When there was no shared ordeal, the reverse resulted.[36] The impact of a given induction to work means that when apprentices commit fully to the occupation, it may be because of social or psychological factors, not just because they have invested time and effort in nontransferable technique. Contrariwise, when apprentices fail and drop out of the path into the occupation, it may not be because they have failed to acquire the knack of technique – for they may well have gained transferable skills, knowledge, or connections ("valuables")[37] – but because they have failed to alter their identity or outlook. Tracing what dropouts do next may tell us something about technique and culture of the occupation they rejected, or whose practitioners rejected them.

Learning the culture of the occupation may change the practitioner in all of the six rough types of occupation except perhaps "job," whether a lot or a little. As the authors of *Boys in White* say, "In training for medicine, great emphasis is laid upon the learning of basic sciences and their application in the diagnosis and treatment of the sick. But science and skill do not make a physician; one must also be initiated into the status of a physician; to be accepted, one must have learned to play the part of a physician in the drama of medicine."[38] This is a question not just of playing an outward role, but of conversion: of a dramatic psychological change in one's identity.

Mark Twain documented his own process of conversion on the path into the occupation of steamboat pilot: the initial romantic longing to join the occupation, surges and crises of confidence as the vastness of technique is revealed, moments of loss of faith in the teacher, and eventual mastery of both technique and persona.[39] He dramatized the difference in himself by contrasting how he had seen sunset on the river when still a layman

35   Zurcher, "The Sailor Aboard," 395–97.

36   Lortie, "Shared Ordeal," 263.

37   Geer, "Occupational Commitment," 223–24. Erving Goffman usefully distinguishes between the practitioner's own **commitment**, and the **attachment** of a person to an occupation in the eyes of others. Goffman, *Encounters*, 89.

38   Becker et al., *Boys in White*, 4.

39   Twain, *Life on the Mississippi*, 253–359 (chapters 4–20).

– magically beautiful and majestic – with how he saw it once he became a pilot: "all the romance and the beauty were gone from the river. All the value any feature of it had for me now was the amount of usefulness it could furnish toward compassing the safe piloting of a steamboat." He added, "Since those days, I have pitied doctors from my heart" for being unable to appreciate a woman's beauty, except as signs of health or disease.[40] Twain, a great observer and writer, could remember and record a process that deeply changed him. Most people forget.

That forgetting, the erasure of the process turning an apprentice into a master, applies likewise to the relation between master craftsmen and journeymen in eighteenth-century France. A historian debunking the "secret, mysterious" nature of journeymen's rites of induction into a company points out that most masters had been journeymen and had gone through these rites themselves; the rites were not mysteries to them, and masters even participated in some company activities.[41] But masters could not easily put themselves back into the journeyman's shoes, emotionally and conceptually, so participation in rites could not be an act of solidarity with journeymen.[42] The masters had passed through and out of the journeyman stage: the husk of knowledge remained but emotion and identity had changed.

Boys in White points out that until one is fully initiated into a complex occupation (unless born into it), one has little idea what that occupation is like. "The chooser of a professional occupation makes his first steps toward it on the basis of second-hand images, not of immediate experience; before him is a long blind flight."[43] The images of an occupation in lay popular culture, therefore, will affect the path into the occupation. If laypeople view an occupation with suspicion, the apprentice moving out of lay status must overcome that view sufficiently to start on the path. For instance, Henri Pirenne wrote that peasants, nobles, and clergy alike distrusted the roving medieval merchant, even as they relied on him. Some who became merchants could never quite overcome the dilemma: St. Godric, having earned immense riches in trade, suddenly gave away everything to become a hermit.[44] That is an extreme case of a new occupation. But many an apprentice may struggle with laypeople's views in adopting a new identity and overcoming his/her status dilemma.

40 Twain, *Life on the Mississippi*, 284–85.
41 Sonenscher, "Mythical Work," 42.
42 Sonenscher, "Mythical Work," 36.
43 Becker et al., *Boys in White*, 7.
44 Pirenne, "The Merchant Class," 74–80.

As training proceeds, new knowledge changes not only the apprentice's view of the occupation and himself, but his view of the world. Hughes noted that:

> the learning of the medical role consists of a separation, almost an alienation, of the student from the lay medical world ... in all of the more esoteric occupations we have studied we find the sense of seeing the world in reverse.[45]

Workers in such occupations as healing, astrology, fortune-telling, and others with a high degree of secret technique may continue to experience friction between the culture of the occupation and lay culture, but during apprenticeship that interaction is particularly

> lively – more exciting and uncomfortable, more self-conscious and yet perhaps more deeply conscious. In the process of change from one role [that of the layperson] to another [that of the practitioner] there are occasions when other people expect one to play the new role before one feels completely identified with it or competent to carry it out; there are others in which one overidentifies oneself with the role, but is not accepted in it by others.[46]

Status dilemma and status contradiction are part of the path into the occupation. Rituals, group actions, records of discipline of apprentices, and the like, may point the historian toward this process. The famous study by Robert Darnton of the Great Cat Massacre illustrates aspects of the eighteenth-century French printers' culture, with apprentices and journeymen in the midst of forming their own occupational culture as their hope of moving up to master dimmed.[47] When historians bear these questions and hypotheses in mind, the sources may reveal answers.

At what age did people begin preparation for the occupation?
How long did training last? Who decided that?
Were there distinct phases of entering the occupation?
Did work induction include rites or shared ordeals? What were they?
Do the specifics of induction rituals suggest anything about dirty work, and so on?

---

45 Hughes, "Making of a Physician," 119. Quoted in F. Davis, "Professional Socialization," 235.
46 Hughes, "Making of a Physician," 119. Quoted in F. Davis, "Professional Socialization," 235.
47 Darnton, "Workers' Revolt."

If one left early, what pragmatic advantages might even the incomplete training provide?

For those who flunked out, was there a common fallback occupation? What and why?

What knowledge and dispositions did apprentices and journeymen assimilate?

Did apprentices enter a workspace individually or as a cohort?

How were apprentices taught?

Were apprentices disciplined? For what and how?

What was taught to apprentices, explicitly or implicitly?

Were principles of operation, as well as specific skills, taught?

What did laypeople think about the occupation?

What evidence is there of group identity among apprentices?

Example: The Conversion of Nursing Students

The layered process of conversion, of change to the self, involves both knowledge and belief. Professionals believe in what they know in part because before they knew it, they believed in the teachers who taught it.[48] Fred Davis and his research partners Virginia L. Olesen and Elvi Whittaker offer a vivid illustration of this process based on a five-year study they did in the 1960s. The study focused on young women (they were all women) studying for a professional degree at a school of nursing after two years of a liberal arts education. Davis first contrasts the lay vision of nursing – nurses moved by compassion actively doing specific and straightforward procedures to help sick people feel more comfortable and get well and immediately earning heartfelt gratitude – with three aspects of the professional vision the students must learn.

The occupational culture first redefines the patient. He is not just a person who is temporarily sick, but a client with "health problems" that begin before and continue after the illness crisis. The nurse must understand and may intervene in "the patient's attitudes toward illness, his health practices, and even his social environment."[49] The object of technique, in other words, extends beyond the illness or the body to thoughts, life decisions, and conditions, and the nurse has license to do far more than make the patient comfortable and heal his illness.

Second, replacing the assumption that the nurse simply acts compassionately for the grateful patient, nursing students learn to objectively

48   Camara, *Is There a Distinctively African Way of Knowing*, 29–30.
49   F. Davis, "Professional Socialization," 240.

examine and manipulate both her own and the patient's attitudes. Both previously unquestioned, sacred selves must be, in Davis's phrase, "strenuously 'objectified'."[50] This amounts to **guilty knowledge** on the part of the nurse: rather than believing, as Americans of the period preferred, in each person's unique personality, she subjects personalities, including her own, to comparative analysis.

Third, as in many occupations, the nursing professors insist that real learning is not just a matter of picking up skills, but requires students to learn the principles underlying those skills and to think actively about how to apply them to each situation.[51] Technique, in other words, is elevated from rote skills to knowledge, as a basis for the **license** and even **mandate** the nursing profession claims.

Davis then lays out – with many disclaimers about transferability, blurry lines between stages, and so on – six stages through which the nursing students passed.[52] For historians of other occupations in other place-times, these stages of course pose possibilities, rather than automatically providing answers.

1) Initial Innocence. Entering the course of study with the lay vision summarized above, students are puzzled at being taught so few practical skills (like administering medicine, preparing catheters), reject "all that other stuff on communication and psychological care [as] just so much fluff," and are frustrated when teachers treat the skills they do learn as "small accomplishments." Faced with patients, they fall back on compassion, expressed as if they were kind daughters, and then feel insulted when patients respond in kind. Moreover, each student experiences her worry, confusion, disappointment, and lack of confidence as uniquely hers, because she simply cannot imagine what is wrong.[53]

2) Labeled Recognition of Incongruity. Once mid-term evaluations come in, however, students begin to articulate for themselves and speak to one another about the gap between their expectations and the expressed expectations of their teachers. The option of leaving is thought about and discussed. Those who stay find "other means of accommodation and adjustment."[54]

3) "Psyching Out." This is the emic term that students used to describe how they learned, individually, to figure out "what the teacher wanted" and

50 F. Davis, "Professional Socialization," 241.
51 F. Davis, "Professional Socialization," 240.
52 F. Davis, "Professional Socialization," 241.
53 F. Davis, "Professional Socialization," 242–43.
54 F. Davis, "Professional Socialization," 243–44.

then offer that performance. The best students figure it out by observing what teachers respond enthusiastically to; the second-best by asking; the third-best by imitating the others. But all three groups suffered feelings of inauthenticity and guilt at their own hypocrisy as they performed only for good grades and against their own convictions. "Perhaps to relieve the guilt that attaches to these small betrayals of self, as well as to assure peers that they are not *truly* as they represent themselves before faculty, students will frequently joke among themselves about 'putting on a front'."[55]

4) Role Simulation. Role simulation occurs at the same time as "psyching out": it is the "highly self-conscious, manipulative" performance the students have come to see as required by the institution. Role simulation involves two kinds of "psychological disjunction." First, as mentioned above, the student feels alienated from her true self by putting on an act and may feel guilt about the hypocrisy involved. Even if the performances convince others, the students said things later like "During my first year here all I did was 'play nurse,' I wasn't a real nurse." Second is a disjunction between the student's performance and her worries about others' perceptions of it. But others tend to take one at face value: a good performance will usually convince them. And the more other people believe it, the more the performance seems genuine to the student herself. She comes to see herself as "trustworthy, competent, and legitimate" as others do, and the uncomfortable feelings of hypocrisy, guilt, and inauthenticity dissipate.[56]

5) Provisional Internalization. As students go through this "fake it 'til you make it" process, they integrate the role and thinking unevenly. Vacillating between their laypeople's views and the occupational views they are practicing, they may alternate between strong rejection of the school's doctrines and enthusiastic loyalty to them. Davis further notes that the professional rhetoric or jargon that students may employ before their peers with air quotes slowly comes to provide a new cognitive map for interpreting performance. A second bridge to internalization comes as the group differentiates positive reference models (their teachers) from negative reference models (nurses without university degrees). As students see themselves enacting the nursing behavior of the positive models, they begin to identify with their teachers more strongly.[57] The

---

55 F. Davis, "Professional Socialization," 244–45.
56 F. Davis, "Professional Socialization," 246–48.
57 F. Davis, "Professional Socialization," 248–49.

prejudices of one group of coworkers against another thus arise out of the process of integration into an occupation.

6) Stable Internalization. These behavioral bridges bring the apprentice at last to consistent self-assurance in her role. She can articulate what kind of nursing practice she follows and which she rejects, and why; and, most interestingly, she tends to "reinterpret retrospectively the traumas, personal doubts, and gripes" of the earlier stages. She tends to present her apprentice self as a "miniature version" of herself as a master, erasing the uncomfortable process of alienation and reintegration.[58]

The phases meticulously documented by the sociological observers may appear in historical sources, once we know to look; or historians may find different phases to inform sociological theory.

I sent Davis's article to a mathematician and cryptographer (that is, someone of a highly analytical cast of mind), who had just been ordained as a minister. He responded that he agreed that apprentices focus on actions, rather than on "an internalized experience of being" that was ultimately more central to the culture of the occupation.

> For chaplains and ministers, the tendency at first is also to think of skills – How do I approach a patient and get them to talk about their spiritual life? How do I deliver a sermon effectively? – when in some sense the more important thing is "ministerial presence." One aspect of ministerial presence is often described as "being the least anxious person in the room" (or maybe it would be better to say, the person in the room who gives the *impression* of being least anxious). There are skills to learn in order to have this presence. You need to be aware of your emotions and take them into account in your speech and body language, you need to be able to take any anxiety you feel and put it off for a while, you need to learn how to release it later through some kind of spiritual practice or ritual, and so forth. But the skills are not the visible skills a person might think of when they see a chaplain or minister doing their thing.[59]

One might think that such a complex conversion process would apply only in highly literate occupations and religious occupations. But, as with everything, historians should investigate rather than assume, particularly

---

58   F. Davis, "Professional Socialization," 249–50.
59   Everett Howe, personal communication, August 29, 2020.

since so many occupations have included elements of ritual, magic, and charisma. More important than the requirement of literacy may be, in Bourdieu's phrase in a different context, the "long and slow" process of embedding new dispositions.[60]

> Did technique include teaching others to think differently?
> What lay views of the occupation must apprentices unlearn?
> In what order were skills and abstract knowledge taught to apprentices?
> Did apprenticeship include any of the phases Davis lays out?
> Did apprentices have both positive and negative reference models?
> What might apprentices have to forget as they became journeymen?

Commitment and the Game

Fred Davis concludes his study of conversion in nursing with a directive for sociologists that historians can adopt. We should:

> generate models of professional socialization that are far more faithful to this picture of thinking, feeling, ever-responding and calculating *human* actors groping their way through the ambiguities posed by the confluence of their lived pasts and imagined futures [as opposed to seeing apprentices as] neutral, receptive vessels into whom knowledgeable, expert members of a profession pour approved skills, attitudes, and values.[61]

But historians must also recognize that not all occupations involve conversion; even in professions conversion may not happen. Sociologist Blanche Geer's 1966 study on American students studying to become schoolteachers, for instance, found that the path offered a number of valuables transferrable to other arenas if they did not, in the end, make teaching a permanent career. The career itself was low-paying, often intermittent, with performance seldom observed by high-status others; thus, the commitment of those studying to become teachers was low and they were not "converted."[62]

Even those who choose an occupation and stay in it for a long time may not experience conversion. Individuals' choices, the structure of the institution, general social expectations, or face-to-face interactions with

---

60 Bourdieu, *Language and Symbolic Power*, 51.
61 F. Davis, "Professional Socialization," 251.
62 Geer, "Occupational Commitment."

coworkers or others may create side-bets, ostensibly unrelated to the occupation's standard technique, that commit practitioners to the career for
a stint longer than they intended. So Howard Becker argues in unpacking
the term "commitment," which at the time he was writing was appearing
frequently in sociological literature, "unscathed by so much as a single
reference." Simply because an individual stays in the same occupation for
a considerable time, Becker argues, one cannot assume that the reason lies
in emotional, moral, or rational adherence to the occupation. A person may
keep a job because of a pension plan, or to avoid losing face or gaining a
reputation for untrustworthiness by leaving too quickly. What Becker calls
"side-bets" that might keep a person in line mean that commitment may
grow without the practitioner quite realizing it, let alone intending it.[63]
S/he may end up identifying with an occupation through inertia, and with
no purposeful induction process.

By definition, jobholders do not undergo conversion. They do not deeply
identify with any one line of work. But they can in effect be converted to the
culture of the workshop created by coworkers. A fascinating participant-
observer study by sociologist Edward Davis describes how workers in one
automotive parts supply company divided their time into three categories:
work time, work avoidance time, and free time. The goal was to maximize
"free time" (spent gambling, drinking, smoking marijuana, sleeping, talking
with friends in the workshop, or for the boldest, leaving the premises while
still on the clock) and minimize "work time" spent actually filling orders.
"Avoidance time" was not as good as free time, because one had to look busy.
Workers had nine different strategies for not working, developing new ones
over the course of the study, as well as various ways of emotionally and
socially manipulating their supervisors to diminish their workloads without
risk. Avoiding work was the main activity while on the job; so much so that
new workers, still on probation (from the perspective of the supervisors) and
not yet inducted by threats and sabotage into the work-avoidance mindset
(from the perspective of coworkers), accounted for most of the orders that
were filled on any given day. As Davis explains, "No one in the warehouse
identified with the product." One foreman said,

> The workers are so alienated that they hate this place. Shit, we hate this
> place too. Who gives a shit about car parts? ... The workers ... begin to
> think, "... If I settle for something like this, I must be fucked, but I'm

---

63   Becker, "Concept of Commitment."

not fucked; the job's fucked. That means, the corporation is fucked for offering me this job."[64]

When a worker moved up the hierarchy into the position of foreman, she or he sacrificed any friendship with former colleagues, but took with him or her the knowledge of work-avoidance strategies. Supervisors developed their own strategies in response, since they faced discipline by their own superiors if too few orders were filled or it became obvious that workers were being paid for doing nothing. The game of work-avoidance and the game of "busting" or catching work-avoiders became intertwined and provided all the excitement, pleasure, and pride of the workshop. Another foreman explained:

> When you take away your fear of being fired, you take away your stinger ... If you don't have to fight to live, then half of your drive is gone ... The game now is exciting because it's a fight every day. I could go to work tomorrow and be fired, and that's what I love about it. That's management.[65]

The specifics of *how* to avoid work, how to avoid getting busted, and so on will vary based on technique and object of technique, the layout of the workshop, methods of tracking effort, and other factors. But this was surely not the only workshop in history where new employees were (from the perspective of the boss) subverted, rather than converted, by coworkers. The study points up the sociologists' code of understanding emic values rather than judging workers by our own or their bosses' values. As in participant observation, historians using the Hughes framework as a lens may spot surprises even in well-worked-over sources.

Did practitioners stick to the occupation merely to earn a living, or because they had no choice?
Did the culture of the occupation or the workspace center on work avoidance?
If so, how did work avoidance strategies relate to technique?
How did they inform relations among coworkers or colleagues, with superiors, and with clients?
What games developed among coworkers?
How were newcomers inducted into those games, along with technique?

---

64   E. Davis, *Hidden Dimensions*, 94.
65   E. Davis, *Hidden Dimensions*, 93–94.

The Path Out of the Occupation

Even after a long apprenticeship, new practitioners may suffer bewilderment and "reality shock" when they start their new career.[66] But the fact that work often changes the practitioner's sense of self means that the path out of the occupation can be rough, too. Some occupations have a retirement path; in others, practitioners simply work until they die. Some occupations have an upper age limit based on code or client demand, for instance, "persons in sports, airline pilots, prostitutes, and many types of criminals."[67] On the way out of the occupation a person might turn to teaching the next generation, or do less arduous tasks, especially if work was being done in the home. Emeritus professors teach undergraduates but no longer serve on committees. In the highly commercialized Yangtze delta area of Qing China, old people in farm families continued to work productively at sideline production tasks that would bring in something, if only enough to feed a child. Such tasks included spinning cotton and reeling silk. Under collectivization in the twentieth century, the elderly might raise vegetables as a permitted sideline.[68] These were all tasks that the elderly peasant might have learned as a child, set aside, and then later returned to.

Professions select their recruits carefully, and, if one leaves, the practitioners may, in Hughes's words, "gnash their teeth and tear their hair over a sheep lost from the fold." The US medical faculty that lost a student in the 1950s wondered what they had done wrong, either in admitting or in educating him (occasionally her). In other professional courses of the same place-time, however, students were told on the first day to look around and know that few of those sitting with them would survive until the next year. In such occupations, colleagues and even laypeople may distrust practitioners who leave for reasons other than old age, because the departure casts doubt on the occupation's view of itself as a calling. Rites of passage out may be required – as for priests who return to lay life.[69]

---

66 Zurcher, "The Sailor Aboard," 393.

67 Edward Gross, *Work and Society* (New York: Thomas Y. Cromwell, 1958), 198, cited in E. Davis, *Hidden Dimensions*, 104.

68 Huang, *Peasant Family*, 14, 80, 84, 204. Huang's argument is that, far from increasing capitalist interactions, the development of the textile industry in this area before the twentieth century was a form of "involuted commercialization" in which marginal returns to labor (labor productivity) diminished, rather than increasing, and in which families operated increasingly as an economic unit.

69 Hughes, "Professions," 662–62, 657.

After all, as Bourdieu writes, rites of institution change who a person is and what s/he does. One purpose is to "discourage permanently any attempt to cross the line, to transgress, desert, or quit."[70] Even without a heavy sacred burden, for any practitioner whose self has been greatly shaped by work, retirement may present a personal crisis. Study of the life cycle in any place-time should take work into account.

> Did practitioners experience the occupation as a continuous career or as unrelated stints?
> How much flexibility was there in leaving the occupation?
> Did people age out of it? Willingly or not?
> Did one only improve in technique with experience, or did performance also deteriorate with age?
> Did rituals usher practitioners out of the occupation?
> Did retirees continue to identify with the occupation, for instance by teaching?
> Did retirees move into a related occupation?

Works Cited

Ash, Eric. "Introduction: Expertise and the Early Modern State." *Osiris* 25, no. 1 (2010): 1–24.

Barbieri-Low, Anthony J. *Artisans in Early China*. Seattle: University of Washington Press, 2007.

Bearman, Peter. *Doormen*. Chicago: University of Chicago Press, 2005.

Becker, Howard S. "Notes on the Concept of Commitment." *American Journal of Sociology* 66, no. 1 (1960): 32–40.

Becker, Howard S., Blanche Geer, Everett C. Hughes, and Anselm L. Strauss. *Boys in White: Student Culture in Medical School*. Chicago: University of Chicago Press, 1961.

Berg, Maxine. "Women's Work, Mechanization and the Early Phases of Industrialization in England." In *The Historical Meanings of Work*, edited by Patrick Joyce, 64–98. Cambridge: Cambridge University Press, 1987.

Bourdieu, Pierre. *Language and Symbolic Power*. Translated by Gino Raymond. Cambridge: Polity Press, 1991.

Camara, Mohamed Saliou. *Is There a Distinctively African Way of Knowing (a Study of African Blacksmiths, Hunters, Healers, Griots, Elders, and Artists): Knowing and Theory of Knowledge in the African Experience*. Lewiston: Edwin Mellen Press, 2014.

70 Bourdieu, *Language and Symbolic Power*, 122.

Carter, Ron. "At 85, Legendary Jazz Bassist Ron Carter is Still Going Strong." Interview by Celeste Headlee. *NPR Illinois*, August 19, 2002. https://www.nprillinois.org/2022-08-19/at-85-legendary-jazz-bassist-ron-carter-is-still-going-strong

Darnton, Robert. "Workers' Revolt: The Great Cat Massacre of the Rue Saint-Severin." In *The Great Cat Massacre and Other Episodes in French Cultural History*, 75–104. New York: Basic Books, 1984.

Davis, Edward B. *Hidden Dimensions of Work: Revisiting the Chicago School Methods of Everett Hughes and Anselm Strauss*. N.p.: Xlibris Books, 2011.

Davis, Fred. "Professional Socialization as Subjective Experience: The Process of Doctrinal Conversion among Student Nurses." In *Institutions and the Person: Festschrift in Honor of Everett C. Hughes*, edited by Howard S. Becker, Blanche Geer, David Riesman, and Robert S. Weiss, 235–51. Chicago: Aldine, 1968.

Douglas, Mary. *Thought Styles: Critical Essays on Good Taste*. London: Sage, 1996.

Ehmer, Josef. "Artisans and Guilds, History of." In *International Encyclopedia of the Social and Behavioral Sciences*, vol. 2, 816–21. London: Elsevier, 2001.

Ehmer, Josef. "Work, History of." In *International Encyclopedia of the Social and Behavioral Sciences*, vol. 24, 16569–74. London: Elsevier, 2001.

Fang Qin. "'A Priceless, Civilized Applause': Prostitutes and Charitable Performances in Early Twentieth-Century China." *Late Imperial China* 43, no. 1 (2022): 127–64.

Friedman, Gillian, and Kellen Browning. "July is the New January: More Companies Delay Return to the Office." *New York Times*, October 13, 2020. https://www.nytimes.com/2020/10/13/technology/offices-reopening-delay-coronavirus.html

Geer, Blanche. "Occupational Commitment and the Teaching Profession." In *Institutions and the Person: Festschrift in Honor of Everett C. Hughes*, edited by Howard S. Becker, Blanche Geer, David Riesman, and Robert S. Weiss, 221–34. Chicago: Aldine, 1968.

Goffman, Erving. *Encounters: Two Studies in the Sociology of Interaction*. Indianapolis: Bobbs-Merrill, 1961.

Gold, Ray. "Janitors Versus Tenants: A Status-Income Dilemma." *American Journal of Sociology* 57, no. 5 (1952): 486–93.

Hinchy, Jessica, and Girija Joshi. "Selective Amnesia and South Asian Histories: An Interview with Indrani Chatterjee." *Itinerario* (2021): 1–16.

Huang, Philip. *The Peasant Family and Rural Development in the Yangzi Delta, 1350–1988*. Stanford: Stanford University Press, 1990.

Hughes, Everett C. "Dilemmas and Contradictions of Status." In *Men and Their Work*, 102–15. Glencoe, IL: The Free Press, 1958.

Hughes, Everett C. "Mistakes at Work." In *Men and Their Work*, 88–101. Glencoe, IL: The Free Press, 1958.

Hughes, Everett C. "Personality Types and the Division of Labor." In *Men and Their Work*, 23–41. Glencoe, IL: The Free Press, 1958.

Hughes, Everett C. "Professions." *Dædalus* 92, no. 4 (1963): 655–68.

Hughes, Everett C. "Social Change and Status Protest: An Essay on the Marginal Man." In *On Work, Race and the Sociological Imagination*, edited by Lewis Coser, 171–79. Chicago: University of Chicago Press, 1994.

Hughes, Everett C. "The Making of a Physician." In *Men and Their Work*, 116–30. Glencoe, IL: The Free Press, 1958.

Hughes, Everett C. "Work and the Self." In *Men and Their Work*, 42–55. Glencoe, IL: The Free Press, 1958.

Lortie, Dan C. "Shared Ordeal and Induction to Work." In *Institutions and the Person: Festschrift in Honor of Everett C. Hughes*, edited by Howard S. Becker, Blanche Geer, David Riesman, and Robert S. Weiss, 252–64. Chicago: Aldine, 1968.

Miller, R. L. "Paleoepidemiology, Literacy, and Medical Tradition among Necropolis Workmen in New Kingdom Egypt." *Medical History* 35 (1991): 1–24

Pirenne, Henri. "The Merchant Class." In *Medieval Cities: Their Origins and the Revival of Trade – Updated Edition*, 68–83. Princeton: Princeton University Press, 1980.

Robinson, David M. "Banditry and the Subversion of State Authority in China: The Capital Region during the Middle Ming Period (1450–1525)." *Journal of Social History* (2000): 527–63.

Rule, John. "The Property of Skill in the Period of Manufacture." In *The Historical Meanings of Work,* edited by Patrick Joyce, 99–118. Cambridge: Cambridge University Press, 1987.

Strauss, Anselm L. "Some Neglected Properties of Status Passage." In *Institutions and the Person: Festschrift in Honor of Everett C. Hughes*, edited by Howard S. Becker, Blanche Geer, David Riesman, and Robert S. Weiss, 265–71. Chicago: Aldine, 1968.

Sonenscher, Michael. "Mythical Work: Workshop Production and the *Compagnonnages* of Eighteenth-Century France." In *The Historical Meanings of Work*, edited by Patrick Joyce, 31–63. Cambridge: Cambridge University Press, 1987.

Thomas, Keith, ed. *The Oxford Book of Work*. Oxford: Oxford University Press, 1999.

Twain, Mark. *Life on the Mississippi*. 1883; reprint New York: The Library of America, 1982.

van Vorst, Mrs. John, and Marie van Vorst. *The Woman Who Toils: Being the Experiences of Two Ladies as Factory Girls*. 1902, 1903; facsimile reprint Carlisle, MA: Applewood Books, n.d.

Vienne, Philippe. "The Natural History of Everett Cherrington Hughes: A Master of Fieldwork." In *The Anthem Companion to Everett Hughes*, edited by Rich Helmes-Hayes and Marco Santoro, 93–114. London: Anthem Press, 2016.

Whipp, Richard. "'A Time to Every Purpose': An Essay on Time and Work." In *Historical Meanings of Work*, edited by Patrick Joyce, 210–36. Cambridge: Cambridge University Press, 1987.

Zurcher, Jr., Louis A. "The Sailor Aboard Ship: A Study of Role Behavior in a Total Institution." *Social Forces* 43, no. 3 (1965): 389–400.

V. Self-Regulation and Public Relations (Code and Policy)

Abstract

The shared technique, object of technique, risks of mistakes at work, clients, and social conditions of colleagues in an occupation generated cultural responses beyond shared identity and definitions of dirty work. Two aspects of occupational culture that shape and reflect the social drama of work are "code" and "policy." Code refers to all the formal and informal regulations and expectations that an occupation develops for its members, from expectations about solidarity in demands for remuneration, to induction rituals for apprentices, to norms about keeping secret aspects of technique. Code grows within the larger cultural milieu but may run counter to norms for laymen. Policy is the public face of the occupation: its demands for privileges or particular perceptions by laymen.

Keywords: regulations, unions, production processes, ritual, secrecy, public relations

Understanding the exploitative relations of labor and management, slave and master in terms of large social and economic structures lays the foundation for understanding both the ideological nature of elite-authored texts and the lived experience of workers of all sorts. But historians can also use those sources in combination with occupational sociology to find the more specific ways in which colleagues developed social and cultural norms for themselves and represented themselves to clients and other laypeople. The Hughes framework offers one way to locate agency among the exploited and weakness in the hegemonic.

Schneewind, S.K. *The Social Drama of Daily Work. A Manual for Historians.* Amsterdam: Amsterdam University Press, 2024
DOI: 10.5117/9789048559534_CH05

Policy

> We [sociologists] do not take for granted that the sole [aim] of an organiza-
> tion is what those concerned say it is.[1]

Policy refers to the way the occupational group presents itself to laypeople.
The occupation relates to society in ways that promote practitioners' shared
interests; for instance, as Hughes explains, to real estate agents, "real-estate
law and the land itself are object of technique. If [they] oppose change in
real-estate law, it is not from sentiment, but as a matter of policy."[2] Policy
cannot be unilaterally set by practitioners in an occupation; there must be
some social acceptance of their views, because they are working within the
larger community. A signal of reliability through a **symbol of distinction**
(the monk's tonsure, the cafeteria worker's cap) is no good unless laypeople
can interpret it. Policy is precisely a negotiation of the occupation with the
lay community.

Policy includes demands by the occupation for privileges and efforts to
shape how clients and laypeople perceive it. This might involve a change
in labels, from "personnel" to "human resources," for instance. When
banks failed in the Great Depression, they were slapped with government
regulation from outside, but also developed internal procedures that they
then publicized to reassure clients. When the food industry lobbies for or
against purity and labeling requirements, it is pursuing policy. Policy is any
outward-facing self-representation by a particular occupation.

Policy for the occupation is similar to what Louis Kriesberg calls a workshop's "purpose," usefully distinguished from output. The output, he explains,
is "the goods or service which the producing component [of a workshop]
turns out" – porcelain vessels, repaired limbs, educated graduates, and so
on. "The purpose," by contrast, "is to a large extent the rationale used to
legitimate the organization's activities to significant others." Factory owners
in the USA in the twentieth century, for instance, might have said that "the
purpose of the organization is profit; but the organization's output is not
profits," but rather cars or widgets.[3] The medical school's purpose was to
produce doctors, but doing so involved the output of cared-for patients and
research results.[4] Policy reflects purpose, but different occupations within

1   Becker et al., *Boys in White*, 15.
2   Hughes, "Personality Types," 35.
3   Kriesberg, "Internal Differentiation," 143.
4   Becker et al., *Boys in White*, 13.

the same workshop may not agree on purpose, nor have the same policy. Purpose is to the workshop as policy is to the occupation.

To ask about the difference between output and purpose is to draw attention to rhetoric and ideology that may shape how outsiders view one kind of work, but not reflect practitioners' experience and identity – how they see their own role. Kriesberg gives the example of coal mining. Owners and union organizers agreed that the output was coal, but while owners defined the purpose as profit or as providing coal to as many consumers as possible, labor organizers might well disagree, and "argue that ... providing a decent standard of living for the workers is an essential objective, even if this should mean increasing the cost of coal" – which would mean that some consumers could not afford it or profits went down.[5]

Policy includes "branding" an occupation: saying what it is all about for a lay audience of potential clients and competitors. It includes symbols of distinction, but it also includes aligning the occupation with other high-status features of culture. For instance, over the course of the twentieth century, school teachers, nurses, and realtors all strove to be socially reclassified as "professionals."[6] Seeing that urge in his students led Hughes to recognize that "profession" was a value-laden term, and he changed the title of a course on professions to "Sociology of Work" to encourage objective study of all lines of work.[7] Policy misled even practicing social scientists of the time, he wrote: seeing *themselves* as professionals who had no conflicts of interest with their clients, they accepted at face value the claims of other professionals to have none. Slowly, sociologists uncovered these professions' "feelings of antagonism and resistance" toward their clients and those they knew clients had toward them: feelings that had been concealed. This "common concealment" is part of policy.[8] A skepticism about what practitioners – especially high-status practitioners – said publicly about their occupation was precisely what Hughes and his school brought to the nascent sociology of professions.[9] Skepticism enabled the sociologists to identify gaps between policy on the one hand and the real tensions and conflicts in other elements of occupational culture.

5   Kriesberg, "Internal Differentiation," 145. Kriesberg also offers distinctions among like, common, complementary, and conflicting interests of people within the organization.
6   Hughes, "Professions in Transition," 133. He relates this to **mobility of the whole occupation**. Hughes, "Work and the Self," 45.
7   Chapoulie, *Chicago Sociology*, 181. Bearman, *Doormen*, 11–14, shows that New York doormen in about 2000 similarly wished to define themselves as "professionals."
8   Chapoulie, *Chicago Sociology*, 186.
9   Chapoulie, *Chicago Sociology*, 186.

Policy is the outward face of an occupation, so researchers should question it as they do other forms of ideology – justifications of authority. Likewise, Hughes replaced the value-laden, ideological term "code of ethics" with "colleague code" or just "code" to avoid the tendency to "sort people into the good and the bad" and enable the researcher to see how the rules colleagues develop for mutual protection help them to handle **mistakes at work**.[10] Policy may include publicizing some items of code while hiding others. It certainly includes responding to client fears, including fears that parts of code are being hidden.

> Did the occupation have and express shared interests vis-à-vis laymen?
> Had the occupation experienced a dramatic failure, then changed its public face?
> Did practitioners adopt **symbols of distinction**?
> Did practitioners insist on being labelled, addressed, or treated in certain ways?
> Did workshop owners speak of a purpose that differed from the output workers produced or spoke of?
> What did laymen worry about with respect to the occupation?

Code

Occupational groups often develop code, "a body of rules developed and enforced by the members and with some power to save its members from outside punishment."[11] In the pickle factory, Bessie McGinnis Van Vorst noticed a girl of eleven or twelve years old, so unhealthy looking as to seem "scarcely human." When Van Vorst hurt herself, this "strange little elf" rushed over, all sympathy. Van Vorst comments:

> There is more honour than courtesy in the code of etiquette. Commands are given curtly; the slightest injustice is resented; each man for himself in work, but in trouble all for the one who is suffering. No bruise or cut or burn is too familiar a sight to pass uncared for. It is their common sufferings, their common effort that unites them.[12]

She is arguing that even jobholders had a code of behavior toward coworkers, semi-independent of the ethical values of the community. To determine

---

10   Chapoulie, *Chicago Sociology*, 184.
11   Hughes, "Good People and Dirty Work," 190.
12   Van Vorst and van Vorst, *The Woman Who Toils*, 43.

whether a particular social practice or value in the workshop is code, one would have to show its distinction from practice outside the workshop. Would the strange little elf have rushed to help if Van Vorst had fallen down on the street? If so, her care does not count as code, for like all key concepts in the Hughes framework, code and policy arise among colleagues.

Code is "the occupation's prescribed activity of the individuals within [the occupation] towards each other."[13] Erving Goffman borrows from Hughes the example that a consulting physician will not say anything to embarrass the patient's doctor, and from William Westley the solidarity of policemen before a judge: the two colleagues maintain a "common front."[14] Another example is the way medieval merchants vouched for one another in market-fair disputes.[15] Naturally, colleagues sometimes break code, just as any set of rules will be broken. Code might be imbued with divine authority by placement in the temple of a patron deity, as were the "Fishing Season Prohibitions" designed to deal with disagreements resulting from detached nets and colliding boats along the Zhejiang coast. In the mid-nineteenth century, the Prohibitions were code enforced not just by the god, but by the fishermen themselves. They might drown a colleague for a serious infraction or fine him the cost of an opera performance for a minor one.[16]

Historian John Rule discusses colleague code (without calling it that) among the trades in pre-industrial Britain. The most straightforward example is the agreement not to work for less than the "customary" rate. Journeymen who accepted lower pay might find themselves visited by a group of colleagues, or might "be declared 'unfair' or 'foul' so that honourable artisans would not work alongside them or for their employers."[17] Code may also encompass the form of remuneration, if the occupation could influence that; did one demand remuneration by time or by the piece, for instance? Colleagues might fine those who broke code, or covertly damage the transgressor's tools. Code might limit how much work an ambitious colleague could take on.[18] The degree of specialization within an occupation might also be stipulated by code rather than by management.[19] Code includes

---

13   Hughes, "Personality Types," 35.

14   Goffman, *Presentation of Self*, 90.

15   Pirenne, "The Merchant Class," 76. James Scott extends this insight beyond occupations into an analysis of the "hidden transcripts" and "public transcripts" produced by class relations. Scott, *Domination and the Arts of Resistance*.

16   Muscolino, *Fishing Wars*, 42–44.

17   Rule, "Property of Skill," 112.

18   Rule, "Property of Skill," 112.

19   Mocarrelli, "Attitudes to Work," 95.

any kind of regulation of professional activity created and enforced by practitioners of an occupation themselves.

Code goes beyond technique, object of technique, remuneration, and relations with clients. In the social and cultural realm, code could stipulate participation in celebrations of the patron saint's day and colleagues' funerals. It included induction rites for apprentices and required novice and new journeyman to treat others to beer. It might include patronizing particular pubs and helping colleagues or coworkers financially.[20] Historians, when not (in Rule's phrase) "pour[ing] scorn on notions of a 'golden age'" before industrialization, have sometimes seen all such organization teleologically as the forerunners to trade unions and the like.[21] The sociological framework is less diachronic, focused on understanding work relations at a particular time before talking about change over time. This kind of non-teleological attention to the full scope of colleague interaction provides a firmer baseline for understanding change over time. For instance, historian Emily Honig's study of the different aspects of the lives of factory women in Shanghai, including their shared social, cultural, and religious activities, enabled her to understand the successes and failures of Communist organizers.[22]

The internal regulations of code, formal or informal, must be sufficiently in line with community values to be understood, but instead of social principles of ethical right and wrong, they address occupational specifics. One example is the West African hunter of the mid-twentieth century, who avoided, and expected his colleagues to avoid, killing pregnant animals and mothers with young offspring. This was not an ethical but a practical guideline: hunters did not apply it to "battues" – the flushing out and killing of predators who were endangering communities or to herbivores who were endangering fields and gardens.[23]

Code often determines which parts of technique practitioners should keep secret from clients and laypeople. For Tanzanian Bena blacksmiths in the twentieth century, code included ritual, symbolism, and medicine in their ironworking processes. The iron smelting stage was kept secret from laypeople, but iron refining and smithing were openly carried out near people's homes.[24] It made sense for the occupation to keep the smelting

20   Rule, "Property of Skill," 112.
21   Rule, "Property of Skill," 114.
22   Honig, *Sisters and Strangers*.
23   Camara, *Is There a Distinctively African Way of Knowing*, 17.
24   Camara, *Is There a Distinctively African Way of Knowing*, 13.

stage secret, since it was that transformation of "wild dirt" into workable iron that impressed laypeople so much that they conferred mystic status on the trade. On the other hand, documents recording code are sometimes made public, in which case they become policy: the occupation's outward face. The Hippocratic oath is an example.[25] Policy may include either concealing or revealing the risks inherent in an occupation. Taxi drivers in Boston in the mid-twentieth century did not like their families and other laypeople to know the number of robberies they faced while on the job, even though they were not to blame.[26] Their code included a policy of keeping this risk secret.

How much did colleagues interact with one another?
How would you distinguish colleagues from coworkers for your study?
Did the occupation's norms for itself reinforce hierarchy or egalitarian proce-
dures?
Did those norms govern remuneration? Pace? Specialization?
Did different levels of hierarchy within the occupation have different standard
practices?
How did occupational norms of behavior clash with, how align with, general
social norms?
How did code encourage and how undermine colleague or coworker solidarity?
When colleagues broke code, what happened?
Did code extend to practitioners' family members?
Was code explicitly taught to apprentices, conveyed in rites, or soaked up?
What aspects of the occupation did colleagues expect each other to keep secret?
What parts of code were kept secret?
Which were publicized, becoming policy?
Did code change over time?
What does code reveal about technique?

Code and Technique

Code arises from technique. Mid-twentieth-century Chicago janitors developed code that forbade telling or using the many secrets of tenants that naturally came their way as they separated combustible from non-combustible garbage: discarded mail made each tenant's garbage easy to

25   Another example is found in Bian, *Know Your Remedies*, 132: a list of injunctions to pharmacists, by a pharmacist, was published for the public to see.
26   E. Davis, *Hidden Dimensions*, 110.

identify. The janitors' code also required strict, but indirect, refusals of sexual offers from women in the building. As one janitor reported,

> lots of women try to get you up in apartment just "to talk" or for some phony excuse. When you walk in they are on couch, ask you to sit down, and that means only one thing. When that happens to me and I begin to sweat, I know I better leave. Thing is not to refuse them so they get embarrassed, so I act dumb. I excuse myself and say I forgot about water running some place which I must shut off right away. It's hard to do, but it's best.[27]

It is easy to see that straying from that code would undermine the whole occupation's **license** to come and go as practitioners dealt with radiators, windows, and other objects in need of repair.

Among Hungarian herdsmen in the mid-twentieth century, the helpers comprising teams assigned to individual herds (which belonged to peasants who spent their own time on cultivation) were hired by an older, married, financially secure, and upright herdsman, the *száamadó*, who ranked the helpers and taught the younger men "the skills of herding and correct behavior in accordance with the herders unwritten code."[28] Technique required a strict daily schedule; and in a windstorm or sudden thaw, serious **mistakes at work** could result if everyone did not know his task and follow orders. An established ranking of team members was critical, so, following code, the *száamadó* disciplined junior helpers when they ate out of the pot before senior helpers. But, also following code, he tolerated their stealing animals, which did not affect the work – even though the wider community regarded stealing animals as ethically wrong.[29]

Code is not handed down from on high; it develops organically among colleagues. Therefore, it can be disrupted by a change in workshop organization. For instance, sociologist William Westley shows changes in code in a period in the twentieth century when the US army was rapidly expanding, so that new soldiers were coming in and being cycled through different groupings. That meant that the sergeants did not know their men well. Suddenly many recruits were going AWOL. Before the reform, Westley found that:

---

27   Gold, "Janitors Versus Tenants." For a recent article on French janitors that Vienne describes as "quite in the same mood," see Marchal, "Gardiens."
28   Vincze, "Organization of Work in Herding Teams," 146–47.
29   Vincze, "Organization of Work in Herding Teams," 147–50.

When the men went to town on weekend passes, they would search for girls and, if they found them, were reluctant to come back on Sunday night and would be missing at roll call on Monday morning ... [but] the sergeant would report the men present at roll call. They knew he would do this and would break their necks to get back that day so he would not get into trouble. He, knowing that this was the way they would react, was willing to protect them.

But this changed as the army expanded. The sergeant, not knowing or trusting the new men, reported them AWOL immediately. They expected that, so since they were in trouble anyway, they stayed away, sometimes to the point of desertion. By disrupting the bonding of colleagues up and down the hierarchy within the occupation, the army was depleting its forces.[30] Code develops by negotiation within the practitioners of the occupation and is not determined by higher-ups.

Rules set by superiors may have a great impact on working life, of course, but are not considered code. In fact, Bearman concluded in his study of Manhattan doormen that inflexibly following the written rules of the building robbed doormen of their policy claim to be "professionals" who knew their tenants and their preferences and treated tenants differently according to those preferences, as code demanded. For example, building managers often set as a rule that doormen should challenge all visitors, even those who were clearly entering with a tenant. But that would not only be awkwardly intrusive: it would also signal to tenants that the doorman did not really know them well enough to intuit who were their friends, whereas doormen defined their professionalism as resting precisely on that sort of knowledge. Tenants themselves complicated the problem by shifting their attention away from friends or partners and toward the doorman himself as they entered the lobby, as a kind of "privacy screen" for their friends.[31] Further, efforts by building superintendents to mediate all of the service requests tenants made of handymen, porters, or doormen – since the supers were not always accessible – simply forced building staff and tenants to work around the supers' rules.[32] Code may run directly counter to and be created in opposition to formal rules.

Because code arises from technique, it may not only work around formal rules, but may counter formal hierarchy within the occupation. On a pre-Civil War Mississippi River steamboat, the captain was, formally, the

30 Westley, "Organization of the Army," 204.
31 Bearman, *Doormen*, 105.
32 Bearman, *Doormen*, 133.

master. But because the whole operation, the safety of the workshop, the investment of the owners, the cargo, and the lives of all aboard depended on the delicate navigation through shallows, around bends, past snags, over sandbanks – by day or by night; in rain or in fog – and because the technique the pilot commanded was so specialized and demanding, the captain dared not, even in the most extreme situations, say anything to the pilot about his decisions. The pilot's decisions could not be questioned even by his peers, with whom he alternated shifts. To do so was to break code; and in this case, code was eventually written into the law of the United States, which forbade pilots at work to heed others' commands. "I have seen," Twain wrote, "a boy of eighteen taking a great steamer serenely into what seemed almost certain destruction, and the aged captain standing mutely by, filled with apprehension but powerless to interfere."[33]

Code springs from colleagues' understanding of clients and of technique, and the occupation's need to manage the risk of mistakes at work. It may encompass codes of ethics, and codes of honor (for instance, the steamboat pilot's watchword, never to desert his post), but also shared standards about work that cannot be aligned with right and wrong as laypeople see them.

What does technique reveal about code?
What kind of hierarchy and cooperation did technique require?
Who monitored it?
How were hierarchy or equality ritually expressed within the occupation?
Did members of the occupation break *community* norms, as distinct from code?
What rules did the state or the top brass attempt to impose on the occupation?
Did practitioners follow those rules?
Did those rules support or undermine relations among colleagues?
Did those rules threaten the occupation's self-concept, code, or policy?
Did practitioners expect each other to participate in disobeying top-down rules?
Did code support or undermine hierarchy within the occupation?
How did code articulate or shape relations with clients?

Works Cited

Bearman, Peter. *Doormen*. Chicago: University of Chicago Press, 2005.
Becker, Howard S., Blanche Geer, Everett C. Hughes, and Anselm L. Strauss. *Boys in White: Student Culture in Medical School*. Chicago: University of Chicago Press, 1961.

33   Twain, *Life on the Mississippi*, 313–14.

Bian, He. *Know Your Remedies: Pharmacy and Culture in Early Modern China.* Princeton: Princeton University Press, 2020.

Camara, Mohamed Saliou. *Is There a Distinctively African Way of Knowing (a Study of African Blacksmiths, Hunters, Healers, Griots, Elders, and Artists): Knowing and Theory of Knowledge in the African Experience.* Lewiston: Edwin Mellen Press, 2014.

Chapoulie, Jean-Michel. *Chicago Sociology.* Translated by Caroline Wazer. New York: Columbia University Press, 2001.

Davis, Edward B. *Hidden Dimensions of Work: Revisiting the Chicago School Methods of Everett Hughes and Anselm Strauss.* N.p.: Xlibris Books, 2011.

Goffman, Erving. *The Presentation of Self in Everyday Life.* New York: Anchor Books, 1959.

Gold, Ray. "Janitors Versus Tenants: A Status-Income Dilemma." *American Journal of Sociology* 57, no. 5 (1952): 486-93.

Honig, Emily. *Sisters and Strangers: Women in the Shanghai Cotton Mills (1919–1949).* Stanford: Stanford University Press, 1986.

Hughes, Everett C. "Good People and Dirty Work." In *On Work, Race and the Sociological Imagination*, edited by Lewis Coser, 180–91. Chicago: University of Chicago Press, 1994.

Hughes, Everett C. "Personality Types and the Division of Labor." In *Men and Their Work*, 23–41. Glencoe, IL: The Free Press, 1958.

Hughes, Everett C. "Professions in Transition." In *Men and Their Work*, 131–38. Glencoe, IL: The Free Press, 1958.

Hughes, Everett C. "Work and the Self." In *Men and Their Work*, 42–55. Glencoe, IL: The Free Press, 1958.

Kriesberg, Louis. "Internal Differentiation and the Establishment of Organizations." In *Institutions and the Person: Festschrift in Honor of Everett C. Hughes*, edited by Howard S. Becker, Blanche Geer, David Riesman, and Robert S. Weiss, 141–56. Chicago: Aldine, 1968.

Marchal, Hervé. "Gardiens HLM d'aujourd'hui, concierges d'hier." *Ethnologie française* 35, no. 3 (2005): 513–19.

Mocarrelli, Luca. "Attitudes to Work and Commerce in the Late Italian Renaissance: A Comparison between Tomaso Garzoni's *La Piazza Universale* and Leondardo Fioravanti's *Dello Specchio Di Scientia Universale.*" *International Review of Social History Special Issue* 56 (2011): 89–106.

Muscolino, Micah. *Fishing Wars and Environmental Change in Late Imperial and Modern China.* Cambridge, MA: Harvard University Asia Center, 2009.

Pirenne, Henri. "The Merchant Class." In *Medieval Cities: Their Origins and the Revival of Trade – Updated Edition*, 68–83. Princeton: Princeton University Press, 1980.

Rule, John. "The Property of Skill in the Period of Manufacture." In *The Historical Meanings of Work,* edited by Patrick Joyce, 99–118. Cambridge: Cambridge University Press, 1987.

Scott, James. *Domination and the Arts of Resistance: Hidden Transcripts.* New Haven: Yale University Press, 1990.

Twain, Mark. *Life on the Mississippi.* 1883; reprint New York: The Library of America, 1982.

van Vorst, Mrs. John, and Marie van Vorst. *The Woman Who Toils: Being the Experiences of Two Ladies as Factory Girls.* 1902, 1903; facsimile reprint Carlisle, MA: Applewood Books, n.d.

Vincze, Lajos. "Organization of Work in Herding Teams on the Great Hungarian Plain." In *Work in Non-market and Transitional Societies*, edited by Herbert Applebaum, 143–54. Albany: SUNY Press, 1984.

Westley, William A. "The Informal Organization of the Army: A Sociological Memoir." In *Institutions and the Person: Festschrift in Honor of Everett C. Hughes*, edited by Howard S. Becker, Blanche Geer, David Riesman, and Robert S. Weiss, 200–207. Chicago: Aldine Publishing Company, 1968.

VI. Social Authority (License and Mandate)

Abstract
The very nature of specialization means that clients do not know and cannot know as much about an occupation as its practitioners. If an occupation wins something like a monopoly on managing a particular sphere, society has granted its practitioners "license": they may tell others what to do in that sphere, regardless of social rank. Strong license will include practitioners' monopoly on judging colleagues' success. Some occupations are socially licensed to manage dangerous substances, objects, and forms of knowledge, and along with that burden of responsibility may come the license to live differently from others. An occupation may also win a "mandate" or authority to tell others how to act and *think* about the sphere of specialization.

Keywords: danger, specialization, rank, daily work, ordinary people

An occupation consists in part in the implied or explicit *license* that some people claim and are given to carry out certain activities rather different from those of other people and to do so in exchange for money, goods, or services. Generally, if the people in the occupation have any sense of identity and solidarity, they will also claim a *mandate* to define – not merely for themselves, but for others as well – proper conduct with respect to the matters concerned in their work. They also will seek to define, and possibly succeed in defining, not merely proper conduct but even modes of thinking and belief for everyone individually and for the body social and politic with respect to some broad area of life which they believe to be in their occupational domain.[1]

---

1   Hughes, "Study of Occupations," 25.

Schneewind, S.K. *The Social Drama of Daily Work. A Manual for Historians.* Amsterdam: Amsterdam University Press, 2024
DOI: 10.5117/9789048559534_CH06

License

When an occupation produces objects or serves others with technique encompassing learned skills and esoteric knowledge, clients must accept those services on trust. License refers to an occupation's institutionalized or generally recognized claim to a monopoly or quasi-monopoly on:

  a. doing certain work;
  b. being recompensed for it with money, goods, or services contributing to the practitioners' livelihood;[2] and
  c. determining who is qualified to do it. Only practitioners themselves, they will claim, can determine whether the work is well done.[3]

If laypeople widely accept these claims, the occupation has license.

License varies in form and content. First, there is legal license. Although amateurs may turn their hands to almost any activity, especially when the object of technique is their own property,

> The leaders of an occupation persuade leaders of society that its members possess some technical competence so special and of such importance that the public should be prevented from using any other occupation with the same domain but assertedly lesser competence or integrity.[4]

Examples are present-day engineers, hairdressers, and so on. Physicians in the United States today, for instance, have a documented legal monopoly on performing surgery, granting access to drugs by writing prescriptions, and certifying sick leaves or worker's compensation claims.[5] Professions, as part of their policy, fight for this kind of license to, in Eliot Freidson's phrase, "become a gatekeeper to what is popularly valued," and thus assure a clientele. Even if the layman does not think he needs the professional's expertise, and even if he knows exactly which procedure or drug he wants, to get his form signed or obtain his drug of choice he must go to the physician. Since the physician can, in effect, punish the client by refusing the request, this kind of license is somewhat like the authority of the officeholder, which

2   Hughes, "License and Mandate," 78.
3   Becker et al., *Boys in White*, 5–6.
4   Freidson, "Impurity of Professional Authority," 32.
5   Freidson, "Impurity of Professional Authority," 28.

is backed ultimately by the state's capacity for violence.[6] Legal license also enables an occupation to limit its numbers, so that each individual worker has a better chance to capture client demand. An occupation may also push for measures that keep the clientele from organizing.[7] Legal license was rarer in the past, when states had less capacity to control society.

Second, more common in the past and more interesting, is social license. At a basic level, license means that society (clients and laypeople) recognize an occupation's technique as their possession. An English letter of 1583 called it "as improper and impertinent ... for carpenters and shipwrights to make seawalls and ponds, as it is for makers of seawalls and ponds to build fair houses or make good ships."[8] The category of occupations called "jobs" has no license: society does not recognize that only certain, specially educated people can do those tasks. Shading from jobs into occupations with weak social license are lines of work with technique recognized as difficult and dangerous to the practitioner: roofing, butchering cattle, sailing, and so on.

Third, there are stronger forms of social license that rest not only on the occupation's mastery of skills that endanger the practitioners themselves, but on its mastery of skills and knowledge that endanger clients and others. For instance, pharmacists and healers the world over are socially licensed to understand, handle, and prescribe substances that may poison as well as heal: to cite just one example, the Ming-Qing gentleman-physician had license to dole out poisons to regulate a gentry wife's menstrual cycle, knowing that they might cause abortion.[9] West African blacksmiths, as mentioned, were traditionally licensed to carry out the ritual circumcision of youths transitioning to manhood.[10] Society allows occupations whose knowledgeable guidance it needs to control dangerous things.

Fourth, the license to do dangerous things extends to the license to think dangerous things. Society may permit, may in fact expect, the practitioner to analyze the object of technique in ways that laypeople do not, because of what Hughes calls "orthodoxy and sentiment" – established ideas and deep attachments or revulsions. The doctor, for instance, thinks objectively about death and the body. The priest thinks objectively about sin and immortal life, assessing and handing out penances. (Since these practitioners are humans, they cannot be required to think objectively, without pain, about *their own*

6   Freidson, "Impurity of Professional Authority," 28.
7   Freidson, "Impurity of Professional Authority," 30.
8   Thomas Scott to Francis Walsingham, in Ash, *Power, Knowledge, and Expertise*, 55.
9   Bray, *Technology and Gender*, chapter 8.
10   Camara, *Is There a Distinctively African Way of Knowing*, 12–13.

situations, and therefore "it is unfair to ask the physician to heal himself, the priest to shrive himself, or the teacher to be a perfect parent."[11]) This licensed, objective viewpoint is one kind of **guilty knowledge**, discussed in more detail below.

Fifth, society may also grant practitioners "the right to live one's life in a style somewhat different from that of most people." Hughes notes that, for instance, sailors are indulged when, ashore, they party a bit wildly.[12] Buddhist and Christian monks and nuns across Eurasia – spiritual practitioners with special technique – live oddly: instead of marrying, they live in large same-gender groups, bearing **symbols of distinction** that mark them off from laypeople. As I discuss below, when license includes social permission for technique that in laypeople's hands would endanger not just the client but the social order, the practitioner may be *required* to live differently from laypeople.

We might think of license as protecting clients, but it also protects practitioners: society judges them, while they carry out their occupation, according to standards of the occupation, standards which the practitioners participate in setting. Since roles are filled by persons, license and the requirements that come along with it may extend to the person even when s/he is not working. Moreover, especially in premodern settings where legal license was rare, the process of an occupation or individual practitioners successfully claiming social license was not necessarily straightforward. A French tax collector gained recognition as an expert in engineering when the canal he proposed to finance minister Colbert proved to work and be cost-effective, but had either of those conditions not been met, he would not have been socially licensed as an engineer, and the occupation would not have been strengthened by his success.[13]

The concept of social license developed in a society in which specialization was highly developed. Historians have found that past place-times had lower degrees of specialization, even in medicine. For instance, R. L. Miller points out that physicians in ancient Egypt did not monopolize medical knowledge: it was available in texts that any literate person could read, so that scribes, for instance, sometimes prescribed medicines for others, and construction workers may have practiced medicine on the side.[14] When individuals play different occupational roles, their varying relations with clients must have meant a lower degree of identification with the occupation

11   Hughes, "Professions," 656.
12   Hughes, "License and Mandate," 82.
13   Ash, "Expertise and the Early Modern State," 5.
14   Miller, "Paleoepidemiology," 17.

and other differences from those with a sole occupation. The shape of license and mandate will have differed, too.

> Did laymen know how to do tasks belonging to the occupation?
> Was the occupation licensed by the state?
> Over what technique did it exercise a monopoly or quasi-monopoly?
> Did other occupations licensed by law also seek clients with the same problems, needs, or desires?
> Could the technique endanger anyone?
> Did clients seek advice, before or as well as requesting action?
> What areas of human life did the occupation have to think objectively about?
> Did practitioners signal their occupation with special dress, behavior, taboos, and so on? How did laypeople talk about those aspects of the occupation?
> Who judged results, and how?

Mandate

Practitioners in an occupation socially licensed to monopolize or nearly monopolize actions using their technique on their object of technique "will, if they have any sense of self-consciousness and solidarity, also claim a mandate to define what is proper conduct of *others* toward the matters concerned with their work."[15] License refers to what society has agreed that practitioners of an occupation may do, whereas mandate is a socially accepted claim that practitioners may tell other people what to do and how to think about their area of expertise. Mandate may be implicitly or explicitly denied to an occupation that wants to claim it; for instance, in 1468 it was the Hungarian king who determined which of two astrologers was the better, not their colleagues.[16]

As part of mandate, the physician and the professor do not "let the client decide exactly what service he wants, for only the profession can define his needs."[17] Occupations in the "professional" category usually mingle in their technique practical and theoretical knowledge, manual work whether practical or symbolic (both the priest and the surgeon lay hands on the body) with esoteric understanding that underlies advice given the client.[18]

---

15 Hughes, "License and Mandate," 78.
16 Ash, "Expertise and the Early Modern State," 11.
17 Becker et al., *Boys in White*, 13.
18 Hughes, "Professions," 655.

"Professions *profess*," Hughes wrote: "They profess to know better than others the nature of certain matters, and to know better than their clients what ails them or their affairs."[19] Hughes came to use the label "profession" to talk about occupations with strong license and mandate and a good deal of guilty knowledge.

Claiming that s/he knows what is best for clients, the professional claims their trust, and states that clients cannot truly judge the value and quality of the service she receives. Rather than *caveat emptor*, the motto that expresses mandate is *credat emptor*: let the buyer trust.[20] Physicians, in deciding whether or not one of their number has made a mistake, carry out the discussion beyond the hearing of the client and patient, who might be shocked and upset by hearing their ailments and injuries "discussed as objectively as they must be in deciding whether a professional did, in fact, show competence and whether he acted in accordance with the professional code."[21] Physicians in the US in the twentieth century had very strong license in judging their colleagues, as well as mandate in imposing their judgements on lay understanding. The difference between occupations with mandate and those that have only license relates to what historian Eric Ash (in the context of the early modern consolidation of European state power) proposes as the social construction of a gulf between craftsmen and experts:

> The master stonemasons who built a new fortification wall were merely paid servants of the king; but the engineers who designed the fortification, claimed to understand the geometric principles behind it, knew the latest advances from abroad, and oversaw its construction were truly the experts, for it was they who actually placed the whole art of fortification within the monarch's control.[22]

If we see the stonemasons as possessing license, but the engineers as possessing both license and mandate, this enables us as historians to compare the case with others in other place-times and outside the field of services to the state.

In terms of directing society generally, "The mandate may go no further than the successful insistence that other people stand back and give the workers a bit of elbow room while they do their work. It may, in the case of

---

19   Hughes, "Professions," 656.

20   Hughes, "Professions," 656–57, 660.

21   Hughes, "Psychology: Science and/or Profession," 442.

22   Ash, "Expertise and the Early Modern State," 11.

the modern physician, include a successful claim to supervise and determine the conditions of work of ... nurses, technicians and the many others [in hospitals]." But some occupations successfully claim a broad mandate – the right to tell *other people* what to do, what to think, and even in what terms to think about their technique and objects of technique. Hughes writes: "In the extreme case [mandate] may, as in the priesthood in strongly Catholic countries, include the right to control the thoughts and beliefs of whole populations with respect to nearly all the major concerns of life."[23]

This right to direct clients comes from the detachment of the professional: the practitioner has no vested interest in any particular case but is intellectually interested in all cases that contribute to occupational knowledge.[24] Winning and losing mandate involve struggles the historian can trace; they appear in the process of "professionalization." In determining whether control stems from mandate, the historian must establish whether laypeople permit it, even if grudgingly; control imposed from with the threat of violence is a different matter.

How does mandate work at the level of a single interaction? The occupation's authority – the ability to elicit obedience from clients – may rest on one of several grounds, as Freidson teases out in an elegant essay.

1. The client may obey because he needs some good or service to which the occupation monopolizes access (a drug, a signature on a form), and his obedience may extend only to outward conformity: he still thinks he's right and knows as much as the expert.

2. The client may accept the consultant's advice because it happens to coincide with what he thinks anyway.

3. During their conversation, the consultant may be able to convince the client that the advice he is giving really is good; this is the only case in which "the authority of technical competence" has actually worked, and in which the way clients are persuaded is more or less the way colleagues are persuaded. I would add, however, that consultant may persuade the client on emotional grounds or even through lies (even if the course of action really is what is best for the client).

4. For the professions in particular, the client may obey out of pure faith in the expert as a member of the profession, without asking for explanation and even without asking for a demonstration of competence from the practitioner.

23 Hughes, "License and Mandate," 78.
24 Hughes, "Professions," 660.

5. The expert may have recourse to "the doctrine of free choice," even if it is a fiction because there are no competing colleagues in the community. "The expert may say, 'After all, Mr. Jones, nobody is making you come to me, and I can't force you to take my advice. If you don't want to cooperate, go somewhere else.' In essence, the doctrine of free choice allows the consultant to put the burden of compliance on the client."[25] The practitioner willing to risk losing a client may refer to the client's free choice in order to refuse to persuade or explain, relying on the dignity of his role.[26]

To claim mandate, an occupation that began with technique as a set of practical skills may develop more complex theoretical knowledge, which is controlled as esoteric; those that began as theoretical may develop practical skills or more practical applications of their skills.[27] In either case, the occupation is extending its range.

Both license and mandate may be either narrow or broad, and indeed their boundaries are hard to define, because the two concepts get to the very heart of what society is. Society is fundamentally organized by allowing only some people, in their roles, to do some things. Occupational license always, to some degree, allows the practitioners to act differently from other people, during work and sometimes outside of work. Mandate extends authority by allowing the occupational group to tell other people what to do and how to think about it. As historians, we can try to trace not only the social relations around license and mandate once they have been granted, but also how occupations, through policy, struggle for and win – and sometimes lose again – these forms of social authority.

Did practitioners themselves judge their colleagues' work quality?
Did practitioners allow the client to decide what s/he needed from the practitioner?
Who could listen when colleagues discussed mistakes?
How sharply distinguished were levels of hierarchy within the occupation?
Did technique physically endanger anyone?
Did technique psychologically or spiritually endanger anyone?

25 Freidson, "Impurity of Professional Authority," 31.
26 "It is no accident that, in any profession, one working definition of success is the attainment of such prestige that one need not deal with any [client] who does not come in as a humble supplicant eager to obey: it is the young practitioner and the comparative failure who must cope with the questioning." Freidson, "Impurity of Professional Authority," 30–31.
27 Hughes, "Professions," 657–60.

Did government license practitioners, or did they have informal, social license?
What precautions did practitioners themselves set, and what precautions did
state or society require, to minimize harm?
Were practitioners socially or legally licensed to live their lives, in or out of work,
in ways that were forbidden or scorned for laymen?
For instance, did they wear a uniform, have different family relations, eat dif-
ferent foods, or abstain from certain normal activities, perhaps employing
substitutes?
Did clients and other laypeople obey practitioners in thought or action? Why?
How broad were the matters on which laypeople willingly obeyed?
Did laymen admire or resent the occupation, or express anxiety about its special
knowledge?
Do those feelings show up in culture?

Example: Jazz Musicians

A critical point in license and mandate is who can judge the work of the
practitioner. A "quack" is a member of an occupation who pleases his clients
but not fellow practitioners; while colleagues may judge a task well done
even if it does not please a client.[28] Howard Becker discussed a particularly
sharp conflict between practitioners and clients in a study of jazz musicians
playing in dance halls in Chicago in the 1940s.[29] Since the practitioner is
deeply involved in and the client only casually involved in the activity, Becker
wrote, "it may be inevitable that the two should have widely varying pictures
of the way in which the occupational service should be performed."[30] The
public nature of the musicians' workshop (the dance hall) means that the
conflict was a daily one. The practitioners consider that the client cannot
judge the quality of the output. Since the client is present and can easily
make his or her views felt, practitioners "resent bitterly" the interference (in
the form of expressed views, withheld cash, and song requests).[31]

The musicians required an audience to make a living ("Who pays the bills?
They pay 'em, so you gotta play what they want").[32] They even desired an
audience and its approbation ("I enjoy playing more when there's someone

28   Hughes, "Mistakes at Work," 98.
29   Becker, "Dance Musician."
30   Becker, "Dance Musician," 136.
31   Becker, "Dance Musician," 136, 139.
32   Becker, "Dance Musician," 140.

to play for ... that's what music's for – for people to play and get enjoyment from").[33] But what most of the audience (with rare exceptions) wanted and therefore what club bosses or wedding managers insisted on, was a simplified, corny style that provided a clear dance beat (so hearers knew when to put their left foot out and when their right) and a melody they could hum, or – worse than that – ethnic dances such as polkas. Playing to please the audience was the dirty work of the musicians, although Becker doesn't put it that way. In one case we can even see the musicians pushing that dirty work down the occupational hierarchy to women singers: discussing how one could play jazz and still make a living, one man suggested, "Well, you have to have a sexy little bitch to stand up in front and shake her ass at the [audience] ... You could still play great when she wasn't singing."[34] The authority to decide what constituted great playing, musicians asserted, lay only with them, not with the client.

Likewise, since only other musicians could understand music, the audience's praise, even that of the "jazz fan," was as ignorant and worthless as its criticism. The conflict between *true* music that only one with an innate gift could play ("jazz") and popular pap ("commercial") was agreed on by all the musicians – both those who sacrificed artistic integrity, self-respect, and the respect of colleagues to gain a good, steady livelihood and the acclaim of laypeople by playing in a commercial style, and those who sacrificed fame and fortune by playing for self-respect and the approbation of fellow jazzmen.[35]

Becker noted a number of ways in which the occupational culture of musicians responded to this basic conflict, both in attitudes and in actions. First, musicians developed the idea that they had an innate, mysterious talent: their music could not be taught. Second, because of this gift, musicians should not be controlled. This meant that not only an ignorant client but even a colleague should never try to change another musician's playing on the job. That prohibition was a key article of code. Third, musicians generalized the sense of gift and the right and freedom to believe that they were better than and different from the rest of society, and should thus not be held to conventional morality. They told and treasured stories of unconventionality and refused to discipline one another for such behavior, even when it meant that the whole band suffered.[36]

33 Becker, "Dance Musician," 141.
34 Becker, "Dance Musician," 139–41.
35 Becker, "Dance Musician," 139, 136, 140.
36 Becker, "Dance Musician," 137–38. As with all historical sources, the quotations from musicians reveal complexities that the analysis smooths out. For instance, one musician told Becker that while everyone not a musician was a "square," "professional people – doctors, lawyers, like

Fourth, they separated themselves physically from clients while working. If there was no platform, they would use the piano and chairs to keep themselves apart, and they would avoid eye contact. The rationale Becker gives is that contact would lead to demands by the clients, to the interference that musicians hated most.[37] But the insistence with which the "barricade" was maintained suggests to me that this fear of contact was emotional as well as rational. Historians should not expect to find code set by only rational or only emotional principles. Fifth, and only partly because of their inverted work schedules, many felt isolated from other people and, rather than trying to mitigate that isolation, they enhanced it by their attitudes, clothing, vocabulary (not just technical language but other ways of saying perfectly ordinary things), and behavior.[38]

Becker categorized the musicians (he was one himself) as a "service" occupation and presented their dilemma as one that would face any occupation in which the client is in fairly "direct and personal contact" with the practitioner as s/he works.[39] Becker's analysis may provide questions for historians working not only on entertainers, but on any service practitioner – cook, physician, housemaid, knight, live-in tutor, or governess. Did they face similar dilemmas? The constant irritation of the client's indispensable presence produces intense emotion. Practitioners create and adopt measures to counteract both the interference and the emotion, which become a central part of the culture of the occupation. Since musicians, like professors, identify strongly with their occupation and are, in Hughes's expression "never really off-duty," their occupational culture melds with their personality and is carried into their larger social interactions, in turn affecting the larger culture. (Anyone reading this 1951 article with knowledge of American culture from the 1960s onwards will not doubt that influence.)

When musicians reserved the right to tell others how to think about music and what to do about it (even if the other party was paying the bills), they claimed mandate. And they were frustrated when society rejected the claim, preferring to dance to familiar soupy tunes. Society's granting of license and mandate changes over time and varies by place. Hughes comments, "Social unrest often shows itself precisely in such questioning of the prerogatives of the leading professions. In times of crisis, there may arise a general demand

that – they might not be square ... but outside of show people and professional people, everybody's a f---ing square. They don't know anything" (140).

37 Becker, "Dance Musician," 142.
38 Becker, "Dance Musician," 142–44.
39 Becker, "Dance Musician," 138.

for more conformity to lay modes of thought and discourse."[40] At my moment of writing, the demands of parents and politicians in the USA that teachers conform to the so-called "science of reading," and that librarians remove books from shelves, appear salient examples.

Did the practitioner personally meet the client?
Did they interact in person throughout the provision of the service?
How could the client express dissatisfaction with the service before its completion?
Did clients make suggestions to practitioners as they worked?
Did clients press practitioners to change their technique?
Did practitioners respond to such pressures, and if so, how?
Did they express views about such interference?
What tales did they tell about their relations with clients and laypeople?
How did practitioners and laymen talk about where skill originated? Was skill inborn, learned, granted by a divine power?
Did practitioners live differently from laypeople, in fact or in their self-concept?
Did their working hours differ from those of others?
Did they adopt jargon, clothing, ritual, or other symbols of distinction?

Works Cited

Ash, Eric. "Introduction: Expertise and the Early Modern State." *Osiris* 25, no. 1 (2010): 1–24.

Ash, Eric. *Power, Knowledge, and Expertise in Elizabethan England*. Baltimore: Johns Hopkins University Press, 2004.

Becker, Howard S. "The Professional Dance Musician and His Audience." *American Journal of Sociology* 57, no. 2 (1951): 136–44.

Becker, Howard S., Blanche Geer, Everett C. Hughes, and Anselm L. Strauss. *Boys in White: Student Culture in Medical School*. Chicago: University of Chicago Press, 1961.

Bray, Francesca. *Technology and Gender: Fabrics of Power in Late Imperial China*. Berkeley: University of California Press, 1997.

Camara, Mohamed Saliou. *Is There a Distinctively African Way of Knowing (a Study of African Blacksmiths, Hunters, Healers, Griots, Elders, and Artists): Knowing and Theory of Knowledge in the African Experience*. Lewiston: Edwin Mellen Press, 2014.

40 Hughes, "Study of Occupations," 28.

Freidson, Eliot. "The Impurity of Professional Authority." In *Institutions and the Person: Festschrift in Honor of Everett C. Hughes*, edited by Howard S. Becker, Blanche Geer, David Riesman, and Robert S. Weiss, 25–34. Chicago: Aldine, 1968.

Hughes, Everett C. "License and Mandate." In *Men and Their Work*, 78–87. Glencoe, IL: The Free Press, 1958.

Hughes, Everett C. "Mistakes at Work." In *Men and Their Work*, 88–101. Glencoe, IL: The Free Press, 1958.

Hughes, Everett C. "Professions." *Dædalus* 92, no. 4 (1963): 655–68.

Hughes, Everett C. "Psychology: Science and/or Profession." *The American Psychologist* 7, no. 8 (1952): 441–43.

Hughes, Everett C. "The Study of Occupations." In *On Work, Race and the Sociological Imagination*, edited by Lewis Coser, 21–36. Chicago: University of Chicago Press, 1994.

Miller, R. L. "Paleoepidemiology, Literacy, and Medical Tradition among Necropolis Workmen in New Kingdom Egypt." *Medical History* 35 (1991): 1–24

VII. Technique and Danger (Guilty Knowledge)

Abstract

Practitioners in some occupations must know things that, if misused, could injure their clients in various ways, such as secrets or human weaknesses, or which medicines are poisons. The practitioner must be trusted with that knowledge to do the job, whereas if a laymen held it, he would be presumed to have some guilty purpose. Others, because of their work, view aspects of society objectively that are sacred to laymen, and this, too, is a kind of "guilty knowledge," because to make it public would be to threaten society as a whole. Such occupations often live in distinctive ways or wear outward signs of distinction that advertise that they are licensed to hold and use these dangerous kinds of knowledge.

Keywords: secrets, uniforms, symbols of distinction, social myths, suspicion

The lawyer, the policeman, the physician, the reporter, the scientist, the scholar, the diplomat, the private secretary, all of them must have license to get – and in some degree, to keep secret – some order of guilty knowledge. It may be guilty in that it is knowledge that a layman would be obliged to reveal, or in that the withholding of it from the public or from authorities compromises the integrity of the [person] who so withholds it, as in the case of the police [officer] who keeps connections with the underworld or the diplomat who has useful friends abroad. ... The prototype of all guilty knowledge is, however, a different, potentially shocking, way of looking at things ... Herein lies the whole question of what the bargain is between those who receive a service and those who give it, and of the circumstances in which it is protested by either party.[1]

---

1   Hughes, "Study of Occupations," 26–27, 28.

Schneewind, S.K. *The Social Drama of Daily Work. A Manual for Historians.* Amsterdam: Amsterdam University Press, 2024

DOI: 10.5117/9789048559534_CH07

Guilty knowledge is occupational knowledge that may endanger others. Before turning to its varieties, I will consider how its possession by practitioners of an occupation may be outwardly signaled.

Symbols of Distinction

Because of their expertise, practitioners of some occupations develop dramatically different views of the world from laypeople, who know that and find it uncomfortable. Occupations respond by creating culture, often adopting symbols and patterns of behavior that distinguish them immediately. Such symbols may spring straightforwardly from technique, but they often require a more roundabout explanation, one that lies in a kind of danger that guilty knowledge poses to clients or to society.

Both in artistic representations and in life, laypeople could immediately identify some practitioners' occupations by their dress, hairstyle, or adornment. Symbols of distinction might be things one could doff or don at will, or they might become for practitioners ingrained habits of stance, posture, speaking, facial expression: what Pierre Bourdieu dubbed "hexis."[2] Worship of a patron saint or deity may be a symbol of distinction, as for the fishing communities in late imperial Zhejiang who worshipped Old Man Yangfu.[3] Jargon may be a symbol of distinction: for instance, new sailors in the US Navy had to learn that instead of getting out of bed in the morning they must "heave out and trice up"; that instead of asking permission to smoke they must ask whether "the smoking lamp is lit," and so on. An apprentice who had not yet learnt the lingo faced "stares of chagrin or disgust" from his colleagues when he breached code. The sailors' garb and speech, and the echoes of their culture on shore, mean that laypeople expect and tolerate sailors' wild behavior on shore, as phrases like "drunk as a sailor" suggest.[4]

Symbols of distinction might be granted to an apprentice, journeyman, or new master in an initiatory ritual. For instance, in some places, medieval European students received a book.[5] Other symbols of distinction, too, spring

---

2   Bourdieu, Nice, and Wacquant, "The Peasant and His Body," 582. Bourdieu's insight came from his own experiences in the embodiment of social status, as is clear from Bourdieu, *Sketch for a Self-Analysis*, 89. He attributed his ability to analyze the reality of society to his peasant upbringing (40, 91).

3   Muscolino, *Fishing Wars*, 41–42.

4   Zurcher, "The Sailor Abroad," 397. Hughes refers to this in "License and Mandate," 82.

5   Vienne, personal communication, August 2021.

directly from technique. Eighteenth-century British masons wore special leather aprons and owned their tools. Both aprons and tools were used in production, but also signaled that the masons possessed a "property of skill,"[6] which is roughly equivalent to license. Masons wore their aprons for the same reason that they held ceremonies and shared code about defining outsiders: to claim stonework for themselves alone.

Moreover, symbols of distinction reinforce mandate: the right to tell clients and other laypeople what to do and how to think about the technique and object of technique. We saw this with jazz musicians, but "both the humble janitor and the proud physician," in Hughes's words, contend that laypeople – even clients – lack competence to judge their work; both therefore must "keep their distance" from individual clients to prevent any presumption that they understand the practitioner and his technique.[7] But what form does "keeping one's distance" take? Formal language? Payment up front? A gruff or a smooth exterior? A uniform? All these are symbols of distinction. Although drawn from technique, to be legible they must also derive from other elements in the larger cultural repertoire of their place-time; to which, in turn, they contribute.

Precisely because symbols of distinction were public and even stereotyped, they are relatively easy for historians to find. They include rites and ceremonies of many kinds, songs and oaths, "a galaxy of historic founders, innovators, and other heroes, the saints or gods of the trade; and a wealth of remembered historic or legendary events, which justify its present claims."[8] An example is Master Jacques of the French journeymen's companies. He left no documentary trace, but oral tradition hailed him for several centuries as a patron of the rites of the companies, including not only technique-related contests of skill, but also drunken inductions, a female innkeeper delegated as the "mother" of the companions, brawls between rival groups, public parades of companions wearing astonishing quantities of ribbons, and so on.[9] Saints of medieval European trades are well known; they were also common in Ming China, where, for example, an apotheosized official named Gao Yao was "the professional god for the prison staff."[10] Symbols of distinction may affect any aspect of the occupation, including the way

---

6   Rule, "Property of Skill," 104–6. The idea behind this term is that the practitioner's qualifications had cost him as much time, effort, and money as purchasing land or houses would have.
7   Hughes, "Sociological Study of Work," 425.
8   Hughes, "Study of Occupations," 31.
9   Sonenscher, "Mythical Work," 37.
10   Y. Zhang, *Religion and Prison Art*, 2–3.

the practitioner receives his remuneration: medieval university teachers collected fees from students in a box shaped like a lemon.[11]

Symbols of distinction consolidate the occupational sense of shared identity, but the historian should not assume that this is their primary social function. For the phenomena named in the Hughes framework are generated by tensions and dilemmas in the social drama of work.

> How did contemporary culture portray practitioners?
> Did practitioners have special clothing hairstyles, taboos, and so on?
> Did practitioners live or speak differently from other people?
> Did symbols of distinction relate obviously to technique?
> If so, why? Did those aspects of technique worry or reassure clients or laymen?
> How were those symbols of distinction explained emically?
> Did laypeople practitioners or laymen tell stories about practitioners who mis-used technique? If so, what do the details suggest?
> Did the occupation have a patron saint or god? Did it have a founding myth?
> How did practitioners keep individual laypeople at a psychological or physical distance?

Flavors of Guilty Knowledge

On seeing symbols of distinction, therefore, the historian should ask not only about technique and object of technique, code and policy, license and mandate, but also about guilty knowledge. In fact, the social permission to hold guilty knowledge is often a key element of license. Examples include the familiarity of exorcists with the ways of demons and the familiarity of crime-solving detectives and magistrates with the ways of criminals. If a layperson knew as much about demons as an exorcist, or as much about crime as a police detective, s/he would be assumed to be in league with demons or criminals. Pharmacologists know, and to serve society must know, how to use drugs to help people, so they also know how to use drugs to harm people. Anyone *not* licensed to know how to affect lives and bodies with drugs who had this knowledge would be presumed to have bad motives – to be guilty. Hence the term "guilty knowledge." The term does *not* mean that the practitioner feels guilty about his/her knowledge. Nor does it mean that the client feels guilty about consulting the practitioner. It means a wide variety of things that are all linked to

---

11   Huisman, "L'étudiant au Moyen Âge," 52.

dangers, whether to the client, laypeople generally, or society and its sacred truths.

With the license to hold knowledge that endangers society comes the attendant burden of acting in ways that convince laypeople that the practitioner "does not yield to the temptations of his privileged position."[12] Symbols of distinction, therefore, are a form of policy; for instance, the doctor's white coat advertises: "I deal in your blood and gore, but I am not bloody and gory – I am clean and do not misuse my knowledge for harm." The Roman Catholic priest hears everyone's sins, assigns penance, and doles out absolution. He must know a lot about sin to distinguish different degrees of sin. He must read forbidden books, or how could he know which books to forbid? To show that he will not abuse his knowledge and power, the Church sets him apart with celibacy and black uniform, deviations from normal lifestyles that laypeople would not admire, perhaps would not even tolerate, in other laypeople.[13]

The first kind of guilty knowledge is professional secrets. The social worker, the hairdresser, the prostitute, the doorman, the lawyer: all know things that the client must trust they will keep secret. But as with all aspects of occupational technique, what counts as professional secrets may not be predictable. Ron Carter refused to answer any of a reporter's questions about the famous musicians who had hired him to play bass with them. He said at first that it was because he didn't want her to leave anyone out, but he continued that he didn't want to talk about them, and since he considered the personal inseparable from the professional, he could not comment on what they were like to make music with without it reflecting on whether they were good or bad people.[14]

A second kind of guilty knowledge is magic or ritual intertwined with the practical work of production. The Hungarian *számadó* cured sick animals and protected them with magic, as well as hiring, training, and managing the herdsmen.[15] Bronislaw Malinowski pointed out that "Magic and practical work are [among Trobriand gardeners] inseparable from each other, though they are not confused." Both were done throughout the growing year, neither could be neglected, and everyone had to participate in both as well as paying the specialized ritualist, the *towosi*. The *towosi* not only did the magic, but also

---

12 Hughes, "License and Mandate," 80; Hughes, "Study of Occupations," 26.
13 Hughes, "License and Mandate," 80; Hughes, "Study of Occupations," 26. In "Bastard Institutions," 197, Hughes argues that deviations from the norm, such as celibacy, may be socially tolerated when they have an institutional home but not in a lone individual.
14 Carter, "Legendary Jazz Bassist."
15 Vincze, "Organization of Work in Herding Teams," 147.

announced when each horticultural task would begin, chastised the lazy, and praised the steady.[16] Knowing that he who can cure can injure, that he who can nourish can blight, we recognize magic as guilty knowledge and are not surprised to find that ritualists live differently from others. The *szamadó*, for instance, unlike the herdsmen he managed, had to be married and "morally irreproachable."[17] The *towosi* had to abstain from eating certain foods (usually those that played a role in his garden magic), to fast on days on which he carried out rituals, and to perform yet another rite before he could eat of any new crop.[18]

Herding and gardening seem dramatically different, yet the Hughes framework enables us to see why the garden magician and the *szamadó* have not only license (they are the experts who determine what is done when, and are the only ones to perform certain rituals to fend off mistakes at work) but also mandate (they tell others what to do and how to think about their area of expertise). Because the *towosi* and *szamadó* were licensed to hold the guilty knowledge of how to control garden fertility/animal health, both had to demonstrate that they would not misuse that knowledge by adhering to a special lifestyle; and because their activities were so central, society also granted them mandate. As Malinowski puts it, the Triobriand people were "prepared to admit that [the *towosi*] should also control the work of man ... Public praise from the *towosi* [was] a highly appreciated reward and a great stimulus to the perfect gardener."[19] The guilty knowledge of the ritualist simultaneously gives him/her social power and controls his/her behavior.

A third way to think about guilty knowledge is that a client may feel that something that the practitioner is doing *for* him or her is being done *to* him or her. Hughes gives the examples of people with mental illness confined in a hospital by doctors, and of short-term patients suffering indignities at the hands of hospital workers.[20] Discipline necessary to properly carry out the task the practitioner has been hired to do (a schoolteacher keeping a classroom in order, for instance) can easily cross a line into cruelty, at least in the perception of the client. Hughes notes that "the opposite of service is disservice, and that the line between them is thin, obscure, and shifting."[21] Because the practitioner's knowledge is felt to endanger someone, it is part of guilty knowledge in the terminology of the Hughes framework.

16   Malinowski, "Trobriand Gardeners and Their Magic," 162.
17   Vincze, "Organization of Work in Herding Teams," 147, 150.
18   Malinowski, "Trobriand Gardeners and Their Magic," 166.
19   Malinowski, "Trobriand Gardeners and Their Magic," 167.
20   Hughes, "Social Role," 69.
21   Hughes, "Social Role," 70. Becker elicited a hair-raising description of one teacher's technique of knocking a child dizzy while leaving no mark. Becker, "Social-Class Variations."

Fourth, guilty knowledge includes general knowledge – not about specific clients, but about the clientele in general – of human weaknesses. For instance, sellers of luxury goods in many times and places know that their clients want to show off or to enjoy fancy, silky, colorful fabrics and shiny, smooth, glistening metals and gems in defiance of practicality. Embroiderers and dyers partake of this guilty knowledge: they must know how to please customers, even when it means tapping into titillation and desire for colors that clients were not legally permitted to wear. In Ming China, for instance, there were many yellows that *just* missed being imperial yellow.[22] Vendors of pornography or its less offensive cousins understand the objects of lust. And so on. This professional knowledge endangers society because practitioners can stir up desires in customers. Moralists the world over have understood this principle perfectly well, and thus have objected to novels and other such slippery slopes. Knowledge of human weakness, even when socially licensed, could be misused: it is guilty knowledge.

Fifth, practitioners must look at their object of technique dispassionately. They must be permitted to think about and discuss things that clients hold dear in objective terms. Hughes explains:

> The prototype of all guilty knowledge is a way of looking at things different from that of most people and consequently potentially shocking to the lay mind. Every occupation must look in a relative way at some order of events, objects, and ideas. These must be classified. To be classified they must be seen comparatively. Their behavior must be analyzed and, if possible, predicted. A suitable technical language must be developed so that colleagues may talk among themselves about these things. This technical – therefore relative – attitude will have to be adopted toward the very people one serves; no profession can do its work without license to talk in shocking terms about its clients.[23]

For example, we permit doctors to discuss our bodies and even our minds in ways that, were laypeople to do it, would deeply distress and humiliate us; we permit lawyers to discuss – behind our backs, as well as to our faces – our strained relationships with family members in ways that we would condemn as vicious gossip if the talk were among acquaintances at a cocktail party.

---

22   As suggested by Maura Dykstra, Yuanfei Wang, and Ina Asim in the MISC meeting, January 2021.
23   Hughes, "License and Mandate," 81–82. For a slightly different formulation see Hughes, "Study of Occupations," 27.

Struggles over mandate may come from society's reluctance to permit dispassionate analysis of its basic, sacred tenets.[24]

Sixth, society may license an occupation to hold knowledge that leads the professional to viewpoints that endanger society. This kind of guilty knowledge may prove to be the one that reveals the most about how the social drama of work has shaped historical cultures generally. Occupations that have developed a theory of the world or the cosmos are licensed to discuss dispassionately not only aspects of individual lives that people hold dear (one's body, one's soul) but ideas on which the whole social order rests. Academics, for instance, claim the right to reconsider and even debunk national myths, and they claim that license even when laypeople find it distinctly dangerous. Hughes gives examples from the Cold War, in which "detachment appears to be the most perilous deviation of all, hence the one least to be tolerated."[25] Bourdieu gives another example in his account of his attempt to give an inaugural lecture about the inaugural lecture as a rite of institution: until he had begun speaking he did not recognize, in his words,

> the supreme social barbarism ... of suspending belief, or, worse, calling it into question and threatening it in the very time and place where it is supposed to be celebrated and strengthened ... [This] constituted a challenge to the symbolic order, an affront to the dignity of the institution which demands that one keep silent about the arbitrariness of the institutional rite that is being performed.[26]

Code required that the ritual work of academia be exempted from the objective analysis with which academics approached other social topics. Bourdieu, as a sociologist, was licensed to hold the guilty knowledge that all human rituals are arbitrary historical products, but that did not prevent his auditors from feeling endangered by his wielding of that knowledge with reference to their own practices.

---

24 Becker pointed to this phenomenon in sociology itself. Mid-twentieth-century American sociologist C. Wright Mills aroused opposition, Becker suggests, not just because he was a "smart-aleck," but because "interpreting the events of daily life in a university department or research institute as sociological phenomena is not palatable to people who run such institutions or to those who live by them and profit from them; for, like all institutions, universities and institutes have sacred myths and beliefs that their members do not want subjected to the skeptical sociological view." Becker, "Professional Sociology," 177.

25 Hughes, "Study of Occupations," 28. For the danger to society posed by sociologists and others who compare societies, religions, statuses, etc., see Hughes, "Improper Study of Man," 170.

26 Bourdieu, *Sketch for a Self-Analysis*, 109–10.

How might routine duties to clients hurt or embarrass them?

What sorts of secrets did the practitioners need to know about clients?

What sorts of crime, sin, pollution, evil, or harmful forces did practitioners manage?

How did the occupation understand, classify, and manipulate bodies, the social order, or central social beliefs?

Did the occupation speak in technical language about things sacred to others?

How did practitioners express authority over clients or other laypeople?

What did practitioners have to know about human weaknesses?

What insight did practitioners have, by virtue of technique, into key social myths?

Example: Master Jacques of the Journeymen's Companies

Practitioners in some occupations, therefore, must know secrets and weakness of clients, of all humans, of an institution, or of a whole society. Some practitioners must know about what they condemn for others, from sin to sugar: they must know it intimately so they can fight it. At the same time, they must convince others that they do not partake of the forbidden themselves and will not misuse their dangerous knowledge. To hold guilty knowledge without being considered guilty, and to mitigate the suspicion that lurks in all lay relations with professionals requires potent symbols that set the profession apart, including rituals, costume, and special ways of living. Practitioners licensed to hold guilty knowledge must behave so uprightly that others accept that they can control the guilt of others without revealing it. They must earn the right to adhere to the codes of professional confidentiality. Symbols of distinction mark the license to hold dangerous knowledge and channel the inevitable social unease about such knowledge; they limit the behavior of practitioners and advertise that they will not misuse it.

Let's follow up on Master Jacques and ask: what guilty knowledge did journeymen in the trades possess by social license? One might guess that a locksmith is socially licensed to know how to pick a lock. But research shows that this is not the guilty knowledge at stake. Here is the argument: aside from luxury artisans who worked in glass or gold, Michael Sonenscher says, "the rudiments of most trades were available to a large number of potential practitioners." Even experienced itinerant journeymen were not finely distinguished by specific technique, but roughly into those who worked with wood, leather, or iron.[27] Practitioners had only a weak claim to license to monopolize technique when skills were so widely shared. Sonenscher writes:

> Work in many trades did not require rare abilities or esoteric techniques. The ritual of the *companonnages* – the initiatory ceremonies, the pitched battles, the feats of prowess in arts which too many of them could master – were an inverted acknowledgement of the wide dissemination of ordinary abilities. They made it possible to transform similarity into difference in a world in which too many people could do the same thing.[28]

Sonenscher argues explicitly against the assumption among historians that journeyman's associations (*companonnages*) consolidated group identity. On the contrary: the associations created "a complex world of ephemeral distinctions." Affiliation to the *companonnage* distinguished the "true artists," who would work for no less than thirty *sous* per day, from ignorant apprentices and scabs who would work for as little as twenty. The symbolic inequalities generated by journeyman affiliation to the *companonnage* enabled masters to offer non-monetary incentives that would not drive wages up, when they needed extra workers for a rush job or the best workers to meet a client's high standards.[29] The associations divided practitioners, rather than uniting them, Sonenscher argues.

So, if not shared license to understand locks (or weapons, etc.), what guilty knowledge did the rites signal? Eighteenth-century Europe still accepted the ideology of the Great Chain of Being: not only every creature, but every rank and place in the human part of the cosmos (not yet conceived of as "society") was divinely ordained and necessary. For an individual to leave his place was to subvert order; likewise, those in higher places were there by right.[30] But these journeymen had no fixed place in the social order; they jostled along as best they could, turning to soldiering at times, and were easily replaced.[31] Without the itinerant journeymen's rites, there would have been

---

27 Sonenscher, "Mythical Work," 54–55. The quality of work could also be difficult to use to draw distinctions: at least one contest of technical prowess between two stone-cutters ended in a tie after three months of effort (52).

28 Sonenscher, "Mythical Work," 56.

29 Sonenscher, "Mythical Work," 51, 57–58. Masters could then quickly fire these additional workers (tailors, for instance, were employed in workshops for a mean of two weeks and a median of just over two weeks).

30 Lovejoy, *The Great Chain of Being*, 206.

31 Sonenscher, "Mythical Work," 42.

no indication that the social order was just. The rites covered up the trades' guilty knowledge that the social order was the work not of a just god, but of one who played with dice. Guilty knowledge is not just about hair dye or poison, but about the deep-seated doubts and worries of a particular society.

The Dilemma of Routine and Emergency

Speaking of the sixth kind of guilty knowledge, Hughes writes, "Sometimes, an occupation must adopt this objective, comparative attitude toward things which are very dear to other people or which are indeed the object of absolutely held values and sentiments"[32] – that is, things that are sacred either to individuals (such as our own bodies, minds, and emotions) or to communities or societies as a whole, such as religious values. "The professional may see the present in longer perspective than the layman, ... as a link in a causative chain of events. The emergency may appear greater to the professional than to the layman."[33] An example of the professional perceiving a more alarming threat than the layperson is the explosion of the Ming imperial gunpowder workshop on May 30, 1626, when a violent and destructive conflict between two court factions was at its height. To ordinary folk, this was a unique and dramatic disaster. To scholar-officials, learned in history and licensed to interpret events and set policy, the explosion portended failings in government that threatened the whole nation.[34]

But "in another sense" and at the same time, Hughes continues, the emergency "may appear *less* crucial" to the professional than to the laypeople, "since the professional sees the present situation in comparison with others; it is not unique."[35] While the authors of the official report of the Tianqi explosion historicized it and related it to national affairs, they themselves were immediately safe, while for laypeople who had suffered losses of home and life the explosion was the end of the world, or close to it.

Often what is an emergency to the layperson is, and must be, routine to the practitioner. Out of this emerges an aspect of "guilty knowledge" likely to affect the broader culture: the dilemma of routine and emergency. Necessarily, practitioners see the object of technique differently from the way laypeople do. At one level, this is straightforward: the boatbuilder

---

32 Hughes, "Study of Occupations," 27.
33 Hughes, "Study of Occupations," 28.
34 N. Feng, "Mushroom Cloud."
35 Hughes, "Study of Occupations," 28.

can judge good wood, whereas a client cannot. But further, practitioners must view analytically and objectively objects of technique that are sacred to laypeople.[36] The surgeon cannot be sentimental about your hand; if you have gangrene, she will cut it off. A real estate agent cannot share the client's sentimentality about a family home: he rightly views it as a piece of property with a certain market value. The object of technique is the body or the house; the technique is healing or selling. He has seen hundreds of bodies; she has sold hundreds of houses. The work is routine.

But to the client, the hand and the home are sacred, in the sense of being unique and irreplaceable, so the moment of threat or transition evokes tremendous emotion. Removing the hand or selling the home is an emergency. The client wants the expertise of the practitioner and tries to hire the one with the most practice and expertise, who will view objectively what to the client is sacred. But at the very same time, the client recognizes and emotionally reacts against the coldblooded analytical skills he is paying for. To the real estate agent, the home is just a house. The doctor, somewhere in her mind, is thinking, "It's just your hand, let's cut it off and save your life from the gangrene." She says, instead, "I am deeply grieved that we have no choice but to amputate. You know, there are all sorts of good artificial limbs now, and with therapy you will regain a significant degree of function. You will hardly notice the difference." Since roles are held by persons, this dilemma creates personal emotional tension between client and practitioner. But since the dilemma occurs over and over, that emotional tension takes a cultural and social form.[37]

The precise forms of emotional tensions, and how they are managed, shape and are shaped by culture and society. Manhattan doormen knew a lot about the personal lives of tenants. Tenants knew that; they wanted doormen to know them well enough to treat their friends, their deliveries, and so on in the particular way they desired (let Mrs. A right up but warn me about Mr. B); yet they also found the doorman's knowledge uncomfortable. They could not neutralize that discomfort as those with servants had done in earlier times, by considering them "socially dead" – of no interest in the client's world – because of the American myth of classlessness. Instead,

36 The obvious example is the doctor who has seen thousands of cancer cases and treats the disease in a person's body as just one of those, instead of as the uniquely horrifying experience of that individual as his health and life slip away. But all professions view sacred things analytically, which can shock people. For instance, history teachers are licensed to teach critical thinking, including the ugly sides of their nation's past, which may shock their clients (students or parents) and other laypeople. They claim the right to teach that, and society – sometimes – recognizes that claim.
37 For additional comments see Hughes, "Mistakes at Work," 92.

even though they typically knew nothing about the doorman's life, which was quite different from theirs, they talked about doorman as being "part of the family" – like a pet, Peter Bearman writes.[38] The metaphor licensed the doorman's intimate knowledge and tenant dependency, without creating a reciprocal obligation on the part of the tenant. "Tenants want to feel they are distinct, and ... doormen want to know whom their tenants wish to see and not to see," in order to provide "particularized – that is, professional – service."[39] The client wants an experienced, professional doorman, with the objectivity that that entails; yet at the same time, they resent the doorman's analytical knowledge of their lives and selves. So, the guilty knowledge of doormen is a special case of the dilemma of routine and emergency. Asking about different ways of handling the tensions around the guilty knowledge of practitioners will help historians see the occupations they are studying in close relation to the society of their place-time.

What kinds of situations brought clients to practitioners?
How might the client view the practitioner's object of technique as sacred?
How does the practitioner's proper response to the client's emergency threaten that sacred object of technique?
How does the practitioner view that sacred object of technique analytically?
What kind of emotional response did the client want from the practitioner?
How did the client phrase or imply that demand?
How did the practitioner respond in the special language of the occupation?
How might special language and other cultural forms have developed precisely to phrase that response?

Fraud and Corruption

Occupations may also have ways of working that are part of colleague code but look to outsiders like crime, and thus get labeled "corruption." This is not guilty knowledge in the sociological sense. To pass ethical judgement on the actions and thoughts of the players in the social drama of work is alien to the analytical spirit of occupational sociology. Of course, people do cheat, but historians should not make assumptions about what counted as cheating to practitioners or clients. Ethical rights and wrongs, what

38   Bearman, *Doormen*, 6–7.
39   Bearman, *Doormen*, 11.

regulations permit, and even what the law permits, not only change over time but are perceived differently by people in different roles.

A study of adjustments that both managers and employees made as a manufacturing company reorganized points out that there were workarounds that neither side perceived as corruption. For instance, some workers, still on the clock, were released nominally for union meetings as a cover for doing extra work outside the company.[40] But workarounds may be required to get the job done. A sociological study of the relations among privates, sergeants, and their superiors in the US Army in about 1956 revealed this. The sergeants met every morning for coffee and figured out how to get their tasks done in ways that bent the rules, because the rules would have blocked action. "A man who needed a truck the next day would persuade the motor pool sergeant to declare it out of commission until he called for it. Arrangements would be made to have lost equipment declared lost [only] when it was [plausibly] expendable during the next field exercise."[41] Although the sergeants benefited from such arrangements to get their tasks done, the officers above them did, too – as one of them found to his cost when he insisted on going by the book. When he was then caught short of supplies his superiors demanded, his sergeants punished him by going by the book, too.[42] Likewise, Louis Zurcher's study of the Navy follows Erving Goffman in considering as "secondary adjustments" the ways sailors bent the rules to trade radio parts for meals or grow beards that created a sense of individuality. Sailors created informal systems outside the formal rules.[43] Workarounds or secondary adjustments naturally require a protective strategy of secrecy, as Edward Davis points out.[44]

Of course, every occupation has its bad apples who will cheat clients; code may include ways to discourage or manage dishonesty. But what the historian should remember is that, as the authors of *Boys in White* point out, "There is no organization in which things look the same from all positions."[45] And it is not the historian's job to take sides.

---

40 Dalton, "Reorganization and Accommodation," 23.
41 Westley, "Organization of the Army," 201.
42 Westley, "Organization of the Army," 202–3.
43 Zurcher, "A Sailor Aboard," 398–400. Primary adjustments are the ways the individual changes his behavior to fit in with the requirements of an institution, submitting to its discipline to do what it expects. So, "secondary adjustments" refers to unauthorized ends or means that individuals adopt to circumvent the institution's rules and assumptions. See Goffman, *Asylums*, 189.
44 E. Davis, *Hidden Dimensions*, 115–17.
45 Becker et al., *Boys in White*, 15.

Workers might see as legitimate what managers considered theft. Circumstances of forced labor for the state, or in which workers could not choose another job or leave freely, or in which managers denigrated and underpaid workers, might be especially likely to see thefts from workshops. US sailors justified taking ship parts or tools for their own hobbies with the word "cumshaw" (from the Chinese "ganxie" or "Thanks!"), which expressed (in sociologist Zurcher's words) the attitude, "By gosh I deserve it, because I have certainly done enough for them!"[46] The managers' and workers' different views of "cumshaw" naturally involved tension.

In extreme cases, managers organized the workshop and workflow *primarily* around preventing theft. One example comes from Tudor England: the danger that Henry VIII's kitchen staff would pilfer spices and exotic fruit dictated the spatial arrangement of kitchen workshop. At Hampton Court, each kitchen office (bakery, buttery, spicery, etc.) had one door, and they all opened onto one closed courtyard with the feasting hall at one end and a gatehouse at the other, where clerks checked workers going in and out.[47] In the imperial porcelain manufactory in sixteenth-century Jingdezhen, the cobalt used to create blue designs on white pottery was precious, because it was mined a thousand miles away. After days of pounding and purifying with water and magnets, the cobalt was sealed in locked boxes. The officials who managed the work gave each painter a half-day's supply of cobalt in the morning and another half-day's supply at noon. Even so, painters might mix cheaper blues into their paint and steal the cobalt, so each vessel they painted was tracked by their seat number until it had emerged from the kiln – for only at that point could the off-color blue reveal the cheat.[48] Clients' concern about fraud could reshape workspace at greater scales than the individual workshop, too: in 1327, Edward III required all goldsmiths to live in Cheapside, near him, so that it was easy to check up on them.[49]

Straight-up cheating and fraud are less interesting within one occupation than when an adjacent occupation's technique includes detection. For instance, Anne Gerritsen shows that minor government clerks had the task of weighing the firewood supplied to the Chinese imperial porcelain kilns, determining whether it belonged to the category "water fuel," that is, pine logs floated down the river, or the superior category "boat fuel," which was good and dry because it had been transported by boat. Water

46 Zurcher, "The Sailor Aboard," 399.
47 Oledzka, *Medieval and Renaissance Interiors*, 96.
48 Gerritsen, *City of Blue and White*, 65–66, 163.
49 Oledzka, *Medieval and Renaissance Interiors*, 135.

fuel, although useable for some things, would spoil the whole expensive kiln load of imperial porcelain.[50] Clerks who mistakenly, or under pressure, accepted and paid for water fuel as boat fuel, or mixed loads, were endangering the output of the whole enterprise. The wood suppliers' technique naturally included knowing all about different kinds of wood, but the clerks' technique, too, included being able to distinguish types of wood. Clerks' technique entailed being able to identify cheating in mixed loads and they may have had to be able to identify cheaters among the wood suppliers by their demeanor.

Should we consider the woodman's ways of cheating as part of their technique? The answer might be yes, if the knowledge was widespread in the occupation and if code included not ratting each other out. But some occupations necessarily have high rates of failure; for instance, the sensitive and varied raw materials, the high heat, the hand labor, and other factors in Chinese imperial porcelain production meant that mistakes, or failures in firing, were inevitable, and supervisors responsible for filling large orders from the throne had to plan additional production to compensate for those inevitable mistakes. The failed wares or the extra successes could then be sold to different kinds of customers; was such a response "fraud"? Gerritsen points out that "Words like 'mistakes' and 'fraud' create too much of a binary distinction between the two, when in the practical culture of work, it was probably more fluid and in fact, that fluidity was necessary for the overall successful outcome."[51]

Historians sometimes throw the word "corruption" around as if its meaning were clear and transhistorical, even attributing major historical changes like the fall of regimes to its acidic power. Sociology suggests that historians should look for and consider understandings generated, not only within specific place-times, but within specific occupations.

> Did practitioners and managers agree to break rules handed down from on high?
> Were such workarounds necessary to get the job done?
> Did they have to be kept secret from clients or others?
> How precious or saleable was the object of technique or tools?
> Did practitioners take objects from the workshop?

---

50   Gerritsen, *City of Blue and White*, 146, 154–55. Another case of "mixed loads" is when the painters mingled good Yunnan cobalt with cheaper blues, pocketing the good stuff to sell or to use in a private workshop.

51   Anne Gerritsen, personal communication, June 7, 2021.

How did the power of the boss relate to state power or social authority?

Could workers refuse to take the job?

Could workers leave the job?

Were workers legally protected from abuse?

Were wages or terms of service fixed by the state or another power?

Did the boss recognize or denigrate the skills of the practitioner?

How did theft prevention affect the organization of workspace or time?

Did potential theft or rule-breaking by one occupation constitute the object of technique for coworkers?

Works Cited

Bearman, Peter. *Doormen.* Chicago: University of Chicago Press, 2005.

Becker, Howard. "Professional Sociology: The Case of C. Wright Mills." In *The Democratic Imagination: Dialogues on the Work of Irving Louis Horowitz*, edited by Louis Filler, chapter 10. New York: Routledge, 1994.

Becker, Howard. "Social-Class Variations in the Teacher-Pupil Relationship." *The Journal of Educational Sociology: A Magazine of Theory and Practice* 25, no. 8 (1952): 451–65.

Becker, Howard S., Blanche Geer, Everett C. Hughes, and Anselm L. Strauss. *Boys in White: Student Culture in Medical School.* Chicago: University of Chicago Press, 1961.

Bourdieu, Pierre. *Sketch for a Self-Analysis.* Translated by Richard Nice. Cambridge: Polity, 2007.

Bourdieu, Pierre, Richard Nice, and Loïc Wacquant. "The Peasant and His Body." *Ethnography* 5, no. 4 (2004): 579–99.

Carter, Ron. "At 85, Legendary Jazz Bassist Ron Carter is Still Going Strong." Interview by Celeste Headlee. *NPR Illinois*, August 19, 2002. https://www.nprillinois.org/2022-08-19/at-85-legendary-jazz-bassist-ron-carter-is-still-going-strong

Dalton, Melville. "Reorganization and Accommodation: A Case in Industry." In *Institutions and the Person: Festschrift in Honor of Everett C. Hughes*, edited by Howard S. Becker, Blanche Geer, David Riesman, and Robert S. Weiss, 14–24. Chicago: Aldine, 1968.

Davis, Edward B. *Hidden Dimensions of Work: Revisiting the Chicago School Methods of Everett Hughes and Anselm Strauss.* N.p.: Xlibris Books, 2011.

Feng, Naixi. "Mushroom Cloud Over the Northern Capital: Writing the Tianqi Explosion in the Seventeenth Century." *Late Imperial China* 41, no. 1 (2020): 71–112.

Gerritsen, Anne. *The City of Blue and White: Chinese Porcelain and the Early Modern World.* Cambridge: Cambridge University Press, 2020.

Goffman, Erving. *Asylums: Essays on the Social Situation of Mental Patients and Other Inmates*. Chicago: Aldine Publishing Company, [1961] 1962.

Hughes, Everett C. "Bastard Institutions." In *On Work, Race and the Sociological Imagination*, edited by Lewis Coser, 192–99. Chicago: University of Chicago Press, 1994.

Hughes, Everett C. "The Improper Study of Man." In *On Work, Race, and the Sociological Imagination*, edited by Lewis Coser, 159–70. Chicago: University of Chicago Press, 1994.

Hughes, Everett C. "License and Mandate." In *Men and Their Work*, 78–87. Glencoe, IL: The Free Press, 1958.

Hughes, Everett C. "Mistakes at Work." In *Men and Their Work*, 88–101. Glencoe, IL: The Free Press, 1958.

Hughes, Everett C. "Social Role and the Division of Labor." In *Men and Their Work*, 69–77. Glencoe, IL: The Free Press, 1958.

Hughes, Everett C. "The Sociological Study of Work: An Editorial Foreword." *American Journal of Sociology* 57, no. 5 (1952): 423–26.

Hughes, Everett C. "The Study of Occupations." In *On Work, Race and the Sociological Imagination*, edited by Lewis Coser, 21–36. Chicago: University of Chicago Press, 1994.

Huisman, Michel. "L'étudiant au Moyen Âge" [Students in the Middle Ages]. *Revue de l'Université libre de Bruxelles* (1899): 45–67.

Lovejoy, Arthur O. *The Great Chain of Being*. Cambridge, MA: Harvard University Press, [1936] 1964.

Malinowski, Bronislaw. "Trobriand Gardeners and Their Magic." In *Work in Nonmarket and Transitional Societies*, edited by Herbert Applebaum, 161–67. Albany: SUNY Press, 1984.

Muscolino, Micah. *Fishing Wars and Environmental Change in Late Imperial and Modern China*. Cambridge, MA: Harvard University Asia Center, 2009.

Oledzka, Eva. *Medieval and Renaissance Interiors in Illuminated Manuscripts*. London: British Library, 2016.

Rule, John. "The Property of Skill in the Period of Manufacture." In *The Historical Meanings of Work,* edited by Patrick Joyce, 99–118. Cambridge: Cambridge University Press, 1987.

Sonenscher, Michael. "Mythical Work: Workshop Production and the *Compagnonnages* of Eighteenth-Century France." In *The Historical Meanings of Work*, edited by Patrick Joyce, 31–63. Cambridge: Cambridge University Press, 1987.

Vincze, Lajos. "Organization of Work in Herding Teams on the Great Hungarian Plain." In *Work in Non-market and Transitional Societies*, edited by Herbert Applebaum, 143–54. Albany: SUNY Press, 1984.

Westley, William A. "The Informal Organization of the Army: A Sociological Memoir." In *Institutions and the Person: Festschrift in Honor of Everett C. Hughes*, edited by Howard S. Becker, Blanche Geer, David Riesman, and Robert S. Weiss, 200–207. Chicago: Aldine, 1968.

Zhang, Ying. *Religion and Prison Art in Ming China (1368–1644): Creative Environment, Creative Subjects*. Leiden: Brill, 2020.

Zurcher, Jr., Louis A. "The Sailor Aboard Ship: A Study of Role Behavior in a Total Institution." *Social Forces* 43, no. 3 (1965): 389–400.

VIII. Mistakes at Work

Abstract

Although historians often focus on how work is done by the best practitioners under the best conditions, the risk that something will go wrong in any task is real. That risk creates both generic and specific tensions between practitioner and client that create stereotypes, including the charisma of certain occupations. The emotions that swirl around possible failure – whether or not anyone is really to blame (some diseases cannot be healed) – also underlie relations among colleagues and coworkers. Subject to the same risks of mistakes and the same clients' emotions, colleagues react as a group, ritualizing processes to define success and failure in in ways that protect their authority and create their identity. Mistakes and worry thus underlie work culture as much as do success and ambition.

Keywords: daily work, emotion, culture, failure, charisma, ritual

Back when I was a cub reporter at *The Peoria Journal Star*, I was moping around the office kicking myself over some ridiculous thing I got wrong. One of the veteran reporters pulled me aside, "Hey, Vecsey," he said. "Look: Doctors bury their mistakes. Lawyers lock theirs away. But reporters print theirs for the whole damn world to see."[1]

When the woodmen supplying imperial kilns succeeded in passing off a mixed load as boat fuel, that constituted, for the clerks, an instance of the key concept called "mistakes at work." All occupations share the problem of mistakes and failures. Work entails physical, financial, social, and psychological risks. The risk of mistakes at work underlies many of the concepts already covered (code, policy, license, mandate, guilty knowledge, symbols of distinction, the dilemma of routine and emergency) and interacts with others (technique, clients and colleagues, the path into the occupation,

---

1   Vecsey, "Because of an Editing Error."

Schneewind, S.K. *The Social Drama of Daily Work. A Manual for Historians.* Amsterdam: Amsterdam University Press, 2024
DOI: 10.5117/9789048559534_CH08

hierarchy within the occupation).[2] In some occupations, the risk to the practitioner is considerable; one sociologist wrote about his experiences as a flagger marking ground for crop-dusters, as a dynamite man in California water control, and driving a cab in Boston.[3] In other cases, the overt risk is greater for the client, but failure may of course endanger the practitioner and even the whole occupation. The reason for the centrality of mistakes at work is precisely the emotional burden of those risks, which strains all the social relations around work, not only with clients and laypeople, but also with coworkers and colleagues.

Mistakes at work include a whole range of actions. They may include the practitioner injuring himself; injuring a client; creating bad conditions (bad lighting, bad smells, a flood, etc.) in the workshop for everyone; or breaking with code even if there are no discernible effects. In some fields they are irretrievable; in others they can be corrected. A fictional carpenter expressed his love for his own object of technique:

> In wood, you must work with care, and respect, and love. For wood has soul and spirit, and is not at the mercy of triflers. One slip of your chisel in carelessness or ignorance, one shave too many with your plane, and your work is ruined, and fit only for burning. But with iron, you shall beat and beat, and only an angriness of sparks, like the spitting of a toad to answer you, and if you make a mistake, back on the fire with it, a leaning on the elbows, and here it is again, poor spiritless stuff, ready to be beaten again.[4]

Mistakes must be handled, sometimes by code that hides the "inner workings of the occupation from public view."[5] Generally, colleagues share the social and emotional strain of the risk of mistakes, so they make collective decisions about how to manage them. As Hughes put it, colleagues "compose a collective rationale which they whistle to one another to keep up their courage, and ... build up collective defenses against the world."[6] As they build those defenses – code and policy – and clients build their own, occupational dynamics contribute significantly to the culture of the place-time.

---

2   Hughes, "Mistakes at Work," 90. If the reader wants to read just one Hughes article, I suggest this one.
3   E. Davis, *Hidden Dimensions*, 97–102.
4   Llewellyn, *How Green Was My Valley*, 411.
5   Solomon, "Sociological Perspectives on Occupations," 9.
6   Hughes, "Mistakes at Work," 90–91. Hughes explains this by an analogy to insurance, arguing that colleagues are spreading the risk around psychologically.

In what ways could practitioners fail?

What kinds of mistakes could they make?

How serious were the results of mistakes or failures and for whom?

How much choice did clients have in practitioners?

How much choice did practitioners have in clients?

If clients recommended particular practitioners to other laymen, how did they praise them?

Did clients make donations to practitioners, above the agreed-upon terms?

Did they honor them in the social terms of that place-time?

Flow and Error

Psychologist Mihaly Csikszentmihalyi has written about the state of "flow" achieved by highly skilled practitioners. In a passage reminiscent of the Daoist classic *Zhuangzi*'s famous chapter on Cook Ding, who had butchered so many cattle that his knife no longer became blunt, Csikszentmihalyi says:

> One of the people I interviewed was an old man in Manhattan and his job was making the best lox and bagels in that part of the city. He sounded like some of the poets or the Nobel Prize-winning physicists talking about his work. He says: "I get to work at 7 o'clock in the morning – get a delivery of four or five huge salmons, and have to fillet them for selling them with the bagels. I take the first one – drop it on the counter, and watch how the skin moves – that tells me where the bone structure of the fish is – like a three-dimensional x-ray so I can see inside – how the flesh trembles when it falls. So then I know what's inside and take one of these five knives that I keep sharpening and start slicing – make sure to waste as little of the meat as possible, make the cuts as thin as can be, and do it as fast as I can. Those are the three things I want to achieve. And at the end of the day, I usually feel wow – I don't think anyone could do so thin, without wasting, as fast as I can.[7]

The idea that one can find happiness as well as success by losing oneself in the flow of work is very appealing. The "tacit knowledge" of the practitioner – in historian Eric Ash's words, "an enigmatic combination of techniques, experience, and skill that is essentially indefinable and irreducible" – is easy to romanticize precisely because, as Ash says, its unknowability means that

7   Csikszentmihalyi, "Getting into the Flow."

it "is not open to historical or social analysis."[8] Historians should push as far as they can to understand the components of any occupation, Ash writes, but recognize that they may not be able to understand everything. In particular, the joy of another's work may be hard to fathom.

Cabinet-maker Peter Korn, while accepting much of Csikszentmihalyi's description of flow, also highlights the anxiety of work. He writes, "in my experience, the possibility of failure is always present in the workshop. Success and failure are magnetic poles to which I orient my compass at every moment to determine whether or not to take (or persist in) a given course of action."[9] Moreover, in some occupations, the excitement and pleasure of the work go hand-in-hand with the danger, as expressed to me by an arborist removing an enormous eucalyptus that had fallen on my house, and in the excitement or worry at a rough crossing in an ancient Cypriot pottery model of a ship filled with sailors.[10]

All practitioners make mistakes. Difficult chemical operations, extreme environments, and tricky technique make mistakes more likely; mistakes occur more often when workers get out of practice or out of shape. But mistakes are normal – in fact required – for learning. Experience lowers the risk of mistakes, but not to zero. In fact, Hughes argued that the more often a practitioner does a task in a workday, the more likely a mistake becomes. If a top surgeon does ten times more operations than a resident (journeyman), his incidence of error in each one would have to be less than one-tenth of the resident's rate of error for him to make fewer mistakes in total. Some technique requires more constant practice and thought, and some is more vulnerable to chance.[11] Technique normally includes, in the words of historian Eric Ash, "the ability to learn on the job, and especially to cope with the surprises and unexpected setbacks one is virtually certain to encounter."[12] Since most occupations require bundled skills, a practitioner might be naturally good at one (say, those requiring hand-eye coordination) yet naturally less talented at others (say, people skills). Even the practitioner who is nearly flawless at one skill may handle another clunkily, so relations with coworkers are essential to complete success.

8   Ash, "Expertise and the Early Modern State," 9.
9   Korn, *Why We Make Things*, 54.
10   Karageorghis, *Everyday Life in Ancient Cyprus*, 49. See also 187, where a painted white-ware vase depicts one sailor rowing, one managing the anchor, and a third trying to get back into the ship to escape a large fish.
11   Hughes, "Mistakes at Work," 89.
12   Ash, "Expertise and the Early Modern State," 6.

What technique did the occupation require?

What mistakes and failures were possible?

Is there evidence that practitioners experienced flow states?

How much concentration did tasks require?

Were mistakes at work so likely to be fateful that they created a lot of stress?

Would some of the occupation's bundled skills be easier for people with particular personality traits?

Mistakes, Colleagues, and Coworkers

The risk of error affects relations among colleagues who are coworkers. Senior members of the occupation may use their seniority to control workflow in a way that minimizes their own mistakes: either pushing tough cases down the hierarchy within the occupation or consistently taking the tough cases themselves to maintain their skill at the highest level.[13] Mistakes relate to and may influence paths into and out of the occupation. Hughes points to complaints by interns and residents (journeymen on the path into the occupation). Placed in a hospital to learn by doing, they complained that the leading surgeons took "all the interesting cases, not merely out of charity, but to keep their level of skill up to the point of least risk for the few patients who [could] pay a really high fee."[14] The surgeons' role as teacher was clashing with their role as practitioner and their wish to reduce their mistakes and garner high remuneration.

Sociologists have found that most workers complain that they could do their job better if it were not for interference from those playing other roles in the occupational system.

> Teachers could teach better were it not for parents who fail in their duty or school boards who interfere. Psychiatrists would do better if it were not for families, stupid public officials, and ill-trained attendants. Nurses would do more nursing if it were not for administrative duties, and the carelessness of aides and maintenance people.[15]

Ming magistrates complained about the stupid people of their jurisdictions or blamed failures on the corrupt clerks and runners in the county government offices. As always, we ask what lies behind these complaints. One answer is that

13   Hughes, "Mistakes at Work," 89.

14   Hughes, "Mistakes at Work," 89.

15   Hughes, "Social Role," 75.

as the division of labor changes, the people playing various roles are working with a changing script. They have different conceptions about what the tasks of each role should be, or, even more fundamentally, about who should decide on those tasks. They may not even agree on the output of the workshop.[16]

Even when the division of labor is stable, those lower in the institutional hierarchy, in Hughes's words,

> bring into the institutional complex their own conceptions of what the problem is, their own conceptions of their rights and privileges ... Like most humans, they do not completely accept the role-definitions handed down from above, but in communication among their own kind and in interaction with [clients], work out their own definition.[17]

Those lower in the hierarchy of the occupation have a different impact on shared occupational culture or (depending on where one draws the line) develop their own occupational culture. To understand any institution entails considering it from the perspective of all participants.[18] This seems an obvious point, but it is often overlooked by historians, who may describe the state from the point of view of the ruler or ministers and not lowly clerks or taxpayers. Recently, historians have been adding animal coworkers into the picture as agents as well as victims.[19] Managing relations with coworkers who are not human can also be difficult, as we see in an ancient Cypriot seal representing a man trying to keep two bulls apart.[20]

Sociologists found that those working at lower levels (i.e., all but the very top level) shared "a common dignifying rationalization": namely, that "We in this position save the next higher position above from their own mistakes."[21] An example is the sergeants studied by William Westley. Over morning coffee, "They would discuss how to cover up for someone who was in trouble. There was much talk about the care and control of officers." Officers, the sergeants believed, did not know how to look after their own interests by figuring out

16   Hughes, "Social Role," 75–76.
17   Hughes, "Social Role," 76–77.
18   Hughes, "Social Role," 76–77.
19   Braden, *Serve the People.*
20   Karageorghis, *Everyday Life in Ancient Cyprus,* 54–55. The Appendix (227–35) discusses textual evidence for over twenty occupations in ancient Cyprus, including doctors, scribes and teachers, actors, sculptors, architects and builders, weavers, fullers, shipbuilders, murex fishermen, bronzeworkers, silversmiths, chariot makers, bowyers, potters, barbers, bakers, cooks, perfume makers, merchants, and priests.
21   Hughes, "Work and the Self," 45–46.

how to work around Army regulations to get the work of the Army done. Sergeants did it for them, and as the officers tacitly approved, the arrangements "grew up pragmatically as a way of working together. It was a product of time and common experience in which the men came to share the same views and know each other well. Yet with time it gained the qualities of a moral order."[22] (This is code: rules about technique that the occupation itself develops.)

Although these sergeants talked among themselves about how to manage their superiors' mistakes at work, other cases are often dealt with by stonewalling. Silences, as well as communication, contribute to occupational culture.

> That people can and do keep a silence about things whose open discussion would threaten the group's conception of itself, and hence its solidarity, is common knowledge. It is a mechanism that operates in every family and in every group which has a sense of group reputation ... This common silence allows group fictions to grow up.[23]

Colleagues often release emotional tension around mistakes by confidentially discussing their worries, as well as their questions about their own competence, the occupation's output, the folly of superiors and inferiors within the work institution, and so on.[24] But among colleagues, acknowledgement of mistakes may also occur by "subtle gestures," mastery of which is part of learning the occupational culture. These gestures make open discussion of some errors unnecessary among colleagues – a first step toward building a code of silence within the occupation. Since only colleagues understand, any degree of transparency, with its accompanying implication that the layperson can judge success or failure, will meet strenuous opposition. This may be especially true when a failure has become a matter for public discussion.[25] Individual practitioners might think of benefiting in the short term by criticizing a colleague, but this must be counterbalanced by the risk of admitting that outsiders have a role to play in judging one's work; that dilemma is probably reflected in colleague code. Hughes notes that if the discussion of mistakes no longer occurs even among colleagues, "public discussion may be doubly feared; for in addition to questioning the prerogative of in-group judgement, the outside inquisitor lifts the veil from the group's hidden anxieties."[26]

22 Westley, "Organization of the Army," 201–2.
23 Hughes, "Good People and Dirty Work," 184.
24 Hughes, "Dilemmas and Contradictions of Status," 108.
25 Hughes, "Mistakes at Work," 94–95.
26 Hughes, "Mistakes at Work," 95.

How much repetition did each skill require for a low rate of error?
Did individual practitioners at all levels of the hierarchy within the occupation get enough practice?
Besides insufficient practice, what other contingencies might lead to failure?
If coworkers did not share a language, only technical jargon, did that language suffice in crisis situations or did coordination break down?
Whom did practitioners complain about hampering them and on what grounds?
Did those lower in the hierarchy say they saved their superiors from mistakes?
Among colleagues, were mistakes discussed openly, subtly acknowledged, or dealt with silently?

Danger and Charisma

Those hidden anxieties are sharper when occupational mistakes matter more to the practitioner, the client, the valuable object of technique, or coworkers. That is so from the first step on the path into the occupation. As Hughes points out, "In occupations in which mistakes are fateful and in which repetition on living or valuable material is necessary to learn skills … there is a special set of problems of apprenticeship." Apprentice barbers must practice with real razors on real heads, and a Ming joke demonstrates the social anxiety around that: every time his razor slips and nicks the customer's scalp, an apprentice puts a finger over the wound to staunch it. As he runs out of fingers, he laments, "It would take the Thousand-Armed Bodhisattva Guanyin to do this job!"[27]

The client is lamenting, too, and more dramatically. But despite the danger, the client seeks out the practitioner. An occupation's having a clientele may stem in the first place from a layperson having failed to fix a problem. As Eliot Freidson writes,

> When the suburban householder has taken apart a defective fixture and cannot get it back together again to work even as badly as before, or when the ailing soul has dosed himself only to feel worse than he felt originally, he is inclined to seek the aid of someone else.[28]

The layperson's failure leads him to delegate to the practitioner not only the hope of success, but also the risk of failure, along with the burden of

27 Feng M., *Xiao fu*, 147.
28 Freidson, "Impurity of Professional Authority," 27.

guilt or shame for mistakes.[29] The practitioner shoulders that burden, but the client's worries are not over. S/he must trust the practitioner, yet in the nature of the case cannot fully judge the practitioner's quality until the fateful decisions have been taken, and perhaps not for a long time, depending on the occupation. So the client, and laypeople generally, feel anxiety about "the danger that the advice given a [client] may be wrong, or that work done may be unsuccessful or cause damage."[30] The need to trust coupled with the inability to verify cause a complex swirl of feelings around hiring a specialist.

One result is social charisma. We are accustomed to associating charisma with political leaders, religious practitioners, and the like, but it is part of many occupations. How does this come about? On the one hand, it stems from taboos and mystifications purposely created by practitioners, as discussed above. But its home is the mind of the client, who most obviously suffers from mistakes and failures. The practitioner knows that sometimes things will go wrong, but observation shows that the client often wishes to believe absolutely in "the charisma of skill." Ray Gold, in studying construction work,

> found that the housewife likes to believe that the plumber she calls in is perfect, not merely *relatively* good. He keeps the mysterious entrails of her precious house in order. How much more does one want to believe absolutely in one's dentist, lawyer, physician, and priest.[31]

The plumber's charisma is one example of how occupational sociology enables researchers to screen out elite bias.

Mistakes at Work Create Culture

One could say that failures may result from causes other than mistakes: a teacher may have done everything right and still have to fail a student; a hairdresser can do only so much to make dead-straight hair look naturally curly. But knowing how to anticipate and guard against chance is part of technique, whether that involves using back-up systems or accurately gauging factors beyond the practitioner's control, like war or weather, lazy students or limp locks. The occupation itself, within and contributing

29 Hughes, "Mistakes at Work," 91.
30 Hughes, "License and Mandate," 82.
31 Hughes, "Mistakes at Work," 91–92.

to the parameters of the larger culture, defines which factors are out of practitioners' control. Colleagues deal with the emotional burden of likely errors and failures by sharing both collective defenses against accusations by laypeople and collective ways to stave off their own self-doubts.[32] Which factors in failure, for instance, can practitioners not control and therefore not be blamed for? That will vary by place-time, as occupations build their defenses out of available ideas and practices.

But the risk of error in occupations not only draws on, but also contributes to culture more broadly. This means that there is necessarily a diachronic dimension: mistakes are made and responded to as culture changes over time. The risk of mistakes at work contributes to taboos, ritual, deities, and occupational identity, among other aspects of culture.

Explanations for failure may create taboos. In twentieth-century East Africa, smelters protected their smelting sites by claiming that menstruating women could cause the process to fail. The historian can look around for cultural ideas that might underlie the specifics here – for instance, Camara suggests a correlation with the idea of bringing forth raw materials from the "womb" of Mother Earth.[33] But potters also did that, and potters *were* women; there is no logical reason that such a belief would bar menstruating women from the site. A liminal analysis of pollution might suggest the danger of fluids breaching boundaries where the miraculous transformation of dirt into iron was occurring, but that, too, is an abstract, post-hoc explanation, and one that could keep women away from *any* activity: indeed, in the early modern Arab-Islamic world women worked in many trades, but rarely in food preparation, and menstrual pollution is offered as a reason.[34] If we begin with the workshop, and colleagues' recognition that mistakes will happen and smeltings fail for reasons that practitioners did not fully understand, we can see the need for an all-purpose explanation that is hard to prove wrong. If the reason given for failure in this all-male occupation is the presence of a woman who may not even have known that her period had started, that strengthens the need for all coworkers to observe code by excluding women. This explanation of failure also strengthens the likelihood that clients will grant the occupation mandate, accepting that blacksmiths have the right to tell them to keep away from smelting activities, and to explain why.[35]

32   Hughes, "Mistakes at Work," 90.

33   Camara, *Is There a Distinctively African Way of Knowing*, 14.

34   Hofmeester, "Jewish Ethics and Women's Work," 159.

35   See P. Cohen, *History in Three Keys*, 119–45: by blaming failures of their magic on the presence of women, particularly menstruating women, Boxers tightened their hold on the urban population through regulations designed to prevent that interference.

In fraught situations such as a sea voyage, practitioners' attempts to avoid mistakes at work may further affect the larger culture through supplication to divine beings. Passengers on Japanese ships prayed to Buddhist and Shinto deities before embarking, but also, influenced by sailors, to the Chinese god Mazu and to Christian spirits.[36] A deity or saint who assured clients a safe experience in the workshop might well be adopted outside that workshop, too. Meanwhile, the passengers – whatever their social status – have accepted that sailors know better than they do which deities matter on the sea.

One mode of both swaying the client and protecting oneself from the psychological and social risks of failure is the development of ritual. Workers develop a particular set of steps for each task – this is code. They consider that if they have followed all those steps, that in itself is success, regardless of whether (say) the pupil learns or the patient recovers.[37] The ritual and art of an occupation – Hughes offers the example of young lawyers who write elaborate briefs that judges will not read – may be in themselves admired, not only by colleagues, but also by "the simple client." In most historical societies, the risk of mistakes at work was defended against by a deeper ritualization: magic of various kinds.

Ritualization provides an answer to a key question that relates to both license and mandate: "Who has the right to say what counts as a mistake or failure?" In any case short of the precisely and accurately measured tolerances of the highest-tech factories, there is debate. Practitioners generally accept only the verdict of colleagues, not laypeople or clients. "The simple client may be dazzled" by elaborate and artful ritual productions like long legal briefs, but he also distrusts the complexities of "the art and cult of the law" and resents having to financially support that cult.[38] Because the client is precisely a person who does not have mastery of technique and does not understand the object of technique well enough to be persuaded by informed, rational argument, as one's colleagues could be, professionals "minimize the role of persuasive evidence" in swaying clients to follow their advice.[39] Rather than persuading, and rather than judging success by the client's criteria, the practitioner judges success by whether all the right steps were followed.

High risks mean high levels of ritualization. Code may ritualize tasks more fully at the levels just below the top of a hierarchy of related occupations.

36 Shapinsky, *Lords of the Sea*, 42–43.
37 Hughes, "Mistakes at Work," 96–97.
38 Hughes, "Mistakes at Work," 96–97.
39 Freidson, "Impurity of Professional Authority," 27.

Those on whom the highest practitioner relies – the lieutenants – know that the boss may pass the buck and that he has greater resources to protect himself than they do. Outranked by the doctor, nurses and pharmacists are punctilious. "Pharmacists," Hughes writes, "are said often to become ritualistic wipers and polishers, flecking infinitely small grains of dust from [their] scales."[40] Of course, a pharmacist's scale *should* be clean: there is a rationale in technique and object of technique for the germ of what blossoms into occupational culture. If we look at ritual in the occupations of past place-times for both the rational germ and the hothouse of emotions and social tensions that brought it to fruition, we will understand a lot about the people we are studying – and their culture.

Identity itself can become a way to deal with the risk of mistakes at work. To dilute the risks of failure, a practitioner says not "I fix pipes," but "I am a plumber"; not "I improve students' minds and abilities," but "I am a teacher." A practitioner who has gone through the ritual steps established by code has done the job, even if the pipes leak or the student remains cloddish. Since ritual is performance, and since the disagreements over failure go to the heart of professional autonomy and of individual and occupational dignity and identity, it should be clear why we refer to "the social drama of work." As in a drama, it is roles that make up the social system.[41]

And when a client identifies the practitioner as an expert and puts full faith in the occupation, surrendering his own judgement and agency, that deepens the divide between practitioner and client in ways that may resonate in the broader culture. Peter Shapinsky quotes *The Tosa Diary*, a personal account of a sea voyage from about 900 by a member of the Hei'an court elite. At that time, the court elite were in the process of divorcing the culture of the archipelago from the sea and adopting a terracentric identity based on Chinese models. Ki no Tsurayaki wrote: "As for the weather, all we could do was to depend on the captain and the crew. For men unused to these journeys, it was a great source of worry. Women laid their heads on the floor of the ship and cried." Shapinsky argues that "The premodern practice of delegating maritime responsibilities away to 'sea people' may have heightened the feeling of powerlessness of dealing not only with the ocean and the weather but also with seafarers themselves."[42] The practitioner-client relation intensified the cultural change of the period.

40 Hughes, "Mistakes at Work," 97.
41 Hughes, "Mistakes at Work," 98.
42 Shapinsky, *Lords of the Sea*, 42–43.

What safeguards were in place against the occupation's mistakes at work?

What rituals and taboos developed around the work?

How did practitioners show concerns about mistakes at work?

Who decided whether a mistake had been made?

Who decided whether failure was the result of a mistake?

What steps did code prescribe for each task?

Which of those steps seem purely pragmatic and which require further thought?

What taboos surrounded work and who enforced them?

Whom did workers complain about?

What spirits or other external forces could they blame failures on, and what

steps could they force laypeople to take to prevent future mistakes?

How did practitioners define success and how did clients?

Example: Mistakes in !Kung San Hunting

Mistakes happen in all kinds of work. Hunters master the patterns of movements of game animals, the plants that draw them at particular seasons,
how to create smells and drink potions; rub bodies, clothes, and weapons
with lotions; and spray powders around sites of camping and ambushing.
Hunters learn to mentally prepare themselves for success in the hunt.[43] Yet
with all this knowledge, at times the !Kung San hunter stalking a gemsbok
may move carelessly, make a sound, get upwind of the animal, or in trying
to stay downwind lose sight of the spoor. He may forget to leave the bulk
of his kit with his comrades before approaching the animal on his belly. He
may watch its tail rather than its ears for signs of alarm. He may become
impatient with wriggling forward on his belly and rise to his knees. He may
have strung his bow too loosely the previous evening and miss the first
shot, alarming the animal into galloping away, or he may have neglected
to oil his bow, so that it cracks when he draws it.[44] The !Kung San in the
1960s spent hours discussing what, where, and when to hunt. Why? To avoid
possible mistakes at work. When hunting the ant-bear such mistakes can
be deadly; less seriously, in up to half the cases in which they wound an
animal, they fail to bring it in to eat.[45] The possibility of error appears in

43   Camara, *Is There a Distinctively African Way of Knowing*, 17–22.

44   I am imaging possible mistakes based on the technique described in Richard B. Lee, "Hunting
among the !Kung San," from his *The !Kung San: Men, Women and Work in a Foraging Society*,
part of which is reprinted in Applebaum, *Work in Non-market and Transitional Societies*, 73, 81.
Lee's three years of fieldwork took place in the 1960s.

45   Lee, *The !Kung San*, 211, 216, 221.

many of the statistics and observations from Richard Lee's study of work among the !Kung, yet overall, Lee concludes that the !Kung carefully and purposefully used cultural practices to maintain an egalitarian society in the face of great differences among men in their success in the central activity of hunting.[46]

In other words, in this society in which the economy was not marketized nor work specialized (all men hunted), features of dealing with mistakes at work still arose. There was code: one does not boast of one's own prowess; one denigrates the achievements of the best fellow practitioners and explains away the failures of the worst; and the most successful take frequent days off, on which they are fed by others.[47] There was clear spreading of work risk: ownership of the meat went to the maker of the arrow, and arrows circulated widely, including among women, who never hunted. Lee explains why: The owner had to manage the meat distribution. Along with prestige, that process brought with it "the risk of accusations of stinginess or improper behavior if the distribution [was] not to everyone's liking." Trading arrows "diffuse[d] the responsibility for meat distribution and spread the glory (and the hostility) around."[48]

What do we gain by slapping labels like "code" and "mistakes at work" on Lee's facts about the !Kung San in the 1960s? It means we can compare them to all other human groups and specify both similarities and dissimilarities. It avoids labels like "primitive," and progress narratives that employ terms like "developing" or "pre-capitalist." It puts analysis of the !Kung San hunter of the 1960s, the US Senator of the 2020s, and the Chinese silk weaver of the 960s on the same level.

Further, using these terms raises new questions about !Kung San working lives and lets us use the insights about their work to raise questions about other societies. Questions about the !Kung San might include considering the women as clients, which might lead to more emphasis on their complaints about men not bringing home enough meat: "Good-natured (and not so good-natured) accusations of men's laziness at hunting were a common refrain."[49] In the face of this client complaining about mistakes at work, the practitioners (hunters) had developed clear colleague policy: a presentation that anyone could be lucky or unlucky and that the hunt required the contributions of all. Questions about other societies might include, in situations in which significant teamwork among practitioners

46   Lee, *The !Kung San*, 243–44.
47   Lee, *The !Kung San*, 244–47, 249.
48   Lee, *The !Kung San*, 247–48.
49   Lee, *The !Kung San*, 220, 235–36.

is required, whether code requires batting down the arrogance of the best with denigrating jokes, or whether some ritual bolsters the self-confidence of the worst practitioners. When this happens, does it erase the high prestige of the best member of the group, or does going along with such behavior increase his prestige, adding social approbation for being "a team player" to his glorious performance? When someone – say a department chair – has acquired resources (research funds, perhaps) to hand out, does she form a committee to do so precisely to deflect the possible hostility, even at the cost of diminishing her own glory? Historians of any one place-time can use the Hughes framework to gather new questions about work from any other place-time.

> In what areas of life must the layperson trust practitioners?
> Precisely what could go wrong with technique?
> How could a mistake harm a client or object of technique?
> What failures might result, even if practitioners made no mistakes?
> What precautions did practitioners take or prescribe?
> What rules did the occupation make for itself, written or not?
> Were there rules that seem excessive, irrational, or ritualistic?
> Working back from the rules, what areas of anxiety appear?

Works Cited

Ash, Eric. "Introduction: Expertise and the Early Modern State." *Osiris* 25, no. 1 (2010): 1–24.

Braden, Peter. *Serve the People: Bovine Experiences in China's Civil War and Revolution, 1935–1961.* Ithaca: Cornell University Press, forthcoming.

Camara, Mohamed Saliou. *Is There a Distinctively African Way of Knowing (a Study of African Blacksmiths, Hunters, Healers, Griots, Elders, and Artists): Knowing and Theory of Knowledge in the African Experience.* Lewiston: Edwin Mellen Press, 2014.

Cohen, Paul. *History in Three Keys: The Boxers as Event, Experience, and Myth.* New York: Columbia University Press, 1998.

Csikszentmihalyi, Mihaly. "Getting into the Flow: A Q&A with Dr. Mihaly Csikszentmihalyi." Interview by James Suillivan. *Brain World Magazine*, January 11, 2020. https://brainworldmagazine.com/getting-into-the-flow-a-qa -with-dr-mihaly-csikszentmihalyi/

Davis, Edward B. *Hidden Dimensions of Work: Revisiting the Chicago School Methods of Everett Hughes and Anselm Strauss.* N.p.: Xlibris Books, 2011.

Feng Menglong. *Xiao fu* 笑府 *Treasury of Laughs* [Feng Menglong's Treasury of Laughs: A Seventeenth-Century Anthology of Traditional Chinese Humor]. Translated by Hsu Pi-ching. Leiden: Brill, 2015.

Freidson, Eliot. "The Impurity of Professional Authority." In *Institutions and the Person: Festschrift in Honor of Everett C. Hughes*, edited by Howard S. Becker, Blanche Geer, David Riesman, and Robert S. Weiss, 25–34. Chicago: Aldine, 1968.

Hofmeester, Karin. "Jewish Ethics and Women's Work in the Late Medieval and Early Modern Arab-Islamic World." *International Review of Social History Special Issue* 56 (2011): 141–64.

Hughes, Everett C. "Dilemmas and Contradictions of Status." In *Men and Their Work*, 102–15. Glencoe, IL: The Free Press, 1958.

Hughes, Everett C. "Good People and Dirty Work." In *On Work, Race and the Sociological Imagination*, edited by Lewis Coser, 180–91. Chicago: University of Chicago Press, 1994.

Hughes, Everett C. "License and Mandate." In *Men and Their Work*, 78–87. Glencoe, IL: The Free Press, 1958.

Hughes, Everett C. "Mistakes at Work." In *Men and Their Work*, 88–101. Glencoe, IL: The Free Press, 1958.

Hughes, Everett C. "Social Role and the Division of Labor." In *Men and Their Work*, 69–77. Glencoe, IL: The Free Press, 1958.

Hughes, Everett C. "Work and the Self." In *Men and Their Work*, 42–55. Glencoe, IL: The Free Press, 1958.

Karageorghis, Vassos. *Aspects of Everyday Life in Ancient Cyprus: Iconographic Representations.* Nicosia: A. G. Leventis Foundation, 2006.

Korn, Peter. *Why We Make Things and Why It Matters: The Education of a Craftsman.* Boston: David R. Godine, 2013.

Lee, Richard B. "Hunting among the !Kung San." In *Work in Non-market and Transitional Societies*, edited by Herbert Applebaum, 69–83. Albany: SUNY Press, 1984.

Lee, Richard B. *Hunting among the !Kung San.* Cambridge: Cambridge University Press, 1979.

Llewellyn, Richard. *How Green Was My Valley.* New York: Touchstone/Simon and Shuster, 2009.

Shapinsky, Peter D. *Lords of the Sea: Pirates, Violence, and Commerce in Late Medieval Japan.* Ann Arbor: Center for Japanese Studies, University of Michigan, 2014.

Solomon, David N. "Sociological Perspectives on Occupations." In *Institutions and the Person: Festschrift in Honor of Everett C. Hughes*, edited by Howard S. Becker, Blanche Geer, David Riesman, and Robert S. Weiss, 3–13. Chicago: Aldine, 1968.

Vecsey, David. "Because of an Editing Error." *The New York Times*, January 3, 2021. https://www.nytimes.com/2021/01/03/insider/editor-errors-corrections.html

Westley, William A. "The Informal Organization of the Army: A Sociological
Memoir." In *Institutions and the Person: Festschrift in Honor of Everett C. Hughes*,
edited by Howard S. Becker, Blanche Geer, David Riesman, and Robert S. Weiss,
200–207. Chicago: Aldine, 1968.

IX.   Pace and Discipline

Abstract
Much scholarship on work has focused on questions of pace and time discipline. A contrast that has often been made between the extreme discipline of the assembly line and the relaxation of work in non-market societies exaggerates the difference between modern and premodern times and between commercialized and less commercialized societies. By looking at pace through the lens of sociology, we can add texture and detail to portrayals of the work experience in any place-time, and center workers as subjects. We can also reconsider how the experience of working as a group might affect both production and experience positively or negatively.

Keywords: time, pace, factory, workshop, labor, management

Sociologist William Grossin wrote that "every activity generates its own time."[1] A great deal of historical work has been done on time within the workshop, including a debate about how and when the discipline of the clock came to govern working lives.[2] The transition certainly happened in various ways: even in twentieth-century industrial settings, managers continued to delegate time control to the floor, while workers found ways around time discipline.[3] As Grossin suggests, technique underlies time-management in any occupation, but it does not determine everything, precisely because technique resides in people. Who regulates pace, and with what results, is a complex question.

---

1   Conference paper cited in Whipp, "A Time to Every Purpose," 215.
2   Thompson, "Time, Work-Discipline, and Industrial Capitalism."
3   Whipp, "A Time to Every Purpose," 222–23.

Schneewind, S.K. *The Social Drama of Daily Work. A Manual for Historians.* Amsterdam: Amsterdam University Press, 2024
DOI: 10.5117/9789048559534_CH09

The Assembly Line and the Anthropologist

The introduction of the industrial factory has loomed over all historical discussions of pace ever since E. P. Thompson hypothesized that its long, regular hours, measured by the clock, revolutionized people's relation to time.[4] The discipline of the assembly line intensified the traumatic change. Richard Brown, a worker in a US car factory in the mid-twentieth century, reported:

> My job cycle took 1.2 minutes and was repeated 389 times a day. I had to move the axle from the rear line, push it ahead on a double hook, turn it, tighten the control knobs and undo the brake cable. I hated that line ... I used the same muscles over and over, not my whole body. At the end of the day I was worn out and in pain ... If you get a little ahead, say 1.1 minutes on a 1.2 cycle, and try to light a cigarette, these efficiency guys would give you more work. You are a slave to the line.[5]

Brown later took up construction work because "he did not want to work at a job where he had no control over his time and his movements."[6]

This side of the industrial age has been contrasted with hunter-gatherer societies and agricultural societies, usually with a palpable sense of nostalgia. In those societies, work was self-governed and more or less continuous: "Even when people are sitting around talking or visiting they are working – making an arrowhead, shaping a tool, or constructing a carrying device."[7] Mayo villagers in Mexico in 1948 spent about the same amount of time working as men on a job in Washington, D.C., anthropologist Charles Erasmus and his wife concluded from closely tracking their activities; but unlike in Washington, "each adult Tenían is his own boss and can work or rest as he feels inclined."[8] In non-market economies, Herbert Applebaum writes,

> People work when the land needs to be tilled, when crops must be harvested, when animals have to be milked, and when the time of day or the coming of a new season makes it opportune to hunt, trap or fish. Discipline is not absent from work in non-market economies. A !Kung San

4   Thompson, "Time, Work-Discipline, and Industrial Capitalism."
5   Nash, "Anthropology of Work," 52–53.
6   Nash, "Anthropology of Work," 52–53.
7   Applebaum, *Work in Non-market and Transitional Societies*, 66.
8   Erasmus, "Work Patterns in a Mayo Village," 177.

hunter might have to be on the trail of a giraffe for two weeks, tracking from early morning to dark; during harvest time, peasants work from dawn to dusk, fourteen hours a day; village blacksmiths, once they place their iron in the fire, must work at it so it will not fail.[9]

Applebaum contrasts "flexible and varied" task-oriented work and "rigid and strictly regulated" time-oriented work.[10] Kapauku farmers in New Guinea in the 1950s measured work by the task ("I will clear the land from this line to that fence"), and when colonialists came in and paid them by the hour, "they deprive[d] the [worker] of the initiative and pleasure derived from work and planning, and turn[ed] him into a slow, unreliable worker."[11]

But the assembly line and the farm are not simple opposites in terms of pace and discipline. Rather, the details of work culture that are so central to people's waking hours vary within workshops in unpredictable ways.

How precisely was work time measured, and by whom?
How did practitioners talk about time?
Who set the pace of work? Was it set for individuals or for a group?
How was the pace set? Was hostility or harmony the keynote?
Was work measured by task or by time?
Who decided which tasks to do when?
Were there fixed hours of work, by custom if not by contract?
Did work time or task vary by season?
How did the time of day affect tasks being done?

Rethinking Pace

The distinction between, on the one hand, pre-industrial, task-oriented self-management, and on the other, industrial, time-oriented work for a boss, has sometimes been overdrawn. In the early eighteenth century, employers required British hatters to produce a certain amount, but they could come and go from the workshop on their own say-so.[12] Even factory production had a degree of flexibility; the familiar picture of unskilled workers punching a relentless time-clock developed slowly.

9 Applebaum, *Work in Non-market and Transitional Societies*, 17.
10 Applebaum, *Work in Non-market and Transitional Societies*, 17.
11 Pospisil, "Organization of Labor among the Kapauku," 181.
12 Rule, "Property of Skill," 109.

Richard Whipp describes how, as late as the 1920s, the pottery production of Staffordshire was subdivided into tiny functional departments, some with only four to eight workers. Many had no official time clock and no standard workday: "We have no set time for stopping and starting here … the Boss troubles no more about one's coming and going," wrote R. Sirrat, a molder. Tasks were parceled out within the workshop by the practitioners themselves to equalize the workload. Each task ran on a different time: making slip for coating vessels, for instance, took two to three hours, while firing a kiln took two days. The different times led both to down time, which the workers called "play" and used for family matters, and to conflict among workshops blaming one another for bottlenecks.[13] The enterprise needed the flexibility of experts, such as fitter Colin Sedgly, who wrote in 1919 about the years it took to learn how to fit together some five thousand vessel shapes out of the sections in which they were made. Whipp concludes, "The tiny workshops therefore became saturated with their own codes which arose spontaneously among workers in order to regulate such an unsynchronized production process."[14] A similarly pragmatic flexibility took different forms in the Jingdezhen porcelain industry on the other side of the world, including work and workers moving between imperial kilns and private kilns, contrary to the logic of bureaucratic control.[15]

The imperatives of capitalism have made the level of effort, especially the pace of work, a focus of study. But the human feelings in work relations may win out over capitalist rationality. When one factory gave female paint sprayers the right to set their own pace of work, they worked faster than everyone else and earned more than more highly skilled male workers, who complained, as did middle managers who felt it was their right to make those decisions. Although granting this autonomy had made workers *more* productive, it was withdrawn.[16] From the other side, in some workshops in the early twentieth century, those who worked fastest were decried by coworkers as "hogs" or "boss's pets."[17] Code aimed to keep them in line.

Again, while the difference between piecework and hourly wages has been explored from an economic perspective, the human dynamics of different kinds of measurement also affected people's experience of work, their

13   Whipp, "A Time to Every Purpose," 226–28.
14   Whipp, "A Time to Every Purpose," 227.
15   For the British imitation of Chinese porcelain production work organization, see Ledderose, *Ten Thousand Things*; Gerritsen, *City of Blue and White*, 194.
16   Karsh, "Human Relations versus Management," 40, citing William F. Whyte, *Money and Motivation* (New York: Harper, 1955), 90–96.
17   Tomczik, "He-Men," 705.

colleagues, and thus their place in the world.[18] Bessie McGinnis Van Vorst's early participant study of factory girls took her through many different work environments in which piecework and timed work, along with the personality of the boss, made a significant difference in the mentality of the workers. Having been switched from time to piecework, and doing the latter in a group of three whose output and recompense were divided evenly, she commented,

> There is a stimulus unsuspected in working to get a job done. Before this I had worked to make the time pass. Then no-one took account of how much I did; the factory clock had a weighted pendulum; now ambition outdoes physical strength. The hours and my purpose are running a race together ... With an ache in every muscle, I redouble my energy after lunch.[19]

When Van Vorst was assigned to the cafeteria, by contrast, she was immediately depressed by the endlessness of the work: dishes washed were immediately dirtied again, "and when we have finished the work stands ready to be done over the next morning with peculiar monotony. In the factory there is stimulus in the feeling that the material which passes through one's hands will never be seen or heard of again" – despite the mindboggling effort to have "innumerable human beings with distinct tastes and likings, abilities and failings" turn out products that were completely identical.[20] Van Vorst's memoir is good evidence of how different factory workers were in some ways, yet how much they shared in others: enough that we may ask about commonalities.

More than one factor may affect level of work. Adam Tomczik writes that "Pride worked well enough to make lumberjacks into hard workers," and he documents how "hustlers" who set a fast pace for coworkers were admired as heroes. But he also argues that lumberjacks worked without gloves or socks and that their caps were small; if they did not work hard and continuously to generate body-warmth, they would lose fingers, toes, and ears.[21] So there were both a carrot and a stick motivation for continuous work. The historian should recognize pride in work, but not romanticize it.

As Tomczik's comment suggests, the level of effort affects and creates stress, too. Anne Gerritsen points out in *City of Blue and White* that the

18 For a complex case, see Dalton, "Reorganization and Accommodation," 19–22.
19 Van Vorst and van Vorst, *The Woman Who Toils*, 41.
20 Van Vorst and van Vorst, *The Woman Who Toils*, 51, 71.
21 Tomczik, "He-Men."

historian can learn from the material evidence – sherds – of failed firings of porcelain vessels. Firings failed because the clay was inadequately prepared or too many vessels were crammed into the kiln; this shows that workers were under tremendous pressure to produce quickly, whether from imperial agents or from merchants.[22] The stress they experienced was an aspect of their life that went beyond pay or punishment. Knowing from the sociologists that the pace of work is often an issue not only between managers and other workers but also among workers, we may look for evidence of struggles over pace that informed the reality of daily working lives.

> Was work remunerated by task or by time?
> Did a task, once begun, have to be completed in one go?
> Could one practitioner pick up from another mid-task?
> Who planned the work of the day: the worker or a manager?
> How did practitioners fit family business into their workdays?
> If the pace of work was sometimes set by the individual practitioner, sometimes by the boss, and sometimes by the group, which pace was fastest and why?
> Did practitioners do more or less work than the boss wanted?
> What kinds of repetition and what kinds of creativity or variety did the work involve?
> Did the occupation have heroes or model workers? Warning examples?
> How did the physical reality of technique affect pace?
> How did shortcuts affect the quality of the product?

The Group and the Pace

Many scholars have discussed the "restriction of production," or working more slowly than the boss wants.[23] Many scholars, especially those working for companies, assumed that while the outstanding individual setting his own pace of work would aim high, a pace of work determined collectively would be slow. Anthropologist June Nash learned that workers on an assembly line had figured out shortcuts to buy themselves a little time. When they struck and their managers temporarily took to the line, workers feared that the managers would figure out the shortcuts and, when they returned to their managerial roles, eliminate them.[24] Bosses who began as workers

---

22 Gerritsen, *City of Blue and White*, 1, 228–30.
23 Hughes, "Work and the Self," 47–48.
24 Nash, "Anthropology of Work," 51.

are harder to fool and may be less sympathetic; one of Van Vorst's coworkers said she had left a previous job when her pay was cut in half by a boss who had begun as a workman himself: "They're the worst kind," she said.[25]

But Max Weber wrote that a group might aim at a high level of effort.[26] Anthropologists have shown that communality can motivate individuals to work harder, not only for themselves but for others.[27] The mowing scene in *Anna Karenina* also illustrates this. The old man chosen as leader, whose long experience enables him to make the most efficient movements and move quickly despite his age, sets the pace not only for the other peasants but even for the landowner, Levin, who is participating.[28] Similarly, an anthropologist of work observing Haitian farmers in the 1930s as they collectively cleared a field for one member of the community wrote:

> As workers gather, their work is supervised by one individual who sees that the pace is adequate. The workers, each with a hoe in hand, form a line while drums mark the rhythm for the songs and set the beat for the hoes. The stimulus of group effort on the workers is such that in a single afternoon a field of several acres can be cleared ... by a work force of sixty to sixty-five men.[29]

Communal work may add to hard labor the pleasures of sociality and competition for the prestige of being the best (fastest, most careful, or most competent) worker, so that more, not less gets done.[30] Van Vorst wrote of the pickle factory: "Companionship is the great stimulus. ... [Without] the encouragement of example, it would be impossible to obtain as much [work] for each individual girl as is obtained from them in groups of tens, fifties, hundreds working together." In nearly every job Van Vorst took on, she found that her fellow-workers not only stimulated, but patiently taught and encouraged her.[31] Conversely, colleagues higher in the hierarchy of the occupation may hinder work, for instance by commandeering tools.[32]

---

25 Van Vorst and van Vorst, *The Woman Who Toils*, 141.

26 Becker et al., *Boys in White*, 11–12.

27 Applebaum, *Work in Non-market and Transitional Societies*, 3.

28 Tolstoy, *Anna Karenina*, 268–71.

29 Melville J. Herskovits, *Life in a Haitian Valley* (1937), paraphrased in Applebaum, *Work in Non-market and Transitional Societies*, 9.

30 Herskovits, *Life in a Haitian Valley*, quoted in Applebaum, *Work in Non-market and Transitional Societies*, 14.

31 Van Vorst and van Vorst, *The Woman Who Toils*, 33.

32 E. Davis, *Hidden Dimensions*, 55: the head of pathology gave the microscope assigned to a pathologist's assistant to a medical resident who needed it; the result was that pathologist's assistant's proper task was taken from him.

Thus, in addition to pressure or inducement from clients or other bosses, coworkers may hinder or help one another, and speed up or slow the pace of work. Cultural aspects of the occupation, such as singing, should not be reduced to functionalist explanations like setting the pace. A Texas prisoner of the 1960s, doing forced labor, explained at length the benefits of singing at work.[33]

> Did pace affect remuneration or reputation?
> Did workers compete for speed or quality? Who judged?
> How was pace regulated? Did it involve music?
> What kinds of shortcuts did practitioners develop and why?
> How did practitioners teach newcomers about shortcuts or foot-dragging tech-
> niques? Was the atmosphere in the workspace cooperative?
> How did bosses learn about shortcuts or slowdown techniques, if they did?
> Who watched the clock?
> Did tasks take different amounts of time?
> If that led to bottlenecks, how did coworkers respond?
> Could expert workers leave to work elsewhere?
> How did practitioners and managers respond to top-down directives for
> change?
> Did gender play a role in pace regulation?
> Did songs or rituals commemorate speed?

Works Cited

Applebaum, Herbert, ed. *Work in Non-market and Transitional Societies*. Albany: SUNY Press, 1984.

Becker, Howard S., Blanche Geer, Everett C. Hughes, and Anselm L. Strauss. *Boys in White: Student Culture in Medical School*. Chicago: University of Chicago Press, 1961.

Dalton, Melville. "Reorganization and Accommodation: A Case in Industry." In *Institutions and the Person: Festschrift in Honor of Everett C. Hughes*, edited by Howard S. Becker, Blanche Geer, David Riesman, and Robert S. Weiss, 14–24. Chicago: Aldine, 1968.

Davis, Edward B. *Hidden Dimensions of Work: Revisiting the Chicago School Methods of Everett Hughes and Anselm Strauss*. N.p.: Xlibris Books, 2011.

33 In *Wake-up Dead Man: Afro-American Worksongs from Texas Prisons* (1972), quoted in Thomas, *Oxford Book of Work*, 157–59.

Erasmus, Charles J. "Work Patterns in a Mayo Village." In *Work in Non-market and Transitional Societies*, edited by Herbert Applebaum, 168–79. Albany: SUNY Press, 1984.

Gerritsen, Anne. *The City of Blue and White: Chinese Porcelain and the Early Modern World.* Cambridge: Cambridge University Press, 2020.

Hughes, Everett C. "Work and the Self." In *Men and Their Work*, 42–55. Glencoe, IL: The Free Press, 1958.

Karsh, Bernard. "Human Relations versus Management." In *Institutions and the Person: Festschrift in Honor of Everett C. Hughes*, edited by Howard S. Becker, Blanche Geer, David Riesman, and Robert S. Weiss, 35–48. Chicago: Aldine, 1968.

Ledderose, Lothar. *Ten Thousand Things: Module and Mass Production in Chinese Art.* Princeton: Princeton University Press, 1998.

Nash, June. "The Anthropology of Work." In *Work in Non-market and Transitional Societies*, edited by Herbert Applebaum, 45–55. Albany: SUNY Press, 1984.

Pospisil, Leopold. "Organization of Labor among the Kapauku." In *Work in Non-market and Transitional Societies*, edited by Herbert Applebaum, 180–85. Albany: SUNY Press, 1984.

Rule, John. "The Property of Skill in the Period of Manufacture." In *The Historical Meanings of Work,* edited by Patrick Joyce, 99–118. Cambridge: Cambridge University Press, 1987.

Thomas, Keith, ed. *The Oxford Book of Work.* Oxford: Oxford University Press, 1999.

Thompson, E. P. "Time, Work-Discipline, and Industrial Capitalism." *Past & Present* 38 (1967): 56-97.

Tolstoy, Leo. *Anna Karenina.* Translated by Constance Garnett. N.p.: Quality Paperbacks, 1991.

Tomczik, Adam. "'He-Men Could Talk to He-Men in He-Man Language': Lumberjack Work Culture in Maine and Minnesota, 1840–1940." *The Historian* 70, no. 4 (2008): 697–715.

van Vorst, Mrs. John, and Marie van Vorst. *The Woman Who Toils: Being the Experiences of Two Ladies as Factory Girls.* 1902, 1903; facsimile reprint Carlisle, MA: Applewood Books, n.d.

Whipp, Richard. "'A Time to Every Purpose': An Essay on Time and Work." In *Historical Meanings of Work,* edited by Patrick Joyce, 210–36. Cambridge: Cambridge University Press, 1987.

X.   The Family Workshop

Abstract

In the past, production often occurred within the family unit, and occupations were passed on from parent to child. Since the family was also
a key site for the production and transmission of culture (conceptions and
practices of gender differentiation, religion, consumption, stories and
songs, etc.), historians can illuminate culture and society by investigating
how the social drama of work occurred at home as well as outside. Did
senior family members push occupational dirty work off on juniors? Did
patriarchal family ideology, gender differentiation, and apprenticeship
practices develop in order to minimize tension between coworkers?
If family identity and religious practice managed occupational guilty
knowledge and shaped colleague code, what changed when work was
no longer shared?

Keywords: gender, religion, family production, daily work, ordinary people,
patriarchy

Anthropologists have shown that in many less-marketized societies, including some industrializing societies, the family was the producing and
managing unit in a wide variety of occupations. This does not include merely
close kin. The lines between bondage and kinship vary by place-time and
context, and servants embedded in other people's families experienced the
domestic space as a public site of labor.[1] As Bernard Karsh comments, "The
family is not a collection of independent creative individuals; it is a very
highly structured system of discrete roles ... [which] every culture clearly
prescribes."[2] And those roles centered on work.

---

1   On bondage as a form of kinship, see for instance Hinchy and Joshi, "Selective Amnesia," 7.
2   Karsh, "Human Relations versus Management," 38.

Schneewind, S.K. *The Social Drama of Daily Work. A Manual for Historians.* Amsterdam: Amsterdam University Press, 2024
DOI: 10.5117/9789048559534_CH10

Family members not only shared the proceeds of production, but also carried on the work communally. In some cases, tasks were divided by age and gender; in others the whole family worked on a task: clearing weedy growth from a field, harvesting grain, or roofing a house, for instance.[3] Among the Gadulia migratory blacksmiths in Northern India in the early 1960s, all family members learned blacksmithing as children, but the actual work was divided. An old man or woman or a child operated the bellows; two or three adults did the hammering; and one man, normally the head of the household, held the piece on the anvil with a pair of tongs and told others where and how to hammer, whether to add air, and so on.[4] (Note that the division of labor is very similar to that depicted in Figure 2; see p. 55 above.)

When tasks are apportioned by age and gender, specifying basic variables like technique and object of technique will help determine whether this work is best conceived of as comprising different occupations, different levels of hierarchy within the occupation, or stages in the path into the occupation. In the case of the blacksmiths, a male child might move first to hammering and then to the position of principal artisan, but a female child would not make it beyond hammering before she switched, in her old age, to bellows operator. Conceivably, a parent could be operating the bellows at the instruction of a son: and recognizing that work tensions are likely would lead to questions about family dynamics.

The different calculations involved in family work and their economic results have been extensively studied. Among the Gadulia blacksmiths, P. K. Misra reports, "all available persons in a household share in the work. The actual number of persons employed is never included in assessing the costs of the items made."[5] Likewise, historian of late imperial China Philip Huang has argued that because family members had to be fed no matter whether they worked efficiently or not, work was done even when marginal returns on an individual worker's output were extremely low. He likened this to agricultural involution, calling the result in the Yangzi delta "involutionary growth" that stymied "modernization."[6] But looking beyond the question of remuneration and its effects on the economy, historians could ask how the family-based organization of work affected culture. Since the producing family, like any organization or workshop, is a culturally structured system of roles, we can look for dirty work, code, policy, and all

3   Applebaum, *Work in Non-market and Transitional Societies*, 4.
4   Misra, "Gadulia Lohars," 129.
5   Misra, "Gadulia Lohars," 130.
6   Huang, *Peasant Family*, 80, 88. A debate followed in which I am not taking sides.

the rest within the producing family, and further ask how those aspects of the social drama of work interact with other, ideological models of family roles and interactions.

Francesca Bray, studying early modern Chinese families, discusses how the senior first wife's role as the head of home-based work (i.e., both domestic work and production for household use, taxes, and the market), meant that not only her daughters-in-law but also her husband's concubines were under her management.[7] What effects did these overlapping family and work roles have on creativity, worker engagement, and family loyalty? Karsh writes, "It can be argued that an employer has no right to probe either the conscious or the unconscious feelings of workers. There is no evidence to support the premise that the goals of individual workers are, or should be, the same as an employer's."[8] But the Chinese parent *did*, in ideological constructs, have the right to probe children's feelings and to assume that goals were shared. To what extent did parents and children working together share goals? When feelings were probed, how did children respond? Was the edifice of filial piety built and maintained precisely to keep the family workshop running smoothly?

"The family is often the scene of sharp differences among and between its members," Karsh notes, and "it sometimes takes a loud and vigorous quarrel between a man and his wife [for] the marriage to continue as a constructive and compatible enterprise. Third-party mediators are sometimes used."[9] There are other solutions to family work tensions. In the USA in the late nineteenth century, large numbers of young people left home for factory work: participant-observer Bessie McGinnis Van Vorst commented, "It is easier to submit to factory government which commands five hundred girls with one law valid for all, than to undergo the arbitrary discipline of parental authority."[10] Of course, Van Vorst did not meet the girls who happily stayed home. The historian should investigate, not take for granted, the feelings of those in other place-times who had no escape.

Another solution to family tension appears in the apprenticeship system of West African blacksmiths: while boys' training began at home at a very young age, it was completed at another family's forge. This was not a universal practice for all occupations, however. For griots, the oral historians, advisors, bards, and censors of the West African kingdoms, the family connection was

7   Bray, *Technology and Gender.*
8   Karsh, "Human Relations versus Management," 39.
9   Karsh, "Human Relations versus Management," 42.
10 Van Vorst and van Vorst, *The Woman Who Toils.*

the guarantee of accuracy and the basis for license and mandate – including reprimanding rulers in public – so all apprenticeship took place within the family.[11] Technique and object of technique, as well as the basis of claims to license and mandate and other relations with clients, may determine how tensions in the family workshop were managed in different place-times. The historian should not seek answers in ideology about the family until s/he has explored all other avenues of explanation, precisely because ideology shouts loudest in the written record.

Recognizing that the social drama of work (with its tensions over who does what when and how and who decides) affected the family workshop illuminates one major historical question. Almost every past human society has divided work by gender, invoking some version of "Adam delved and Eve span." Once such arrangements are in place, ideology may grow up around them, as Marx teaches.[12] And early socialization into the rules about roles means that emotional attachments to them are powerful.[13] It is important to note, as Herbert Applebaum does, that "the only hard and fast rule about the sexual division of work is that there are no hard and fast rules." When the need arises, family members cross gender lines to cook, hoe, or operate the bellows for blacksmithing.[14]

Widows, in particular, often take on the husband's business: examples range from a famously wealthy mine owner in Han China, to widows in eighteenth-century India who managed small and large tax-exempt hold-ings, to widows in eighteenth-century Britain who ran businesses in toy, button, and buckle manufacture, japanning (lacquering), plumbing, glazing, brass founding, pewter making, ironmongering, and so on.[15] In Jewish communities in the early modern Arab-Islamic world, the expectation that the husband spend his time studying Torah meant that not only widows but wives worked as spinners, weavers, dyers, embroiderers, doctors, fortune-tellers, ritualists, real estate agents, moneylenders, landlords, brokers, and merchants, among other occupations, both inside and outside the home.[16]

In addition to this flexibility, societies have developed different gendered work rules, so the specifics cannot be explained by biology.

---

11   Camara, *Is There a Distinctively African Way of Knowing*, 10–11, 33–36. Griots advertised their reliability within their recitations: "My word is pure and free of all untruths; it is the word of my father; it is the word of my father's father."
12   As research has found for racist ideology, too. Kendi, *How to be an Anti-Racist*, 230.
13   Applebaum, *Work in Non-market and Transitional Societies*, 14.
14   Applebaum, *Work in Non-market and Transitional Societies*, 14.
15   Chatterjee, "Monastic Governmentality"; Berg, "Women's Work," 86.
16   Hofmeester, "Jewish Ethics and Women's Work," 157–62.

But why is family work so often gendered in the first place? Recognizing that divided responsibility for tasks can reduce friction in enterprises, it makes sense for husband and wife working together to have different tasks, so that the family can continue. In Japanese rural society, conversely, people recognized that good sexual relations between husband and wife were necessary to keep the enterprise centered on a particular piece of land passed down through generations going.[17] It seems likely that not only ideology of gender difference, but also the differentiation of tasks within the family that generated that ideology, sprang from the social drama of work, and from the tensions in the first human workshop: the home.

Who belonged to or lived with the family in the occupation?

Did practitioners learn and carry out work in the family home?

Did the occupation's technique include a wide variety of tasks?

Were those tasks apportioned according to age (relating to path in the occupation) or gender (possibly differentiating occupations or establishing hierarchy within the occupation)?

How did the family remunerate working members?

Did workers in the family home belong primarily to different occupations?

If so, how did the work of the individual relate to the strategy of the family as a whole?

Or, if a whole family worked together in an occupation, how did the hierarchy of the occupation interact with family hierarchy?

Who apportioned tasks?

Who set the pace?

Does the ruling ideology of the place-time suggest tensions around work?

Could junior members of the family work elsewhere, yet still be considered to be contributing to the family?

Even if workers would return home, did they apprentice elsewhere?

If work was normally gendered, when and how were exceptions made and who decided?

Did age or seniority add nuance to gendered division of labor in the family?

17   Bernstein, *Haruko's World*, 141.

Works Cited

Applebaum, Herbert, ed. *Work in Non-market and Transitional Societies.* Albany: SUNY Press, 1984.

Berg, Maxine. "Women's Work, Mechanization and the Early Phases of Industrialization in England." In *The Historical Meanings of Work*, edited by Patrick Joyce, 64–98. Cambridge: Cambridge University Press, 1987.

Bernstein, Gail Lee. *Haruko's World: A Japanese Farm Woman and Her Community.* Stanford: Stanford University Press, 1983.

Bray, Francesca. *Technology and Gender: Fabrics of Power in Late Imperial China.* Berkeley: University of California Press, 1997.

Camara, Mohamed Saliou. *Is There a Distinctively African Way of Knowing (a Study of African Blacksmiths, Hunters, Healers, Griots, Elders, and Artists): Knowing and Theory of Knowledge in the African Experience.* Lewiston: Edwin Mellen Press, 2014.

Chatterjee, Indrani. "Monastic Governmentality, Colonial Misogyny, and Postcolonial Amnesia in South Asia." *History of the Present* 3, no. 1 (2013): 57–98.

Hinchy, Jessica, and Girija Joshi. "Selective Amnesia and South Asian Histories: An Interview with Indrani Chatterjee." *Itinerario* (2021): 1–16.

Hofmeester, Karin. "Jewish Ethics and Women's Work in the Late Medieval and Early Modern Arab-Islamic World." *International Review of Social History Special Issue* 56 (2011): 141–64.

Huang, Philip. *The Peasant Family and Rural Development in the Yangzi Delta, 1350–1988.* Stanford: Stanford University Press, 1990.

Karsh, Bernard. "Human Relations versus Management." In *Institutions and the Person: Festschrift in Honor of Everett C. Hughes*, edited by Howard S. Becker, Blanche Geer, David Riesman, and Robert S. Weiss, 35–48. Chicago: Aldine, 1968.

Kendi, Ibram X. *How to be an Anti-Racist.* New York: One World, 2019.

Misra, P. K. "The Gadulia Lohars: Nomadism and Blacksmithy." In *Work in Non-market and Transitional Societies*, edited by Herbert Applebaum, 127–33. Albany: SUNY Press, 1984.

van Vorst, Mrs. John, and Marie van Vorst. *The Woman Who Toils: Being the Experiences of Two Ladies as Factory Girls.* 1902, 1903; facsimile reprint Carlisle, MA: Applewood Books, n.d.

XI. Conclusion

Abstract
An example of stonemasons in early modern Italy shows how the Hughes
framework can help bridge the gap between sources written by the elite
and the lives of working people in the past. Historians can identify practitioners (and their colleagues), coworkers, and clients for a given occupation;
specify technique, object of technique, workshop, hierarchy within the
occupation, and paths into and out of the occupation; and see more about
them in historical sources through the lenses of the key Hughes concepts
of dirty work, code and policy, license and mandate, guilty knowledge
and symbols of distinction, and mistakes at work. Shared vocabulary will
facilitate comparative work in the history of occupations.

Stonemasons in Early Modern Italy

When historians have to rely mainly on texts by members of the literate
elite, concepts in the sociology of occupations can help us bridge the gap
between intellectual history and common thought in the place-time. I will
conclude with one example.

Luca Mocarelli has compared two sixteenth-century thinkers' approaches
to stonemasons. Augustinian scholar Tommaso Garzoni (1549–1589) admit-
ted that stonemasons are needed because they build houses but complained
that their work was not precise and they would drag out a stint just to make
more money; "thus as a penance they frequently fall from the roof, or the wall
or the stairs, and break their necks." Physician-surgeon Leonardo Fioravanti
(1517–1588), by contrast, praised stonemasons as next to architects, and
described their various techniques. He pointed out that "in no other case
will a man so willingly pay others, as when he is having a sumptuous and
magnificent house built ... yet since this is what he wants to do, the art of
the stonemason is necessary."[1] The two views are quite different.

---

1   Mocarelli, "Attitudes to Work," 102–5.

Schneewind, S.K. *The Social Drama of Daily Work. A Manual for Historians.* Amsterdam: Amsterdam University Press, 2024
DOI: 10.5117/9789048559534_CONC

Mocarelli discusses the two texts as serving the purposes of the two men and reflecting their identities. Garzoni aimed to guide the ruler to make nobles more purely noble (focusing on honor, to the exclusion of thinking about merchandise) and plebians more purely plebian (with no interest in titles, only profit) and assumed that scholarship and high culture were superior. He studied the trades dispassionately, revealing the tricks and failings of commoners "without trying to find any meaning in their work." Fioravanti, according to Mocarelli, observed workers directly, praised them all, wanted dignity for all, and in ordering occupations by utility rated highly not just the farmer and breeder, but also the blacksmith and carpenter, because so many other trades depended on theirs. The writers' different views of stonemasons did not simply spring from their intellectual differences, however, for with respect to tailors, Garzoni thought they offered everyone a chance at beauty and dignity, while Fioravanti commented that such distinctions of dress were meaningless and said that a tailor's work entailed only "draping a piece of cloth over someone and cutting away the excess, thus the garment is made." If we put the two texts together, instead of just pointing out their differences, we can learn more. The concepts introduced in this manual suggest a way to do that with respect to stonemasons.

Putting the two observations together, we see that the client wants a fancy house, and he wants everyone to know that he paid a lot for it, as a reflection of his own worth – so says Fioravanti. But of course, he doesn't want to be cheated and he wants the house to be finished in a timely way. The lowly stonemason (Garzoni categorizes him as "serving" others, a characterization that the stonemasons themselves, if they shared the pride of other craftsmen throughout history, might reject) controls the time and the money, because the client does not know enough to build the house, nor how long each task and phase should take. He must rely on the stonemason to tell him that. The client has to trust him, yet he cannot trust him. Garzoni's focus on the potential trickery of making the task last longer and cost more than necessary expresses the distrust of clients and potential clients. (Even the monastery where Garzoni resided and wrote relied on stonemasons for building and repairs, and religious orders, like secular clients, wanted buildings that expressed their dignity and worth.)

The stonemason's technique is physically dangerous, and Garzoni invokes a moral universe that will punish cheating masons by having them fall from the places understood to be most dangerous. But the stonemason is also licensed to possess the guilty knowledge of how much the client is paying for his façade, and where he has cut expenditures elsewhere to make up for it.

The client must trust him to be discreet about that. It stands to reason that Garzoni, who wanted to disentangle "honor" and "profit," would be uneasy about a trade that enabled its clients to convert mere money into prestige. Because he makes this conversion possible, the stonemason possesses a third kind of guilty knowledge – the knowledge that the distinction between noblemen and commoners was not in their God-given natures, but was an outward façade that noblemen worked as hard, and spent as much, to preserve as commoners did to imitate. Putting the two writers together yields a deeper historical understanding of the social world both reflected.

In earlier times, members of the ruling class were often close enough to production processes that they built the specifics, as metaphors, into philosophical texts and guidance for governing. It may make sense for the historian, too, to start with the technique of the occupation under study. But it is possible to start with any of the concepts laid out above, as revealed in one's sources, and work from there.

Even jokes can work as starting points. For instance, a joke reveals a clear Ming equivalent to the dirty work of the mid-twentieth-century jazz musicians in Chicago we saw described above by Howard Becker. In a compilation of jokes made in the early seventeenth century, a country bumpkin demands that the acting troupe his relative has hired to entertain him add battle scenes to the romantic play "Story of a Lute" 琵琶記 (Pipa ji). When they do so at the behest of the host, the ignoramus triumphantly remarks, "This is more like it! I could have held my tongue, but they would have known then that I was not in the business."[2] He is the butt of the joke, and the reader can imagine how embarrassed his relative must have felt before the other guests. But having learned about dirty work, the reader can also imagine how the actors must have resented the member of the audience whose interference destroyed the artistic integrity of their performance. The country bumpkin is quite right to say that the actors will understand him to be asserting professional knowledge – wrongly and offensively.[3] This entry point into the actors' perspective opens questions that may allow us to get beyond self-serving elite descriptions of how they directed and taught their actors.[4]

The new insights from the Hughes framework begin as only questions or hypotheses for the historian. But many of our conclusions about the writing elite themselves are no more than that: take for example Mocarelli's

2   Feng M., *Xiao fu*, 170.
3   Schneewind, "Jokes."
4   As exemplified in Shen, "Private Theatre of the Ming Dynasty."

explanation that Fioravanti and Garzoni differed on stone masons because of their social backgrounds. That cannot be proven, but it is the sort of leap historians make every day. Let's allow those studying the non-elite space for informed speculation, too.

Why Study History through the Social Drama of Work?

In the 1930s it made sense to suggest that the idea comes first and that social understanding is rooted in it. Nowadays the weight of opinion in the history of ideas goes the other way: The social practice roots the idea, and the idea withers if it is deprived of that sustaining soil.[5]

Mary Douglas and Steven Ney are writing about a change in the history of ideas. But in the 1930s, sociologists were already looking at social practice as the origin of ideas and of culture generally. Specifically, the Chicago school of occupational sociology argued that the conditions of work constituted a large part of the conditions of life, and that workers' and their clients' responses to those conditions generated culture and society. Over the long course of human history in most of the world, most people have spent much of their lives in working, whether to support themselves and their families and communities, to pay taxes, or to serve masters who controlled them through violence. Systems that exist at a high level of abstraction, such as capitalism or imperialism, set general conditions of working lives, but do not explain the many variations in people's experiences across the globe. For historians who want to see life close to the ground, asking the questions provided for each of these chapters will help locate the details of the emotional and social aspects of a given occupation in a particular place-time. From there, the historian can trace how aspects of culture arose and were sustained or changed in tandem with changes in work relationships. A bottom-up history of a given society becomes possible.

In every area of the social sciences, shared scholarly vocabulary assists analysis, comparison, and contrast. If historians adopt the terms proposed here for phenomena that occur in working lives worldwide, it will be easier to trace change and continuity over time, and variation and similarity over space. Historians will find that those in the same occupation in different place-times had different as well as similar relations to colleagues, clients, and the laypeople of their surrounding societies. In studying the

---

5   Douglas and Ney, *Missing Persons*, 29.

ordinary people of the past, in all parts of the world, historians who focus on daily work will find sufficient similarities for meaningful comparison and contrast. Similarities across occupations in one place-time will point us to the shared culture of working people, while differences highlight the variety of experience possible under the same regime. This framework illuminates culture and society by showing that aspects of a particular occupation that seem unique often turn out to have counterparts in other occupations.

If we imagine a grid for any one society, in which concepts and questions about occupations occupy the x-axis, and the various occupations the y-axis, we can fill out parts of the grid, lay it flat, and use it as a sieve to sift out elite bias and self-serving misrepresentations in the sources they wrote. Historians who want to trace these new paths into the thinking, experiences, and social relations of the non-elite, and from there locate their influence on culture, will find them in many sources. Reading texts and visual materials, as well as existing historical scholarship, through the lens of the questions and concepts of the Hughes framework, will reveal aspects of technique, dirty work, status contradiction and dilemma, code and policy, license and mandate, guilty knowledge, and the generative worry about mistakes at work that underlay relations among colleagues, coworkers, and laypeople in the workshops, large and small, of all occupations across time and space. For the elite, too, were firmly rooted in the sustaining soil of social practice.

Works Cited

Douglas, Mary, and Steven Ney. *Missing Persons: A Critique of the Social Sciences*. Berkeley: University of California Press, 1998.

Feng Menglong. *Xiao fu* 笑府 *Treasury of Laughs* [*Feng Menglong's Treasury of Laughs: A Seventeenth-Century Anthology of Traditional Chinese Humor*]. Translated by Hsu Pi-ching. Leiden: Brill, 2015.

Mocarrelli, Luca. "Attitudes to Work and Commerce in the Late Italian Renaissance: A Comparison between Tomaso Garzoni's *La Piazza Universale* and Leondardo Fioravanti's *Dello Specchio Di Scientia Universale*." *International Review of Social History Special Issue* 56 (2011): 89–106.

Schneewind, Sarah. "What Do Jokes Reveal about Trust in Ming Work Relations?" *Journal of Chinese Literature and Culture* 9.2 (November 2022): 367-396.

Shen, Grant. "Acting in the Private Theatre of the Ming Dynasty." *Asian Theatre Journal* (1998): 64–86.

Index

actors   58, 185. *See also* entertainers
agricultural societies   168. *See also* farmers;
   non-market economies
amateurs   21–22, 116
anxiety of work   94, 123, 152, 156–57, 163
Applebaum, Herbert   15-16, 29, 50, 69, 161,
   168–69, 173, 178, 180
apprentices and apprenticeships   28, 35, 75,
   83, 86–95, 108, 130, 156, 179–80. *See also*
   hierarchy within the occupation; journeymen; medical students and residents; path
   into the occupation
Arab-Islamic world   158, 180
artisans   20, 29, 68, 89, 107, 120, 137, 178,
   184; blacksmiths   31–32, 54–56, 68, 86,
   108–9, 117, 158, 178–79; carpenters   21,
   30, 32, 36, 42, 55–56, 68, 117, 150, 184;
   coppersmiths   68; goldsmiths   68, 143;
   hatters   82, 169; leatherworkers   68;
   painters   36, 71, 143, 170; smelters   31,
   108, 158; stonemasons   36, 55–56, 120, 131,
   183–86. *See also* textile workers
artists   39, 71
arts (in Hughes's typology), 34–36
Ash, Eric   57, 86, 117–20, 151–52
Asim, Ina   135
assembly line workers   167–69, 172. *See also*
   factory workers
automotive parts supply workers   96–97

Balberg, Mira   69
barbers   30, 62, 68–69, 156
Barbieri-Low, Anthony   86
Barlow, Tani   82
Barr, Allan   72
Bearman, Peter   28, 48, 57, 81–82, 105, 111, 141
Becker, Howard   17–18, 37, 41–42, 50–52, 59,
   63, 88–89, 96, 104, 116, 119, 123–25, 134, 136,
   142, 173
Bena people   108
Berg, Maxine   21, 80
Berger, Peter   16
Bernstein, Gail Lee   181
Bian, He   35, 62, 109
blacksmiths   31–32, 54–56, 68, 86, 108–9, 117,
   158, 178–79. *See also* artisans
Bloom, Phillip   70
bodily aspects of work   36–42, 91, 168, 171
bosses   25, 28, 54, 57–60, 97, 145, 160, 168,
   171–74. *See also* foremen; managers;
   supervisors
Bourdieu, Pierre   71–72, 87, 95, 99, 130, 136
Boys in White   52, 88–89, 142. *See also* healers
Braden, Peter   154

Bray, Francesca   117, 178–79
Brown, Richard   168
Browning, Kellen   86
Buddhism   20, 70, 118, 159. *See also* religion
butchers   69–70, 117

Camara, Mohamed Saliou   28, 31, 39, 86, 91,
   108, 117, 158, 161, 180
cameleteers   54, 68. *See also* transport
   workers
Canada: British Columbia   60
capitalism 98, 170, 186
Caracausi, Andrea   20
carpenters   21, 30, 32, 36, 42, 55–56, 68, 117, 150,
   184. *See also* artisans
Carter, Ron   30, 80, 133. *See also* entertainers
caste system   33, 67, 80
Chapoulie, Jean-Michel   17, 105–6
charisma   156–57
Chatterjee, Indrani   20, 68, 180
Chen, Yunü   49
Chicago-school sociology of occupations   13,
   17, 186
China   27, 31, 37, 72, 81, 179; Jingdezhen   53,
   143, 170; Ming   49, 54, 58, 61, 83, 131, 135,
   139, 153, 156; Ming-Qing   117; Qing   98;
   Shang   21; Shanghai   108; Song
   dynasty   34, 70; Tang   86; Wenzhou   32;
   Yangtze delta   98, 178; Zhejiang   107, 130
choice of occupation, freedom of   34, 37, 58,
   79–80, 84–85, 97, 143, 145. *See also* enslaved
   persons; family (inherited) occupations
Christianity   69, 82, 118, 159. *See also*
   ministers; religion
clients   21, 28–29, 42, 47–51, 58, 104, 108, 116–17,
   121–25, 134, 156–59. *See also* consumers;
   laypeople
coal mining   105
code   19, 35, 51, 53, 59, 62, 75, 82, 87, 103,
   106–12, 125, 150, 155
Cohen, Myron   21
Cohen, Paul   158
colleagues   21, 36, 42, 47–48, 51–52, 58–59, 107,
   110, 155
commercialization of society, level of   28–31,
   50, 98, 167
communal work   50, 172–73, 178
companonnages   137–39
competition at work   51–53, 86, 173–74
construction workers   80–81, 118, 157, 168
consumers   34, 48–50, 105. *See also* clients
conversion (change in identity on path into an
   occupation), 75, 79, 88, 91–97. *See also* path
   into the occupation

cooperation at work   47, 53–54, 56–57, 112, 174.
   See also teamwork
coppersmiths   68. See also artisans
corruption   141–45. See also theft at work
Coser, Lewis   19, 48
cotton-mill workers   41. See also factory
   workers; textile workers
coworkers   21, 47–48, 52–59, 153–56;
   non-human   154
craftspeople. See artisans
Csikszentmihalyi, Mihaly   151–52

Dalton, Melville   142, 171
danger at work   54, 60, 117, 122, 129–37, 150, 152,
   156–57, 161, 184. See also injuries at work
Darnton, Robert   90
Davis, Edward   36, 56, 58, 60–61, 70–73, 75, 81,
   96–98, 109, 142, 150, 173
Davis, Fred   18–19, 36, 90–95
De morbis artificum   38
Deloney, Thomas   81
dieners   60–61, 73. See also healers
direct producing activities   52–53, 58
dirty work   51, 62–63, 67–75 (chapter 3), 124, 185
discrimination   50, 61, 80. See also gender
   dynamics in work; race and ethnicity in
   work
division of labor   29–30, 33, 62, 79–80, 83–84,
   154, 178. See also hierarchy within the
   occupation
doctors   49, 62, 72, 84, 104, 107, 117, 133–35, 140,
   160. See also healers
Donovan, Frances   52
doormen   28, 57, 81–82, 111, 140–41
Douglas, Mary   18, 68, 84, 186
Drewal, Henry John   39
du Maurier, Daphne   39
dyers   69, 135, 180. See also textile workers
Dykstra, Maura   135

East Africa   158
editors   72
Egypt   26, 38, 40, 80, 84, 118
Ehmer, Josef   20, 25, 47, 79, 86
embroiderers   30, 135, 180. See also textile
   workers
emergencies at work   139–41
emotional work   21
emotions at work   13, 53, 56, 75, 89, 94, 125, 140,
   149–50, 155, 158
engineers   116, 118, 120
enslaved persons   15, 21, 34, 58, 79
enterprises (in Hughes's typology), 34–35
entertainers: actors   58, 185; Carter, Ron   30,
   80, 133; musicians   30, 41–42, 123–26
Erasmus, Charles, and his (unnamed)
   wife   29, 168
Europe   62, 82, 131, 138
expertise   57–58, 116, 120–22, 134, 140

factory workers   40–41, 74, 106, 108, 168–69,
   171, 173, 179; assembly line workers   167–69,
   172; cotton-mill workers   41
family (inherited) occupations   33, 83–85,
   98, 177–81 (chapter 10). See also choice of
   occupation, freedom of
Fang, Qin   83
farmers   38–39, 53–54, 98, 133–34, 169, 173. See
   also agricultural society; peasants
Feng, Menglong   156, 185
Feng, Naixi   139
Fervert, Ute   21
Fioravanti, Leonardo   183–84, 186
fishermen   31–32, 107
flow of work   151–53
foremen   26, 96–97. See also bosses; managers;
   supervisors
France   20, 27, 82, 89–90, 118, 131
fraud and corruption   141–45. See also theft
   at work
Friedman, Gillian   86
Friedson, Eliot   116–17, 121–22, 156, 159
Fuller, Michael   17

Gadulia Lohars   31, 178
Gao Yao   131
Garzoni, Tommaso   183–86
Geer, Blanche   88, 95
gender dynamics in work   29, 49–50, 61, 74,
   80–82, 118, 158, 170, 178, 180–81
Gerristen, Anne   53, 143–44, 171–72
Ghosh, Arunabh   72
Goffman, Erving   61, 71, 75, 85, 88, 107, 142
Gold, Ray   71, 75, 82, 110, 157
goldsmiths   68, 143. See also artisans
government officials   55, 58, 131, 139, 143;
   clerks   143–44, 149, 153–54; magis-
   trates   61, 153
Great Britain   107, 131, 169; Birmingham   80;
   England   33, 86, 143; London   38;
   Scotland   21; Staffordshire   170
griots   28, 179–80
Gross, Edward   98
Grossin, William   167
guilty knowledge   33, 35, 42, 51, 87, 92, 118,
   120, 129–45 (chapter 7), 184–85. See also
   occupational knowledge

Haiti   173
hatters   82, 169. See also artisans
hazing   87–88
healers   21, 42, 49, 117; Boys in White   52,
   88–89, 142; dieners   60–61, 73; doctors   49, 62, 72, 84, 104, 107, 117, 133–35, 140,
   160; medical students and residents   73,
   86, 88, 91–95, 152–53; nurses   61, 91–95,
   105; pathologists   60, 73, 173; pharmacists
   and pharmacologists   62, 117, 132, 160;
   physicians   26, 49, 52, 61–63, 69, 88, 107,

116–21, 183; surgeons 30, 61, 63, 69–71, 75, 119, 140, 152–53, 183
Helmes-Hayes, Rick 17
herdsmen 110, 133–34
Herskovits, Melville 173
hierarchy within the occupation 28, 47, 51, 57–63, 110, 124, 153–56. *See also* apprentices and apprenticeships; division of labor; journeymen; masters
Hinchy, Jessica 21, 79, 177
Hofmeester, Karin 158, 180
Honig, Emily 108
Horowitz, Irving Louis 51
Howe, Everett 94
Huang, Philip 21, 98, 178
Hughes, Everett 17–19, 25, 29, 30, 33–36, 48–50, 52, 60–62, 68, 70–72, 75, 81–82, 84–85, 87, 90, 98, 104–7, 115–23, 125–26, 129–31, 133–36, 139–40, 150, 152–60, 172
Hughes's typology of occupations 34–35, 88
Huisman, Michel 20, 132
Hungary 110, 133
hunter-gatherer societies 168. *See also* non-market economies
hunters 108, 161–63, 169

Ilaro 39
India 20, 31, 68, 178
initiation and induction. *See* ritual and rites, initiation
injuries at work 38, 40–42, 150. *See also* danger at work
interpreters 39–40
Italy 183–86

janitors 71, 75, 82, 109–10
Japan 69, 159; Hei'an 160
jargon 130
jobs (in Hughes's typology), 34, 36, 96, 117
jokes 156, 163, 185
Joshi, Girija 21, 79, 177
journeymen 20, 27–28, 62, 82, 86–87, 89–90, 107–8, 131, 137–39. *See also* apprentices and apprenticeships; hierarchy within the occupation; path into the occupation
Judaism and Jewish communities 42, 68, 82, 180. *See also* religion

Kapauku people 53, 169
Karageorghis, Vassos 60, 152, 154
Karsh, Bernard 36, 58, 170, 177, 179
Kendi, Ibram X., 180
Ki no Tsurayaki 160
Ko, Dorothy 32
Korczynski, Marek 67
Korn, Peter 36, 152
Kriesberg, Louis 18, 48, 52, 104–5
!Kung San people 161–63, 168

labor exploitation 13, 21, 103
Lahire, Bernard 58
Langlands, Alexander 38–39
laypeople 19–20, 42, 47–48, 104–5, 108–9, 116, 130–32, 156–57. *See also* clients
Le Goff, Jacques 68–69
leatherworkers 68. *See also* artisans
Ledderose, Lothar 170
Lee, Richard 161–62
license 29, 35, 51, 87, 92, 110, 115–20, 122–23, 125, 131–34, 136; legal 116–18; social 117–19
lieutenants 61, 160
linen spinners 21. *See also* textile workers
lion tamers 54
Llewellyn, Richard 150
locksmiths 27
Lortie, Dan 86–88
Lovejoy, Arthur 138
lumberjacks 26, 60, 143–44, 171

magic 95, 133–34, 158–59. *See also* rituals/ rites; religion
Malinowski, Bronislaw 133–34
managers 58–59, 111, 172. *See also* bosses; foreman; supervisors
mandate 35, 51, 87, 92, 115, 119–23, 125, 131, 134
manufacturing companies 142
Marchal, Hervé 110
market economies 15–16, 28–29. *See also* non-market economies
Marx, Karl 25, 180
Master Jacques 131, 137–39
masters 27–28, 75, 86–87, 89, 120, 138. *See also* hierarchy within the occupation
Mayo people 168
Mazu 159
Meara, Hannah 70
medical students and residents 73, 86, 88, 91–95, 152–53. *See also* healers
Melville, Herman 30
Mexico: Tenía 29, 168
Miller, R. L., 26, 38, 40–41, 80, 84, 118
Mills, C. Wright 136
ministers 51, 94, 98, 117–19, 121, 133. *See also* Christianity; religion
Misra, P. K., 31, 178
missions (in Hughes's typology of occupations), 34–35
mistakes at work 21, 51, 61, 106, 110, 112, 120, 149–63 (chapter 8). *See also* danger at work; injuries at work
Mitchell, David 33
Mocarrelli, Luca 28, 107, 183–85
Muscolino, Micah 32, 107, 130
musicians 30, 41–42, 123–26. *See also* entertainers
myths 16, 129, 132, 136–37, 140

Nash, June   16, 40–41, 168, 172
New Guinea   53, 169
Ney, Steven   186
Nice, Richard   130
non-market economies   16, 28–29, 162, 167–68, 177. *See also* agricultural societies; market economies; hunter-gatherer societies
nurses   61, 91–95, 105. *See also* healers

object of technique   25–42 (chapter 1), 49, 72, 119, 131, 135, 139–40; bundled   29. *See also* technique
occupational culture   28, 37, 41–42, 47, 49, 51–52, 86, 88, 91, 96, 124–25, 130, 154–55, 157–61
occupational identity   15, 35–36, 42, 61–62, 67, 70–72, 75, 79, 85, 87–89, 91–97, 112, 115, 126, 132, 138, 158, 160
occupational knowledge   39, 88–91, 111, 116–17, 121–22, 184–85. *See also* guilty knowledge; skills
occupations: boundaries between   27, 62–63; definition of   20–21; typologies of   25, 33-37
Old Man Yangfu   130
Oledzka, Eva   143
Olesen, Virginia   91
output   48, 56, 104–5, 123, 155

pace of work   167–74 (chapter 9)
painters   36, 71, 143, 170. *See also* artisans
path into the occupation   17, 33–37, 51–52, 61, 75, 79–99 (chapter 4), 153. *See also* apprentices and apprenticeships; journeymen
path out of the occupation   98–99, 153. *See also* retirement
pathologists   60, 73, 173. *See also* healers
peasants   20–21, 98, 173. *See also* farmers
perspective by incongruity   18–19
pharmacists and pharmacologists   62, 117, 132, 160. *See also* healers
physicians   26, 49, 52, 61–63, 69, 88, 107, 116–21, 183. *See also* healers
piecework. *See* task-oriented work
Pirenne, Henri   89, 107
plumbers   157, 160
policy   19, 28, 51, 53, 103–7, 150
porcelain and pottery manufactories   53, 143–44, 170, 172
porters   38, 53, 56, 80, 111. *See also* transport workers
Pospisil, Leopold   54, 169
practitioners, definition of   20–21, 48
priests. *See* ministers
prison guards   68
professional secrets   133. *See also* guilty knowledge
professions (in Hughes's typology), 34–35, 83, 105, 119–20

professors   20, 49, 51, 72, 98, 136. *See also* teachers
purpose (for a workshop), 104–5

race and ethnicity in work   19–20, 32, 35, 37, 42, 61, 79–83, 180
real estate agents   104–5, 140
religion   16, 32, 34, 68, 80, 84, 107, 130–32. *See also* Buddhism; Christianity; Judaism and Jewish communities; magic; ministers; saints; Shinto
remuneration   20–22, 54, 103, 107, 132, 138, 153, 174, 178
reporters   149
retirement   79, 98–99. *See also* path out of the occupation
rituals/rites: and mistakes at work   158–61; as part of guilty knowledge   133–34, 136–39; as symbols of distinction   131; initiation   87–90, 96, 103, 108, 130–31, 138–39; journeymen company   62, 89, 131, 138; of passage   31, 33, 87, 98, 117. *See also* magic
Robinson, David   81
routine   139–41
Rule, John   83, 86, 107–8, 131, 169

sailors   30, 53, 61, 68, 88, 118, 130, 142–43, 159–60. *See also* soldiers
saints   75, 130–32, 159. *See also* religion
Santoro, Marco   17
Schäfer, Dagmar   27
Schneewind, Sarah   21, 35, 62, 185
Scott, James   16, 107
Scott, Sir Walter   25
seasonal work   34, 37
sex workers   29, 69, 83
Shapinsky, Peter   69, 159–60
Shen, Grant   58, 185
Shinto   159. *See also* religion
shipwrights   117
silk-weaving factories   86. *See also* textile workers
skills   14, 25–26, 29, 36, 51, 58, 81, 84, 88, 91–92, 94–95, 117, 122, 131, 153; bundled   30, 32, 34, 152–53. *See also* occupational knowledge
smelters   31, 108, 158. *See also* artisans
social mobility   83–85
soldiers   73–74, 110–11, 142, 154–55. *See also* sailors
Solomon, David   18, 20, 34, 51, 67–68, 74, 150
Sonenscher, Michael   20, 27, 62, 82, 89, 131, 137–38
specialization   28–29, 31, 107, 115, 118, 162
statisticians   72
status contradictions   79, 82–83, 90
status dilemma   62, 82, 87, 89–90
status pain   58, 71–75
status passage   87
steamboat pilots and captains   88–89, 111–12

stonemasons 36, 55–56, 120, 131, 183–86. *See also* artisans
stone quarriers 32
Strauss, Anselm 87
supervisors 55, 60, 71–72, 96–97, 143–44. *See also* bosses; foremen; managers
supporting activities 52–53, 59
surgeons 30, 61, 63, 69–71, 75, 119, 140, 152–53, 183. *See also* healers
Suttles, Wayne 50
symbolic interaction 17
symbols of distinction 51, 87, 104–5, 118, 130–33, 137. *See also* uniforms
száamadó (Hungarian herdsman), 110, 133–34
Szonyi, Michael 38

taboos 16, 69, 119, 132, 157–58, 161
tailors 138, 184. *See also* textile workers
Tanzania 108
task-oriented work 169–72
taxi drivers 109. *See also* transport workers
Taylor, Frederick 58
teachers 49, 59, 95, 105, 140. *See also* professors
teamwork 52, 54–56, 59–60, 110, 162–63. *See also* cooperation at work
technique 25–42 (chapter 1), 48–49, 108–12, 117–19, 130–31, 133, 152; bundled 31, 59. *See also* object of technique
textile workers: cotton-mill workers 41; dyers 69, 135, 180; embroiderers 30, 135, 180; linen spinners 21; silk-weaving factories 86; tailors 138, 184; weavers 27–28, 30, 40, 86, 180; wool cloth manufactories 80–81. *See also* artisans
The Tosa Diary 160
theft at work 143, 145. *See also* fraud and corruption
Thomas, Keith 30, 68, 81, 174
Thompson, E. P., 167–68
Tianqi explosion 139
time-oriented work 169–72
Tolstoy, Leo 39, 173
Tomczik, Adam 26, 170–71
tools 25–26, 30–32, 36, 38–40, 42, 53, 107, 131, 143–44, 173
towosi 133–34
trades (in Hughes's typology), 34, 36, 137–38
transport workers: cameleteers 54, 68; porters 38, 53, 56, 80, 111; taxi drivers 109
Trobriand people 50, 133–34
Twain, Mark 88–89, 112

uniforms 61, 123, 129, 131, 133. *See also* symbols of distinction
United States 34, 49, 61, 68, 70, 73, 80–81, 86, 88, 95, 104, 111–12, 116, 120, 168, 179; Boston 109; Chicago 71, 75, 82, 84, 109, 123; Maine 26; Manhattan 28, 81, 111, 140, 151; North Carolina 41; San Francisco 71; Washington, DC 168
US Army 73–74, 110–11, 142, 154–55
US Navy 53, 61, 88, 130, 142

van Vorst, Bessie McGinnis (Mrs. John), 17, 38, 41, 58, 74, 80, 106–7, 171, 173, 179
van Vorst, Marie 17, 38, 41, 58, 74, 80, 106, 171, 173, 179
Vecsey, David 149
Venice 27
Vienne, Philip 49, 75, 87, 110, 130
Vincze, Lajos 110, 133–34

Wacquant, Loïc 130
wage labor 15
wages. *See* remuneration
waitresses 51–52
Wang, Yuanfei 135
Watson, Tony 67
weavers 27–28, 30, 40, 86, 180. *See also* textile workers
Weber, Max 173
West Africa 28, 31, 86, 108, 117, 179
Westley, William 73–74, 107, 110–11, 142, 154–55
Whipp, Richard 83, 167, 170
Whittaker, Elvi 91
wool cloth manufactories 80–81. *See also* textile workers
work avoidance 96–97
work blockages 56
work culture. *See* occupational culture
work hours/schedule 29–30, 110, 170
work interactions 13
work: study of 15–16; definition of 20–22
workflow 58–59, 143, 153
workshop 25, 29, 40–42, 47–48, 104–5, 107
workshop owners 60, 104–6

Yihao, Qiu 54
Yoruba people 39

Zhang, Kan 32
Zhang, Ying 131
Zhao, Shiyu 38
Zurcher Jr., Louis 53, 61, 88, 98, 130, 142–43